SCIENCE FICTION
SECRETS

BOOKS BY NICK REDFERN PUBLISHED BY ANOMALIST BOOKS

THERE'S SOMETHING IN THE WOODS
ON THE TRAIL OF THE SAUCER SPIES

Science Fiction Secrets
From Government Files and the Paranormal

Nick Redfern

Anomalist Books
San Antonio * New York

An Original Publication of Anomalist Books

Science Fiction Secrets
Copyright © 2009 by Nick Redfern
ISBN: 1933665408

Cover image by Luca Oleastri

Book design by Seale Studios

For information, go to anomalistbooks.com, or write to:
Anomalist Books, 5150 Broadway #108, San Antonio, TX 78209

Contents

For Dave Lea, my best mate

INTRODUCTION

Surely the worlds of science fiction and high-level government secrecy rarely cross paths to any meaningful degree. If that's what you think, you would be wrong. Drastically so. In reality, the exact opposite is the case. And the results are often far, far stranger than anything that the realms of science fiction and fantasy could ever begin to imagine, or indeed have ever imagined. In the pages that follow, you will learn the truly mind-bending answers to some highly intriguing and distinctly thought-provoking questions, including:

- Did the government of the United States of America, as part of a classified operation specifically designed to subtly and carefully prepare the general public for a forthcoming revelation that extraterrestrials really do exist, secretly provide unique assistance to Steven Spielberg in the production of his ground-breaking science fiction movies *Close Encounters of the Third Kind* and *E.T.: The Extra Terrestrial*?

- Why were special agents of the Federal Bureau of Investigation (FBI) so deeply interested in the lives, careers, and activities of sci-fi authors L. Ron Hubbard (who created the Church of Scientology) and Philip K. Dick (of *Blade Runner* fame)?

- What are the strange and convoluted truths linking sci-fi, UFO conspiracies, acclaimed comic-book artist Jack Kirby, and the controversial, so-called Face on Mars?

- How, and why, did *The X-Files* spin-off series *The Lone Gunmen* seemingly appear to eerily anticipate only months in advance the terrible tragedy of 9-11?

- Why were the higher echelons of the U.S. Air Force so secretly interested in, and concerned by, the UFO-related tales of a relatively anonymous 1950s sci-fi movie-maker who ultimately amounted to nothing at all and who died in poverty in the early 1980s?

- Did a nightmarish scenario presented in one of H.G. Wells' science fiction / fantasy novels prompt Soviet Premier Josef Stalin to clandestinely embark upon a secret and diabolical experiment designed to create a super-race of monstrous soldiers that were half-human and half-ape in nature?

- Has the military managed to successfully perfect physical, human teleportation of the type that was most graphically and famously shown in *Star Trek* and *The Fly?*

- And: what has prompted so many people employed by government, military, and intelligence agencies around the world to write science fiction novels following their retirement from the top secret world of officialdom?

The answers to all of these and many more equally intriguing questions of a specifically science fiction nature follow. Very appropriately, they are all quite literally out of this world.

Martian Mysteries

"Hail, twin companionship, children of Mars."

In 1726 Benjamin Motte of England published what ultimately became one of the most well-known and still-warmly-cherished pieces of early science fiction: *Gulliver's Travels*, written by Jonathan Swift. The book, which was originally titled *Travels into Several Remote Nations of the World in Four Parts ... by Lemuel Gulliver*, relates the long-and-winding tale of the seafaring Lemuel Gulliver, who is described within its packed pages as being a middle-aged surgeon and the "captain of several ships." Gulliver also had a distinct flair for foreign languages and a deep passion for exotic locales. Swift's story chronicles the exciting exploits of Gulliver as he hits the mysterious high seas and visits such magical, wonderfully named, far-off lands as Lilliput, Laputa, Brobdingnag, Glubdubdribb, and Luggnagg. (1)

Swift had actually begun the initial work on his renowned saga at least as far back as 1713, but he failed to seriously pursue the idea to any meaningful degree until around 1720. Half a decade later, the manuscript was finally complete, and shortly thereafter it was in the eager hands of Motte, whose publishing house expertly turned the book into an instant bestseller. *Gulliver's Travels* was also a distinctly anonymous bestseller too, due to the fact that it was quickly perceived by the publisher as being very much a controversial satire of British society of the time, and Motte was highly reluctant -concerned, one might say

– to have anyone's name firmly attached to it in any way, shape, or form. Nevertheless, in 1735 the book was re-released by the Irish publisher George Faulkner, when it was included in the collected works of Jonathan Swift. Notably, it was this specific edition of the book that led none other than the renowned author George Orwell (of *1984* fame) to proclaim that *Gulliver's Travels* was amongst "the six most indispensable books in world literature." Praise, indeed. (2)

Although Swift's book is still viewed today as a true and definitive classic of both its time and its genre, it is also a book that is shrouded in deep, dark, and unyielding mystery, and for one prime reason. While on the island of Laputa, Gulliver learns that the nation's scientists have…

…discovered two lesser stars, or satellites, which revolve about Mars; whereof the innermost is distant from the center of the primary planet exactly three of its diameters, and the outermost five; the former revolves in the space of ten hours, and the latter in twenty one and a half; so that the squares of their periodical times are very near in the same proportion with the cubes of their distance from the center of Mars; which evidently shows them to be governed by the same law of gravitation that influences the other heavenly bodies. (3)

This is all well-and-good, of course, since science and astronomy have conclusively shown us that the planet Mars most assuredly does indeed possess two small moons: their names are Phobos and Deimos. The truly vexing and mystifying problem that faces us, however, is that no telescopes existed in the 18th century that were anywhere near powerful enough to provide even the remotest evidence that Mars was home to two such tiny satellites. In fact, the stark and eye-opening reality of the situation is that Phobos and Deimos were not even discovered until 1877, which was 151 years after *Gulliver's Travels* was first unleashed upon an unsuspecting general public.

This, without a doubt at all, begs a highly important and thought-provoking question: from where on Earth (or, perhaps, even off it, one might reasonably be inclined to argue) did Jonathan Swift secure such unknown information about the Martian moons, apparently a century-and-a-half in advance of the world's then-leading scientists and astronomers? It must be stressed that Swift's novel did indeed provide some fairly accurate data at a time when mainstream astronomy and science were still in states of relative infancy: when Phobos and Deimos were eventually discovered (by Asaph Hall at the U.S. Naval Observatory in Washington, D.C., in August 1877), their orbits actually proved to be not too dissimilar to those described by Swift in *Gulliver's Travels*, interestingly enough.

Phobos, for example, is situated some 6,000 km from the surface of Mars, and it revolves around the red planet in a time frame of 7.7 hours; whereas Swift provided his readers with the figures of 13,600 km and 10 hours, respectively. Deimos averages 20,100 km from Mars and orbits the planet in 30.3 hours; in his book, Swift gave estimates of 27,200 km and 21.5 hours. Not precisely spot-on, of course, but, one could argue that such estimates were not bad at all for an 18th century English novelist with no particular expertise in astronomy. (4)

Then there is the classic 1750 story, *Micromégas*, which was penned by the acclaimed Voltaire, and which tells of an inhabitant of the star-system Sirius who, one day, decides to pay a visit to our very own solar system. Notably, Voltaire mentions the two Martian moons in his own tale, too. Without a doubt, it could quite logically and reasonably be argued that Voltaire had carefully digested the pages and the content of Swift's *Gulliver's Travels*, and then simply decided to utilize certain, integral aspects and scenarios of Swift's storyline as a firm basis for his very own out-of-this-world tale. (5)

Unfortunately, and somewhat frustratingly, too, it should

be said, this particular scenario has never been conclusively proven to any meaningful degree of satisfaction. And, as a result of this admittedly intriguing cosmic-mystery, all kinds of strange, warped, and truly odd theories have surfaced. Chief among them is that Swift had been given access to a secret and unique collection of ancient, astronomical texts prepared millennia ago by a long-forgotten race of super-humans, somewhat akin to the legendary and mighty Atlanteans. While another, still more outlandish, theory suggests that Swift himself was actually a Martian, but one secretly masquerading on Earth as a member of the Human Race!

There is a far more plausible and down-to-earth explanation for this genuinely noteworthy puzzle, however. It is an explanation that can be traced back to 1610, and which has its roots in the controversial and now overwhelmingly discredited theory of Celestial Harmony by Johannes Kepler.

Kepler was born in 1571, and as well as being a key and influential character in the scientific revolution of the time, he was a mathematician, an astrologer, an astronomer, and, interestingly enough, a writer of stories of a distinctly science fiction nature. Perhaps best known of all for his Laws of Planetary Motion that were based on his works *Astronomia Nova*, *Harmonice Mundi* and *Epitome of Copernican Astronomy*, Kepler also undertook studies into the realm of optics, and helped to legitimize the telescopic discoveries of his contemporary, the renowned Galileo Galilei. (6)

Without doubt one of the most interesting tomes in the history of science, Kepler's *Somnium* was an early sci-fi-style tale about a roller-coaster-of-a-journey to our very own Moon. Kepler was careful to rely as much as possible upon then-current knowledge and understanding of outer space, astronomy, and the nature of the Moon itself. Unfortunately for Kepler, however, on its initial release his now-legendary book rapidly sunk into overwhelming obscurity. (7)

The mysterious Martian moons: Deimos and Phobos

But, with specific respect to the controversy of Jonathan Swift and the two moons of Mars, Kepler's solid and personal belief was that as the various planets of our solar system progressed ever outwards from the Sun, so did the precise number of natural moons that orbited those same, respective planets. For example, at the time at issue, astronomers were pretty certain in their beliefs and conclusions that both Mercury and Venus lacked orbiting satellites of any kind at all. On the other hand, our planet has one – the Moon; Jupiter, it was generally accepted, probably had four; and Saturn, it was concluded at the time, had five.

And, taking into consideration the fact that Mars is situated between Earth and Jupiter, it seemed wholly logical – during the time-frame in question, at least – to come to a tentative conclusion that if the notion of Celestial Harmony had any validity, then Mars would have two – or, at the very most, three – moons orbiting it. Of course, 20th and 21st century science, astronomy, and space-exploration have demonstrated that both Jupiter and Saturn possess numerous moons, something that completely and utterly negates the possibility of Kepler's theory possessing any degree of validity. But back in 1610, no one at all was in any sort of position whatsoever to definitively refute Kepler's theories, and so Celestial Harmony certainly did seem to make perfect sense at the dawning of the 17th century.

Adding a great deal of weight to Kepler's beliefs and conclusions, in his own mind, at least, was his personal interpretation of a very weird and intriguing anagram that had been devised by none other than Galileo as a means to clandestinely inform the Jesuit Father at the Collegio Romano of a new astronomical discovery. The anagram read: "s m a I s m r m i l m e p o e t a l e u m i b u n e n u g t t a u i r a s."

The correct interpretation of the anagram was actually *Altissimum planetam tergeminum observavi* or: "I have observed the most distant planet to have a triple form." At the time, Saturn was the furthest world known to exist: Uranus, Neptune, and Pluto were still completely and utterly unknown. However, Kepler's own interpretation of the anagram was *Salue umbistineum geminatum Martia proles*, or: "Hail, twin companionship, children of Mars."

As a result, and not surprisingly at all, in fact, Kepler quickly interpreted this as being a reference to the "twin children of Mars," namely, the number of moons that orbited the red planet. In Kepler's own mind, this was yet further vindication for his burgeoning and unique theories.

Although the true meaning of Galileo's anagram finally became clear in the mid-1600s, Kepler's theory of Celestial Harmony continued to circulate and receive some uncritical support; and although it can never be proven to a truly firm degree, it may indeed have been a critical and integral factor in Swift's decision to assert within the pages of *Gulliver's Travels* that Mars possessed two orbiting moons. (8)

Unfortunately, no one has ever been able to provide an absolutely satisfactory answer as to how Swift predicted, with an admittedly fair degree of accuracy for the time period in question too, the number of moons that orbit Mars, their size, and their distance from the planet itself. Perhaps, after all, it really was a matter of chance, coincidence, synchronicity, and / or Swift's personal acceptance of Johannes Kepler's Celestial Harmony.

If not, Swift took a particularly notable science fiction secret of a definitively Martian nature to the grave with him.

■ ■ | | || 2 || | ■ ■ ■

KIRBY CONSPIRACIES

"...education could be accomplished by mass media such as television, motion pictures, and popular articles."

Located in an area of the planet Mars known as Cydonia, and bearing an admittedly striking and eerie resemblance to a human visage, is a truly huge structure that is roughly three kilometers long, one-and-a-half kilometers wide, and lies approximately ten degrees North of the Martian equator. First photographed on July 25, 1976, by the Viking 1 space probe that was orbiting the red planet at the time, this feature was brought to the attention of the public and the media via a National Aeronautics and Space Administration (NASA) press release six days later. The structure – whatever it may or may not one day prove to be – has since become known both universally and famously as the Face on Mars. (1)

Certainly, the overwhelming bulk of all the interpretations of the photograph offered by the mainstream scientific community suggest that the feature is nothing more, or indeed less, than a wholly natural landform, one of the many mesas that certainly can be found all across the length and breadth of Cydonia. But far more intriguing is the theory that posits the Face on Mars may be the ruined remains of an ancient, artificial monument, and one that was possibly built by an indigenous, but now long-extinct, race of intelligent and indigenous Martians. (2)

Photographic evidence secured by the Mars Global Surveyor probes in both 1998 and 2001, and then later, in 2002, by

The "Face" on Mars

the Mars Odyssey probe, however, dealt a distinctly cruel blow to many of those researchers who had excitedly championed the notion that the Face on Mars was without doubt a structure of artificial origins. Indeed, the new pictures seemed to resemble anything *but* a face. (3)

Perhaps inevitably, conspiracy theorists here, there, and just about everywhere, quickly maintained that the ever mysterious "they" had carefully altered, obfuscated, and air-brushed the photographs to specifically lessen their potential impact on the general public, the media, and the world's scientific community. Needless to say, the controversy continues to rumble and reverberate at a steady pace to this very day. But what is particularly fascinating, and decidedly relevant to the subject matter of this book, is that in the same way that Jonathan Swift's *Gulliver's Travels* seemed to somehow strangely anticipate the finding of the two Martian moons, Phobos and Deimos, more than a century before their actual discovery, so the infamous Face on Mars has played a not inconsiderable role in the world of science fiction – fully two decades before its official discovery by NASA in 1976.

Tom Corbett, Space Cadet was a science fiction hit of the 1950s that was based upon a combination of fictional characters that had been created by Robert Heinlein for his 1948 novel *Space Cadet*, and for Joseph Greene's *Tom Ranger and the Space Cadets* series of the same era. No less than eight hardback books, published by Grosset and Dunlap, were published between 1952 and 1956; more than a dozen comic-books were put out by Dell & Prize Comics during the same period; both a daily and a Sunday newspaper strip written by Paul S. Newman and drawn by Ray Bailey ran from September 1951 to September 1953; and a six-month series of radio shows was broadcast in 1952. Not only that but a televised version of the stories ran from 1950 to 1955; first on CBS from October to December 1950, then on ABC until late 1952, and finally on NBC until its ultimate demise. (4)

But most intriguing of all is a 3-D View-Master version of the adventures and escapades of the fictional *Tom Corbett*. Twenty-one, three-dimensional Kodachrome pictures are contained on the three-reels that are titled, respectively, *The Moon Pyramid*, *The Red Planet*, and *The Mystery of the Asteroid*. In the three-part story, a miner, who is busy at work in the vicinity of the Asteroid Belt, uncovers a seemingly ancient artifact: namely, a small, tetrahedral pyramid that appears to be adorned with nothing less than Egyptian-style hieroglyphics. One of the characters in the story, a Captain Strong, concludes that this has to be firm evidence for the existence of a long-extinct civilization that lived on a now-destroyed world which had been situated somewhere between Mars and Jupiter in the largely distant and forgotten past. In the tale, a near-identical pyramid has already been located on our Moon years before, and so, the Space Cadet team quickly heads off to Earth's satellite, taking with them the newly discovered, and seemingly priceless, artifact.

It quickly becomes clear to the whole team that the two items are actually inter-locking parts of one single object that, when combined together, produces a holographic-style image of the planet Mars. The team then travels to the planet, where they locate a huge, 1,000-foot-high pyramid, a variety of obelisk-like structures, and a small, sculpted face with somewhat feline-like features that has been carved out of rock. Not only that, but it looks astonishingly like the Face on Mars that continues to generate so much interest and intrigue to this very day. The story does not end there, however. (5)

In 1958, Harvey Comics produced a comic-book series titled

Race for the Moon. Written and drawn by the renowned and legendary comic-book artist Jack Kirby (who with Stan Lee of Marvel Comics co-created some of the most famous characters in the superhero genre, including the *Fantastic Four*, the *Incredible Hulk*, the *Avengers*, and the *Silver Surfer*), issue two of the series was titled *The Face on Mars* and related the tale of a team of astronauts, led by one Ben Fisher, that launches an expedition to the planet Mars.

On arriving at their destination, Fisher and his colleagues are truly startled to find a monolithic, carved human-like face. Fisher duly scales the gigantic structure and discovers that the eye-sockets are actually nothing less than entrance points to a hidden realm that is buried deep within the mighty form. Inside, and to his complete and utter amazement, Fisher uncovers a lush land that is populated by a band of Goliath-sized alien beings. Without warning, however, marauding insect-style spacecraft attack from far above the land of the giants and rapidly lay waste to the entire Martian world. A remaining Martian, however, embarks on a do-or-die mission to the world of its enemy, which is a planet situated between Mars and Jupiter, and blasts it into overwhelming oblivion, thus creating what today we know as the Asteroid Belt. At this point, Fisher loses consciousness, only to come to the realization upon waking that what he was viewing was actually not an event occurring in real time after all, but a grim vision of a cataclysmic and disastrous war that had occurred millennia before. Or, as he explains it, a "visual history of a race's heroic death and the triumph of a surviving memory." (6)

It has to be said at this point that Kirby's 1958 artistic rendition of the Face on Mars is practically, and eerily, identical to the one that would supposedly not be found by NASA scientists for almost another two decades. (7) On this matter, Richard Hoagland asks: "So, if he didn't get his information from *Tom Corbett* regarding 'ruins of an ancient, war-torn civilization on the planet Mars...presided over by a giant head...' how did Jack Kirby know about the Face?" (8)

Although that particular question remains unanswered, no firm evidence has ever surfaced in support of the notion that Jack Kirby had secret knowledge of the existence of the Face on Mars before the original NASA pictures surfaced in the mid-1970s. Adherents of the theory that Kirby may have had advance knowledge of the Face, however, point towards what they see as intriguing – albeit admittedly fragmentary – supportive data that links three prominent characters in the story: the aforementioned Robert Heinlein, plus Werner von Braun and Willy Ley.

Robert Anson Heinlein was, beyond any shadow of doubt, one of the most influential and renowned authors in the realm of sci-fi; indeed, towards the end of his career he was widely regarded as the "dean of science fiction." In addition, Heinlein is acknowledged as being the very first science fiction writer to succeed in breaking into the mainstream magazine world, with his work appearing in the pages of the *Saturday Evening Post* in the latter part of the 1940s. Heinlein went on to win four Hugo Awards, and was awarded the first Grand Master Award given by the Science Fiction Writers of America for his lifetime achievement to the genre. (9)

Wernher Magnus Maximilian Freiherr von Braun was a leading – albeit highly controversial – figure in the development of rocket technology, in both Nazi Germany and in the United States. German by nationality, he was at the absolute forefront of the Nazi's rocket development program both before and during the Second World War, and entered the United States at the end of the War via the then-secret Operation Paperclip, a Faustian and utterly shameless pact under which the U.S. Government clandestinely recruited a wealth of German scientists (including some who were nothing less than full-blown Nazis), who were all deemed ripe for the picking. Von Braun subsequently became a naturalized American citizen and worked on the American Inter-Continental Ballistic Missile program before joining NASA, where he finally rose to the prestigious rank of Director. Not bad at all, one might say, for one of Hitler's fawning, unrepentant, and subservient minions. (10)

Just like von Braun, Willy Ley was deeply influenced by the Transylvanian rocket theorist Herman Oberth. And, as such, he summarily left behind him a career in paleontology to pursue the then-fledgling science of rocketry. Ley became an important and integral player in such experimentation in pre-war Germany and was a vital component of von Braun's early work. When the Nazis established an admittedly significant foothold in rocketry development and research in the mid-1930s, Ley quickly fled to the safety of the United States, but, on arriving, found to his disappointment, surprise, and dismay that rocketry received little of the serious scientific dedication that could be found in Germany at that time. So, instead, Ley turned his hand to writing for a variety of science-based publications, covering a wide range of subjects, and using his skills to popularize the idea that rocketry and space-travel were issues that should be treated with the utmost seriousness. Ley died in 1969, somewhat ironically barely a couple of weeks before the now-historic launch of *Apollo 11* that took the astronauts Neil Armstrong, "Buzz" Aldrin, and Michael Collins on their historic journey to the Moon. (11)

As noted earlier, the *Tom Corbett, Space Cadet* phenomenon was, in part, based upon Heinlein's 1948 science fiction novel *Space Cadet*. It transpires that both Heinlein and Willy Ley worked as consultants to the television series *Tom Corbett, Space Cadet*. During this same period, von Braun had been hired by the Walt Disney Corporation to act as the chief consultant on three ambitious television programs about outer space: *Man in Space*, *Man and the Moon*, and *Mars and Beyond*. According to the words of Disney spokesman Howard E. Green, the three documentaries were "often credited with popularizing the concept of the government's space program during the 1950s." (12)

Notably, *Man in Space* was so popular (it was watched by a truly astonishing 42 million people in the United States on its first airing alone) that it led none other than then-President Dwight D. Eisenhower himself to contact Walt Disney and personally request his very own copy of the production. When Disney inquired of the president why he wanted a copy, Eisenhower quickly and famously replied: "Well, I'm going to show it to all those stove-shirt generals who don't believe we're going to be up there." (13)

During production of these shows for Walt Disney, von Braun worked with a man named Ward Kimball, who was famous for his on-screen portrayals of the characters Jiminy Cricket, the Cheshire Cat, the March Hare, the Mad Hatter, as well as for redesigning Mickey Mouse in 1938 into his current incarnation. Kimball had joined the Disney Studios in 1934, and rose up in the ranks to become a directing animator on such classic productions as *Snow White and the Seven Dwarfs*, *Pinocchio*, *Fantasia,* and *Peter Pan*. He also directed Disney Oscar-winning shorts *Toot, Whistle, Plunk,* and *Boom* in 1953 and *It's Tough to be a Bird* in 1969. Unknown to many Disney watchers, however, Kimball was also a longstanding student of UFOs and possessed a large collection of books and magazines on the subject, according to Navy physicist and UFO authority Bruce Maccabee, who had the opportunity to meet personally with Kimball in 1980. (14)

It also transpires that, in 1953, a group of scientists, military personnel, and intelligence operatives, collectively known as the Robertson Panel, was convened by the Central Intelligence Agency in an attempt to demystify the atmosphere of intrigue and concern that, in the eyes of the public and the media at least, surrounded the UFO mystery. One of the recommendations made by the panel was that the CIA should embark upon an extensive and in-depth program of "debunking" and "education," in an effort to try and lessen the intrigue and concern over UFOs. Notably, the plan implicated none other than the Disney Company itself. (15)

According to the Robertson Panel's now-declassified files:

The "debunking" aim would result in reduction in public interest in "flying saucers" which today evokes a strong psychological reaction. This education could be accomplished by mass media such as television, motion pictures, and popular articles. Basis of such education would be actual case histories which had been puzzling at first but later explained. As in the case of conjuring tricks, there is much less stimulation if the "secret" is known. Such a program should tend to reduce the current gullibility of the public and consequently their susceptibility to clever hostile propaganda.

In this connection, Dr. Hadley Cantril (Princeton University) was suggested. Cantril authored "Invasion from Mars," (a study in the psychology of panic, written about the famous Orson Welles radio broadcast in 1938) and has since performed advanced laboratory studies in the field of perception. The names of Don Marquis (University of Michigan) and Leo Roston were mentioned as possibly suitable as consultant psychologists.

Also, someone familiar with mass communications techniques, perhaps an advertising expert, would be helpful. Arthur Godfrey was mentioned as possibly a valuable channel of communication reaching a mass audience of certain levels. Dr. Berkner suggested the U. S. Navy (ONR) Special Devices Center, Sands Point, L. I., as a potentially valuable organization to assist in such an educational program. The teaching techniques used by this agency for aircraft identification during the past war was cited as an example of a similar educational task. The Jam Handy Co. which made World War II training films (motion picture and slide strips) was also suggested, as well as Walt Disney, Inc. animated cartoons. (16)

That officials did consult with Walt Disney with regard to collaborating on the production of UFO-themed televisions productions is not in any doubt whatsoever. In 1979, in a lecture delivered to the Mutual UFO Network (MUFON) in San Francisco, California, Ward Kimball stated that at some point during the mid-1950s, Disney was approached by representatives of the Air Force and was invited to lend personal assistance to a documentary production about UFOs. As part of the deal, the Air Force even gave its assurance that it would – somewhat astonishingly – supply film-footage of genuine UFOs in flight, which Disney could include in the production.

Kimball said that there was nothing at all strange about Walt Disney going along with the government and the military's wishes and requests. Kimball recalled how, during the Second World War, the military almost took over Disney's Burbank facilities, where literally dozens of hours of military-training productions and war-effort films featuring Disney characters, like Donald Duck, were shot and produced.

As far as UFOs are concerned, the studio commenced its work, while Walt Disney patiently awaited the arrival of the Air Force's priceless UFO footage. However, at the very last moment, the Air Force mysteriously (and, perhaps, inevitably, it might be argued) withdrew the offer of the priceless footage, and the planned documentary was summarily canceled. (17)

Nevertheless, the fact that (a) Walt Disney was engaged in clandestine operations with the Air Force and the CIA to produce indoctrination-style shows on UFOs; (b) the Disney Corporation's Ward Kimball was acquainted with Wernher von Braun as a result of their work on *Man in Space, Man and the Moon*, and *Mars and Beyond*; (c) von Braun was friends with Willy Ley; (d) Ley and science fiction author Robert Heinlein were the chief consultants on the *Tom Corbett, Space Cadet* series; and (e) Jack Kirby seemed to eerily anticipate the discovery of the Face on Mars long before it was actually found, has led to complex (and, to a degree, somewhat convoluted) assertions that the *Tom Corbett* saga concerning the discovery of ancient pyramid-style designs, obelisks, and even a carved face on the Martian surface was all part of a similar indoctrination plan to subtly prepare the public for the revelation that intelligent life had existed on Mars thousands, or perhaps, millions of years ago. But, whatever the ultimate truth of the matter, the Jack Kirby/conspiracy connections continue.

Written by Roger Zelazny in 1968, *Lord of Light* is an epic novel that sits well in the genres of both science fiction and fantasy, and was awarded the 1968 Hugo Award for Best Novel. The book tells the story of the crew and the colonists of the *Star of India* spacecraft that became stranded on a hostile, far-off planet where, surrounded by distinctly violent alien tribes, they are forced to carve out a place for themselves or die. (18)

In the late 1970s, screenwriter Barry Ira Geller secured the motion-picture rights to Zelazny's *Lord of Light*, and by November 1979 plans were afoot for a full-blown, 50 million dollar production that would commence filming in July 1980 on 1,000-acres near Denver, Colorado. Even more ambitious was a grand idea that Geller would convert the location of the shoot into a huge theme park that was to be called Science Fiction Land, and that it would be approximately three times the size of Disneyland.

In an effort to get the project well and truly on the move, Geller enlisted the skills of Jack Kirby to provide imaginative renditions of both the theme park and the movie-sets that were then incorporated into a promotional package to be used to secure funding. Kirby's artwork on Marvel's comic books *The Fantastic Four*, *The Incredible Hulk*, and, particularly *The Inhumans* and the "ancient astronauts"-themed *The Eternals* graphically displayed the exact type of imagery that sat very well within the fantastic world of *Lord of Light*. (19)

Unfortunately, the project was constantly beset by legal problems, and neither the movie nor the theme park ever came to fruition. However, there is a far stranger aspect to this particular story. In 1979, when a crisis erupted in Iran and a number of U.S. hostages were held at the American Embassy in Tehran, six U.S. State Department employees carefully managed to evade their captors and made their cautious and secret way to the Canadian Embassy – where they were to remain for almost three months.

In an effort to get the six home, the best minds of the CIA came up with an ingenious plan: to pretend that the six were innocents who were merely part of a Canadian-based film company that was making a movie in Iran – and to walk them straight out of Tehran's airport and onto a plane home. Faked passports and credentials were carefully created for the six, even plans to disguise them with wigs and make-up were discussed, and the operation was quickly put into action.

John Chambers, who had worked on the 1968 science fiction movie *Planet of the Apes*, was secretly enlisted for his make-up and special effects skills, as was Bob Sidell, who had also been employed on *Planet of the Apes* and had subsequently worked with Steven Spielberg on *E.T.: The Extra-Terrestrial.*

Antonio J. Mendez, a former employee of the CIA who successfully created, planned, and executed the clandestine operation in question, said: "Because *Star Wars* had made it big only recently, many science-fiction, fantasy, and superhero films were being produced. We decided we needed a script with 'sci-fi,' Middle Eastern, and mythological elements. Something about the glory of Islam would be nice, too."

Mendez added that John Chambers (whose identity Mendez obfuscates and refers to as "Jerome Calloway" in his own, personal write-up of the affair) "recalled a recent script that might serve our purpose, and he hauled it out of a pile of manuscripts submitted for his consideration."

It was, of course, Roger Zelazny's *Lord of Light*. As it transpired, the secret ruse worked without a hitch: there was no James Bond-style climax to the story with huge explosions, guns blazing, and hot, exotic babes running around in skimpy bikinis. Rather, the group simply breezed their way through Tehran's airport – Iranian officials were evidently quite happy with the bogus passports created by the CIA's finest purveyors of fakery – and boarded a 5:30 a.m. flight first to Zurich, Switzerland, and then another that carried them to safety in the United States. (20)

Once again, and in a strange and decidedly roundabout way, the worlds of high-level secrecy-and-conspiracy and science fiction artist-extraordinaire Jack Kirby had crossed paths.

■ ■ ■ ║║ 3 ║║ ■ ■

THE TUNGUSKA EXPLOSION

*"...the sky split in two and fire appeared
high and wide over the forest."*

Early on the morning of June 30, 1908, numerous people living
in the region of Tunguska, Russia, and specifically in the hills
northwest of Lake Baikal, witnessed what many described as a
large column of blue light moving deliberately across the dawn
sky. Approximately ten minutes later the almighty sound of a
massive explosion shook and truly decimated the area, causing
extensive damage hundreds of miles away from the presumed
impact site of whatever it was that had earlier been seen in the
morning sky.

The event was captured on seismic equipment as far away
as the British Isles. And, in the United States, both the Smith-
sonian Astrophysical Observatory and the Mount Wilson Observatory recorded a marked decrease in atmospheric transpar-
ency in the immediate wake of the event that lasted for a period
of approximately three months. (1)

In the days that followed, Russian newspapers reported
extensively on the event. The July 2, 1908, edition of the *Sibir*
newspaper stated:

In the N. Karelinski village the peasants saw to the North-West,
rather high above the horizon, some strangely bright bluish-
white heavenly body, which for 10 minutes moved downwards.
The body appeared as a "pipe," i.e. a cylinder. The sky was cloud-
less, only a small dark cloud was observed in the general direc-

tion of the bright body. It was hot and dry. As the body neared the ground, the bright body seemed to smudge, and then turned into a giant billow of black smoke, and a loud knocking was heard, as if large stones were falling, or artillery was fired. All building shook. At the same time the cloud began emitting flames of uncertain shapes. All villagers were stricken with panic and took to the streets, women cried, thinking it was the end of the world. (2)

Was an alien spacecraft responsible for the devastation at Tunguska in Siberia in 1908?

Similarly, the *Krasnoyaretz* newspaper recorded the following:

At 7:43 the noise akin to a strong wind was heard. Immediately afterwards a horrific thump sounded, followed by an earthquake which literally shook the buildings. The first thump was followed by a second, and then a third. Then the interval between the first and the third thumps were accompanied by an unusual underground rattle, similar to a railway upon which dozens of trains are travelling at the same time. Afterwards for 5 to 6 minutes an exact likeness of artillery fire was heard: 50 to 60 salvoes in short, equal intervals, which got progressively weaker. After 1.5-2 minutes after one of the "barrages" six more thumps were heard, like cannon firing, but individual, loud, and accompanied by tremors. The sky, at the first sight, appeared to be clear. There was no wind and no clouds. However, upon closer inspection to the North, where most of the thumps were heard, a kind of ashen cloud was seen near the horizon which kept getting smaller and more transparent, and by around 2-3.00 p.m. completely disappeared. (3)

After the initial flurry of excitement, however, the story rapidly vanished into obscurity and did not resurface to any great or meaningful extent until around 1921. It was in that year that Leonid Kulik, who was a Russian mineralogist by profession, visited what is known today as the Podkamennaya Tunguska River Basin, on behalf of his colleagues at the Soviet Academy of Sciences.

At the time, Kulik tentatively concluded that the object that had caused such widespread and overwhelming destruction was a meteorite, and as a result a full-scale expedition duly began in 1927. Interestingly, the Soviet Government agreed to fund the expedition on the grounds that such a huge meteorite would likely have deposited a massive amount of iron in the area. The recovery of the iron itself would surely cover the cost of the expedition and might even prove to be a major boost to the Soviet economy.

On arrival at the scene of the presumed meteorite crash, however, Kulik's team was very surprised to find that there was no impact crater at all. Instead, they found a huge, 50-kilometer-wide area of flattened and burnt trees. Over the course of the next decade, Kulik would initiate no less than three expeditions to the area, in an attempt to determine what had really occurred at Tunguska back in 1908.

In 1930, Kulik recorded the following firsthand testimony from a witness named Semen Semenov:

At breakfast time I was sitting by the house at Vanavara Factory, facing north. I suddenly saw that directly to the north, over Onkoul's Tunguska road, the sky split in two and fire appeared high and wide over the forest. The split in the sky grew larger, and the entire northern side was covered with fire. At that moment I became so hot that I couldn't bear it, as if my shirt was on fire. From the northern side, where the fire was, came strong heat. I wanted to tear off my shirt and throw it down, but then the sky shut closed, and a strong thump sounded, and I was thrown a few yards. I lost my senses for a moment, but then my wife ran out and led me to the house.

After that such noise came, as if rocks were falling or cannons were firing, the earth shook, and when I was on the ground, I pressed my head down, fearing rocks would smash it. When the sky opened up, hot wind raced between the houses, like from cannons, which left traces in the ground like pathways, and it damaged some crops. Later we saw that many windows were shattered, and in the barn a part of the iron lock snapped. (4)

Not until further expeditions took place in the 1950s and 1960s was it determined that large amounts of both nickel and iridium were present at the Tunguska site, both of which can indeed be found in meteorites. As a result, the theory that the Tunguska object was probably a meteorite was the one that gained favor within scientific and academic circles.

Furthermore, experiments undertaken in the mid-1960s by Russian scientists demonstrated that, in all probability, the Tunguska meteorite (if that is indeed what it was) had approached the area at an angle of 30 degrees from the ground – which further reinforced the theory that the object responsible for the devastation had exploded in mid-air, rather than having slammed hard into the ground. Other candidates suggested for the mystery of Tunguska include an asteroid, a small comet, a black hole, or some form of poorly-understood or -defined anti-matter. The most intriguing theory of all, however, suggests that an alien spacecraft exploded high in the skies over Tunguska, and that the Russian Government has secretly and successfully hidden the startling, extraterrestrial truth ever since that fateful day.

As writer and researcher David Darling notes: "According to [Alexei] Zolotov [a prominent Soviet scientist], a spaceship controlled by 'beings from other worlds' may have caused the 1908 explosion. He imagined a nuclear-propelled craft that exploded accidentally due to a malfunction." (6)

Indeed, the possibility that a malfunctioning UFO was the root-cause of the Tunguska event was also addressed at great length in the book *The Fire Came By*, written by John Baxter and Thomas Atkins. (7) On this particular matter, researchers Matthew Wittnebel and Andrew Mann note: "[Baxter and Atkins] say the Earth's magnetic field was disturbed at the time of the explosion, as it would have been by a nuclear blast. Secondly, the pattern of destruction in the shattered forest is more consistent with the shock waves produced by an atomic bomb than with those of a conventional explosion. Other clues were the extreme intensity of the light, and a later discovery of numerous tiny green globules of melted dust, called trinitites, which are characteristic of an atomic blast." (8)

Vladimir V. Rubtsov, Ph.D., a prime proponent of the theory that an alien spacecraft came to grief all those years ago at Tunguska, wrote an article in the May 2001, issue of *Fate* magazine that further demonstrated, in his opinion, that the object had highly exotic, and otherworldly, origins. Rubtsov also specifically comments on the atomic angle:

The hypothesis of a thermal explosion, according to which the Tunguska space body was a meteorite or the core of a small comet that exploded as a result of the rapid deceleration in the lower atmosphere, met with difficulties. A rare mutation among the human natives of the region also arose in the 1910s in one of the settlements near the epicenter. According to Dr. N. V. Vasilyev, medico-ecological examination of the state of health of the native inhabitants reveals population genetic effects similar to those observed in the regions affected by nuclear weapon tests. These facts (as well as the local magnetic storm that started after the explosion) count in favor of the nuclear character of the Tunguska explosion. Maybe we are even dealing in this instance with a novel type of nuclear reaction. (9)

Such stories continue to surface. In August 2004, a Russian team led by Yuri Labvin reported that they had retrieved an "extraterrestrial device" from the scene of the incident. To date, the scientific community is still awaiting the results of Labvin's expedition. (10)

While the idea that an alien spacecraft might have crashed at, or exploded in the air high above, Tunguska in 1908 is certainly provocative, there is one issue that proponents of this particular theory are not at all keen to highlight: its origins can be found not within the worlds of science or high-level government secrecy, but firmly within the realm of sci-fi. It was in 1946 that Soviet Author Alexander Petrovich Kazanstev wrote a novel that was directly inspired by a personal trip he had made the previous year to see the atomic devastation and destruction that was wrought at the Japanese city of Hiroshima.

David Darling notes: "Kazantsev developed the idea that a nuclear-powered spacecraft from Mars on a visit to collect fresh water from Lake Baikal, had exploded, showering the area in radioactivity." (11)

Similarly, in his debut novel of 1951 titled *Astronauts*, science fiction author Stanislaw Lem utilized the specific scenario of an alien spacecraft exploding over Tunguska as its central, overriding theme. Nearly a decade later, *Astronauts* was adapted into a movie titled *First Spaceship on Venus*, in which Russian scientists stumble upon a "magnetic recording device" at the site of the Tunguska blast, and subsequently determine that the object that exploded there was nothing less than a reconnaissance vessel from the planet Venus. A translation of the recording device reveals that the vessel contained the entire Venusian population, which was coming to Earth with the specific intent of occupying our world. Their goal – as well as their entire race – is brought to an abrupt end, however, with the disastrous destruction of their huge craft. (12)

The fact that Tunguska continues to play a major role in the world of science fiction only ensures that the fine line between fact and fiction becomes even more blurry and indistinct. For example, Donald R. Bensen's 1978 novel *And Having Writ* used the Tunguska story as a springboard for an amusing tale about stranded aliens who are forced to manipulate the technology of early 20th century Earth as part of an attempt to rebuild their stricken craft. (13)

And the novels just keep on coming.

Chekhov's Journey, written by Ian Watson in 1983, presents a scenario in which the playwright Anton Chekhov has personal knowledge of the Tunguska event, which turns out to have been caused by Russian time-travelers from the future. (14) Two years later, Bruce Sterling and Rudy Rucker's story "Storming the Cosmos" depicted a top secret Soviet reconnaissance mission journeying to Tunguska and finding advanced technology that is then incorporated into the Soviet space program. (15)

In the world of science fiction themed comic books the situation is much the same. In the Marvel Comics spin-off of the 1987 movie *Predator,* which starred Arnold Schwarzenegger, the Tunguska explosion is shrouded in mystery but is attributed to either an attempt by the Predators to hide their existence from the Human Race by vaporizing their malfunctioning craft high in the atmosphere, or by the military and governments of

either Russian or America who are firmly determined to prevent the infinitely advanced technology falling into the hands of
the scientific elite of each other's respective nations. (16)

And perhaps inevitably, even *The X-Files* television series
got into the act, too, with a two-part story (titled "Tunguska"
and "Terma"), in which Mulder and his long-time arch-foe,
Alex Krycek, are forced to work together and journey to Tunguska, where they learn that materials recovered at the crash-
site contain a deadly substance known as "Black Oil" that contains a microbial life form capable of infecting, and controlling,
any and all living creatures on the Earth. (17)

All that said, it is highly appropriate to close with the words
of Bill Lee, who worked for the United States' National Reconnaissance Office for more than a decade on such matters as the
Cuban Missile Crisis and the Gary Powers-U-2 Affair, and who
has a personal interest in the Tunguska affair in general and
tales of crashed UFOs in particular:

There's always a chance that maybe extra-terrestrials might
have fallen at Tunguska, and the Russian Government knows this
and kept the secret. But when the picture of exploding atomic
[space]-craft and aliens that the believers paint of this can be
found back in old Russian science fiction stories, you really have
to wonder if people are confusing what they think happened because they think they read it in a scientific periodical or a secret
government file or whatever, with what they might have really
read in an old science fiction yarn. (18)

▌▐ ▐ ▌▌ 4 ▌▌▐ ▐

Planet of the Ape Men

"I want a new invincible human being."

Born on September 21, 1866, in the English town of Bromley, novelist H.G. Wells was the son of a professional cricket-player and a housekeeper, and made an untold number of contributions to the world of science fiction that have, arguably, never been eclipsed. In 1883, after having first been employed as a draper's assistant (an experience that he detailed in his 1905 book, *Kipps*), Wells became a teacher-pupil at Midhurst Grammar School and subsequently obtained a scholarship to the Normal School of Science in London, where he studied biology. In 1887, he elected to leave before obtaining his degree. Wells then taught in private schools for four years, not taking his B.S. degree until 1890. In the following year, Wells settled in London and married his cousin Isabel; he would later leave her, however, for Amy Catherine, one of his students. But the real turning point for Wells came in the year 1893, when he elected to embark upon a career as a full-time writer.

The author of such renowned science fiction classics as *The Time Machine*, *War of the Worlds*, *The Invisible Man*, and *The First Men on the Moon*, Wells was a true prophet, anticipating both the advantages and disadvantages that the Human Race would surely face as both technology and science began to play ever-greater roles in the world and planetary affairs. *The Time Machine* was actually a less-than-subtle parody of British class-divisions, while *The War in the Air* revealed Wells' wholly jus-

H. G. Wells

tified concerns that the development of aircraft would inevitably lead to their use as devastating tools of warfare. It was only a few short years before the carnage of the First World War began, and Wells' fears were finally, and tragically, proven to be utterly correct.

In the aftermath of the War, Wells began to focus his attention on non-fiction, with such works as *The Outline of History*, *The Science of Life*, and *Experiment in Autobiography*. But Wells could never really shake off the concerns he had with respect to what the future might have in-store for the human species. His final book, *Mind At The End Of Its Tether*, was published in 1945 and was a distinctly pessimistic look at the Human Race's future, or rather, its lack of a future. Wells died in London the following year, on August 13. (1)

But perhaps most intriguing – and certainly most relevant to subject matter of this book – was Wells' 1896 science fiction novel *The Island of Dr. Moreau*. As was the case with so many of his other works, this one related in a science fiction format some of Wells' ever-present worries about the ways in which science was advancing and mutating.

The Island of Dr. Moreau tells how, following a catastrophic shipwreck, one Edward Prendick finds himself marooned on an unknown island where, to his horror, he learns of the diabolical "vivisections" of Dr. Moreau. Moreau tells the shocked and dumbfounded Prendick that he has succeeded in achieving what has up until then been presumed completely impossible: namely, the successful transforming of wild animals into strange creatures that are "human in shape, and yet human beings with the strangest air about them of some familiar animal."

Since Prendick is completely and utterly stranded, Moreau and his assistant, Montgomery, eventually decide to confide in him the full and shocking story of their time spent on the island, which involves the man-beasts being forced to adhere to several key laws laid down by Moreau, namely: "Not to go on All-Fours," "Not to Suck up Drink," "Not to eat Fish or Flesh," "Not to claw the Bark of Trees," and "Not to chase other Men." Always, the creatures are required to endlessly repeat: "That is the Law. Are we not men? That is the Law. Are we not men? That is the Law. Are we not men?"

Not content with just playing God, Moreau actually tries to turn himself into a living deity by having the man-beasts worship no one, and nothing, other than himself. Unfortunately, and to his ultimate and tragic cost, Moreau learns that unless he continues to mold, exploit, and control the natural animal instincts of his diabolical creations on a regular basis, they begin to revert to their natural, bestial ways.

As a result, a disturbing undercurrent of revolution begins to stir within the strange world of the "manimals," and Moreau and Montgomery are violently slain by their creations. Prendick is spared, however, and lives for a while with the new rulers of the island until, unable to relate to them after their all-but-complete reversal to animalistic states, he finds an abandoned boat and succeeds in leaving the confines of the island, once and for all. Prendick is shortly thereafter rescued, but his strange tale is assumed to be nothing more than the ravings of a deranged madman driven insane by a near-year-long period of isolation on the island. As a result, the dark and disturbing secret of Dr. Moreau is destined to remain precisely that—a secret.

When Wells wrote *The Island of Dr. Moreau*, England was hotly debating the controversial issue of animal vivisection, and it was largely this issue that prompted Wells to write his novel. And, only two years after publication of the book

– which graphically highlighted in its pages such issues as vivisection, irresponsible and unregulated scientific research, religion, and eugenics – the British Union for the Abolition of Vivisection was created and became a noted and forceful official body. This suggests that perhaps someone recognized that the scenario Wells portrayed might one day become a terrible reality. (2)

A somewhat similar scenario to that portrayed in *The Island of Dr. Moreau* was presented in Pierre Boulle's classic 1963 science fiction story *Monkey Planet*. (3) The book was turned into a famous, Hollywood blockbuster movie five years later starring Charlton Heston: it was called *Planet of the Apes*. In the Oscar-winning production, Heston's character, Taylor, is an American astronaut who travels across space to a planet where talking-apes are the dominant lifeform, and humankind is no more than the equivalent of prehistoric-man that acts as sport, slave, and medical guinea pig for the ape civilization. Only at the end of the movie does Taylor discover the shocking and wholly unanticipated truth: namely, that he has not crossed space at all. Rather, he has actually crossed time; he is back on Earth, an unknown number of millennia in the future, after a devastating nuclear war has obliterated practically every memory and remnant of human civilization – aside from a solitary, and partly-destroyed Statue of Liberty that Taylor finds half-buried in the sands of a new landscape that has been ruthlessly carved by the destructive effects of the mighty atom.

With the success of the first *Apes* movie, four more followed, as did two television spin-offs (one, live-action-based, the other, cartoon-based) and a Marvel comic book. The collective, developing story that is revealed demonstrates that after a catastrophic plague wipes out all of the cats and dogs on the planet shortly before the end of the 20th century, human beings begin to take primates as pets for company, then as slaves who they callously exploit as a result of their own sheer laziness. It is then that things begin to go very wrong for the collective Human Race. The physical appearance of the apes begins to change over time, and they ultimately succeed in developing the power of speech. Inevitably, the apes, grasping their newly found potential, revolt against their human masters. And with catastrophic, worldwide nuclear war looming on the horizon, the inevitable countdown to the end of human civilization, and the birth of a whole new ape-controlled society, begins. (4)

But surely the collective scenario presented in *The Island of Dr. Moreau* and in *Planet of the Apes*, of wild animals becoming more human that bestial, could only ever be considered sci-fi, right? Probably, though not everyone thought so.

Top-secret government files generated in Russia in 1926 under the regime of Premier Josef Stalin reveal the details of an astonishing and shocking story that eerily parallels the scenarios presented in H.G. Wells' *The Island of Dr. Moreau* and Pierre Boulle's *Monkey Planet*. According to the formerly classified records, Stalin had an absolutely crazed idea to try and create an army of half-ape half-man creatures who would be utterly unbeatable and unstoppable on the battlefield.

With this in mind, Stalin told Ilya Ivanov, who was the former Soviet Union's top animal-breeding expert at the time: "I want a new invincible human being, insensitive to pain, resistant and indifferent about the quality of food they eat." Somewhat shrewdly, and perhaps privately anticipating a scenario similar to the catastrophic ending in *The Island of Dr. Moreau*, Stalin added that the creatures should possess "immense strength but with an underdeveloped brain." (5)

Certainly, in the eyes of Stalin, at least, if anyone could make the utterly crackpot project succeed it was Ivanov. A highly regarded figure, he had made his reputation under the Tsar when, in 1901, he established the world's first center for the artificial insemination of racehorses. But more important to Stalin was the fact that Ivanov had already tried to create a "superhorse" by attempting to crossbreed horses with zebras. (6)

Although these crossbreeding attempts failed completely, Moscow's Politburo forwarded Stalin's request to the Academy of Science with the order to build a "living war machine," an order that came at a time when the Soviet Union was ambitiously embarking upon a crusade to turn the world upside down, with social engineering seen as a partner to industrialization.

In addition, Soviet authorities were struggling at the time to rebuild the Red Army after the devastation of the First World War, and there was also intense pressure to find a new labor force, particularly one that would not complain in the slightest. As a result, in the warped mind of Josef Stalin, the secret creation of a super race of hybrid creatures that combined the intelligence of human beings with the physical strength of some of the larger primates, such as gorillas and chimpanzees, seemed to be the absolute perfect antidote to just about every problem facing the Soviet Union.

The Russian scientific community quickly swung into action, and Ivanov was dispatched, with $200,000 in his pocket, to West Africa, where the very first such experiment was planned and executed, namely the impregnation of a number of female chimpanzees with human sperm. Ivanov's now-archived reports reveal that the Pasteur Institute in Paris, France, secretly granted him permission to use their research station in Guinea, West Africa, for ape-breeding research purposes.

As Ivanov advised the Politburo, however: "The biggest problem is to catch living females." As a result, Ivanov's team learned that the answer to this very tricky problem was to burn the nearby trees, and then chase the chimpanzees into cages as they scampered down the trunks. Ivanov also reported, somewhat disturbingly, on the fact that his team had "seized" a number of local African women in the area who were "to be impregnated with ape sperm." Not surprisingly, no pregnancies ever resulted from this unsettling action. More ambitious plans to impregnate female gorillas with human sperm also ended in complete and utter failure.

At the same time, a center for such experimentation in Russia was stealthily established in Stalin's birthplace of Georgia, where the super-apes were to be raised – if impregnation was ever to be successful, of course. Not surprisingly, none of the West African experiments succeeded. Undaunted, however, the Soviets pressed on with an even more controversial plan. Arrangements were made for a number of women "volunteers" in Russia to be impregnated with monkey sperm in an effort to determine whether or not following this particular route might prove to be more successful. Again, it was not. That such experimentation did proceed, however, is not in any doubt; only recently, workmen engaged in the building of a children's playground in the Georgian Black Sea town of Suchumi found a plethora of ape-skeletons, as well as an old abandoned laboratory where some of the dark plans had been undertaken.

In the eyes of the ruthless Stalin, and as a direct follow-on from the resounding failure to create an army of man-beasts, Ivanov was by now in overwhelming disgrace. As a result, Stalin sentenced Ivanov to five years in jail, which was later commuted to five years' exile in the Central Asian republic of Kazakhstan in 1931. He died a year later, however, after falling sick while standing on a freezing railway platform. (7)

And while the whole, strange and secret affair of Russia's super-apes can today be viewed as wholly farcical from beginning to end, there is a serious point to all of this, and it was one that H.G. Wells clearly recognized more than a century ago: that ruthless men without morals, operating in complete secrecy, and with access to advanced science, technology, and impressive budgets, might be the undoing of our whole society. We would do very well to remember the concerns of this science fiction visionary, if only to ensure that one day another Stalin does not secretly try something similar – and finally succeed.

There is a highly intriguing footnote to this story. In 2008, the History Channel's *MonsterQuest* series devoted an episode to Stalin's bizarre project. And although no doubts at all were expressed about the particular nature of Ivanov's experimentation, questions were raised about the extent to which (or not) Stalin had a personal awareness of the experimentation, or if the claims of his direct knowledge and involvement were merely due to media exaggeration and/or misinterpretation.

However, what is not well known is the fact that H. G. Wells visited the Soviet Union in 1934, and, on July 23 actually met and personally interviewed Joseph Stalin. Constantine Oumansky, then head of Russia's Press Bureau of the Commissariat of Foreign Affairs, recorded the conversation, which lasted from 4:00 p.m. to 6:50 p.m. As far as can be determined, the two men did not drift into a discussion of genetically-created, half-human super-apes; their exchange was largely focused upon the then-current state of the world from a purely economic perspective. However, perhaps Stalin – a voracious reader who is known to have enthusiastically read Wells' output – mused upon the possibility of informing Wells that the scenario the science fiction author had presented within the pages of *The Island of Dr. Moreau* was something with which he, Stalin, was secretly quite familiar. Doubtless, Wells would have considered this prime evidence that his very worst fears and nightmares about science really were on the verge of coming all-too-horrifically true. (8)

Project Invisibility

*"Half of the officers & the crew of that Ship
are at Present, Mad as Hatters."*

H.G. Wells' classic science fiction novel *The Invisible Man* was first serialized in *Pearson's Magazine* in 1897 and was published in full-length book form later that same year. The book tells the memorable story of a scientist who comes to the conclusion that if a person's "refractive index" is changed to exactly that of the air, and if his body neither absorbs nor reflects light, then he will become invisible. And, in the book's pages, he does precisely that, and catastrophically so, as the process drives the scientist totally and irreversibly insane. As with *The Island of Dr. Moreau*, the tale of *The Invisible Man* is a cautionary one, specifically designed to warn humankind against the misuse of technology for wholly selfish purposes. It was a tale that also spawned a whole sub-genre within the world of sci-fi. (1)

In 1933, Universal Pictures made a full-length movie version of *The Invisible Man*, which was followed in 1940 by both *The Invisible Man Returns* and *The Invisible Woman*, and in 1942 by *Invisible Agent*. (2) Similarly, the 1987 movie, *Predator*, starring Arnold Schwarzenegger, saw California's most famous mayor pitting his muscles against an alien enemy who has the ability to cloak himself invisible. (3) Likewise, the 2000 movie *Hollow Man*, starring Kevin Bacon, uses Wells' novel as its central plot. (4)

So much for science fiction, but what about the real world?

Certainly, there have been secret attempts on the part of several nations to render their weapons of war invisible, to a degree, at least. The F-117 Stealth Fighter and its cousin the B-2 Stealth Bomber are perfect examples of radar invisibility. But that is without doubt a far cry from literal, optical invisibility. (5) But such research has reportedly been undertaken.

In the 1940s, the U.S. Navy secretly developed a project codenamed *Yahootie*, the purpose of which was to try and create an invisible aircraft. By 1942, the Navy had realized that the crews of German U-boat could often spot their lumbering bombers overhead well in advance of attack and, as result, would quickly dive beneath the ocean waters in plenty of time to avoid destruction. As a result, military planners came up with an ingenious idea: they placed a line of bright lights on both the wings and the propeller hubs of several experimental aircraft, which could be carefully and ingeniously adjusted to correspond with the background light of the sky. Known as isoluminosity, the technique was essentially a means of camouflage rather than actual invisibility. (6)

Interestingly, investigative writer Charles R. Smith noted in 2005 that: "The U.S. may very well possess an advanced version of *Yahootie*…Not only is the aircraft invisible to radar, but also its skin is layered with an array of high-intensity light panels that broadcast the same output as the sky around it. The daylight stealth aircraft may explain the recent reports of UFO sightings over Iran and North Korea and a series of unidentified aircraft sightings inside and around the U.S." (7)

Similarly, the British Ministry of Defense has admitted that it has secretly funded a project known as *Chameleon* that is designed to significantly diminish the contrast between an aircraft and the sky. But some people maintain that the U.S. Navy, at the height of the Second World War, successfully achieved literal, optical invisibility of exactly the type described within the pages of *The Invisible Man*. (8)

In 1975, George E. Simpson and Neal R. Burger penned a science fiction novel titled *Thin Air* that told the story of a Top Secret experiment undertaken by the U.S. Navy in 1943 to render one of its battleships invisible to Nazi ships and aircraft. (9) An identical scenario was utilized in the 1984 science fiction movie *The Philadelphia Experiment*: military scientists succeed in creating the ultimate in camouflage for the Navy. (10)

In both *Thin Air* and *The Philadelphia Experiment*, however, there are catastrophic side-effects: the ship briefly teleports to another location before returning to its original port; many of the crew-members suffer from recurring hallucinations; some vanish into thin air never to return; while others are left completely, and forever, insane.

And while the movie and the novel are entertaining science fiction stories, they are both based upon longstanding rumors and claims that, despite the best attempts of an exasperated and weary Navy to lay them firmly to rest, absolutely refuse to roll over and die. The rumor holds that during the Second World War, the Navy secretly authorized research into a real Philadelphia Experiment that succeeded in making a warship invisible to the naked-eye but with the same devastating physical and mental effects on its crew as mentioned in the movie and the novel. (11)

The Philadelphia Naval Shipyard

Although the Department of the Navy firmly denies that the Philadelphia Experiment occurred in such a fashion, the files of its Office of Naval Research (ONR) do provide an accurate and concise

summary of the story and the subsequent surrounding allegations, demonstrating that the Navy is at least fully conversant
with the claims of cover-up and conspiracy, even if it utterly
denounces each and every one of them. A fact-sheet specifically
prepared by the ONR in response to the mountain of inquiries
that the Navy has received over the years on the Philadelphia
Experiment states:

The majority of these inquiries are directed to the Office of Naval Research or to the Fourth Naval District in Philadelphia. The
frequency of these queries predictably intensifies each time the
experiment is mentioned by the popular press, often in a science
fiction book. The genesis of the Philadelphia Experiment myth
dates back to 1955 with the publication of *The Case for UFO's* by
the late Morris K. Jessup. (12)

Morris Ketchum Jessup was born on March 20, 1900, in
Rockville, Indiana, and served with the U.S. Army during
the closing stages of the First World War, before taking up
a position as a teacher of both astronomy and mathematics at
Drake University, Iowa, and at the University of Michigan, in
the 1920s. In later years, Jessup developed a keen interest in
the culture of the Mayans and the Incas, and ultimately came
to a remarkable conclusion: that these two fantastic civilisa-
tions and their incredible cities could only have come to fruition with the aid of outside help, namely, extraterrestrial visitors. This was a particular theme that Jessup expanded upon
greatly in later years, and in 1956 his thoughts and findings
were published in his celebrated book, *The Case for the UFO*,
which focussed on two key issues: the power source of UFOs
and the utilization of the universal gravitational field as an energy source. (13)

When his research was at its height, Jessup stated: "If the
money, thought, time, and energy now being poured uselessly
into the development of rocket propulsion were invested in a

basic study of gravity, beginning perhaps with continued research into Dr. [Albert] Einstein's Unified Field concepts, it is altogether likely that we could have effective and economical space travel, at but a small fraction of the costs we are now incurring, within the next decade." (14) [The attempts to develop a unified field theory are grounded in the belief that all physical phenomena should ultimately be explainable by some underlying unity.] (15)

The Navy files continue:

Some time after the publication of the book, Jessup received correspondence from a Carlos Miquel Allende, who gave his address as R.D. #1, Box 223, New Kensington, Pa. In his correspondence, Allende commented on Jessup's book and gave details of an alleged secret naval experiment conducted by the Navy in Philadelphia in 1943. During the experiment, according to Allende, a ship was rendered invisible and teleported to and from Norfolk in a few minutes, with some terrible after-effects for crewmembers.

Supposedly, this incredible feat was accomplished by applying Einstein's "unified field" theory. Allende claimed that he had witnessed the experiment from another ship and that the incident was reported in a Philadelphia newspaper. The identity of the newspaper has never been established. Similarly, the identity of Allende is unknown, and no information exists on his present address. (16)

Variously referring to himself as Carl M. Allen and Carlos Miguel Allende, the letter writer maintained, in a bizarre, rambling style full of out-of-place capitals and spelling errors, that it was one pseudonymous Dr. Franklin Reno who had actually succeeded in developing an application of Einstein's theory that was then capitalized upon by the Navy for its Philadelphia Experiment.

According to Allende, the ship used in the experiment was the DE 173 *USS Eldridge*, and that he, Allende, had actually witnessed one of the attempts to make both the ship and its crew optically invisible from his position out at sea onboard a steamer, the *SS Andrew Furuseth*. From the safety of the *Furuseth*, Allende "watched the air all around the ship turn slightly, ever so slightly, darker than all the other air. I saw, after a few minutes, a foggy green mist arise like a cloud. I watched as thereafter the DE 173 became rapidly invisible to human eyes." (17)

On this matter, and in one of his oddly written letters to Jessup, Allende recorded the following:

I wish to Mention that Somehow, also, The Experimental Ship Disappeared from it Philadelphia Dock and only a Very few Minutes Later appeared at its other Dock in the Norfolk Newport News, Portsmouth area. This was distinctly AND clearly Identified as being that place BUT the ship then, again, Disappeared And Went Back to its Philadelphia Dock in only a Very Few Minutes or Less. This was also Noted in the newspapers But I forget what paper I read it in or When It happened. Probably Late in the experiments May have been in 1956 after Experiments were discontinued, I can Not Say for Sure. (18)

As for the crew of the *Eldridge*, Allende had some dark tales to relate:

There are only a very few of the original Experimental DE's Crew Left by Now, Sir. Most went insane, one just walked 'throo' His quarters Wall in sight of His Wife & Child a 2 other crew Members (WAS NEVER SEEN AGAIN). The experiment Was a Complete Success. The Men Were Complete Failures. Half of the officers & the crew of that Ship are at Present, Mad as Hatters. (19)

It is a matter of official record that Carlos Allende did serve aboard the *SS Andrew Furuseth* during the time frame that he claimed to have been exposed to the secret experiment. Crucial to the entire controversy surrounding the *USS Eldridge*, however, is whether or not the case for the reality of the Philadelphia Experiment stands or falls on the word of Allende alone.

As investigator and author Bill Moore, co-author of the 1979 book, *The Philadelphia Experiment*, states firmly: "If the tale of the Philadelphia Experiment is nothing more than a science fiction yarn concocted out of thin air by an unbalanced Allen(de), then it should be impossible to discover any sources of information about the experiment dating any earlier than Allen(de)'s 1955-56 series of letters to Jessup. The very fact that such sources do exist, and that none of them had ever heard of Carl(os) Allen(de)...is sufficient to at least lend serious question to the Allen(de)-as-perpetrator argument, if not to utterly destroy it." (20)

The fact that there are sources other than Allende who assert that the Philadelphia Experiment did occur led to the next strange turn of events in this weird saga, namely, high-level official interest in Jessup's book, as the Navy's files clearly demonstrate.

In 1956 a copy of Jessup's book was mailed anonymously to ONR. The pages of the book were interspersed with hand-written comments which alleged a knowledge of UFO's, their means of motion, the culture and ethos of the beings occupying these UFO's, described in pseudo-scientific and incoherent terms.

Two officers, then assigned to ONR, took a personal interest in the book and showed it to Jessup. Jessup concluded that the writer of those comments on his book was the same person who had written him about the Philadelphia Experiment. These two officers personally had the book retyped and arranged for the reprint, in typewritten form, of 25 copies. The officers and their personal belongings have left ONR many years ago, and ONR does not have a file copy of the annotated book. (21)

If the involvement of the ONR in the story was not enough to have conspiracy theorists salivating like Pavlov's dogs, Jessup's alleged suicide on April 29, 1959, at the Dale County

Park, Florida, most certainly was. To this day rumors continue to circulate among those who believe in the *Eldridge's* disappearing act that Jessup's death may have been a prime example of nothing less than a state-sponsored murder, specifically undertaken as part of an official effort to hide the truth about the strange story of the invisible ship. (22)

The Navy has been very careful not to comment upon the controversy surrounding Jessup's untimely demise. But it does have an opinion with regard to what it believes may really have led to the legend of the Philadelphia Experiment:

> Personnel at the Fourth Naval District believe that the questions surrounding the so-called "Philadelphia Experiment" arise from quite routine research which occurred during World War II at the Philadelphia Naval Shipyard. Until recently, it was believed that the foundation for the apocryphal stories arose from degaussing experiments which have the effect of making a ship undetectable or "invisible" to magnetic mines. (23)

The Navy elaborates:

> Degaussing is a process in which a system of electrical cables are installed around the circumference of ship's hull, running from bow to stern on both sides. A measured electrical current is passed through these cables to cancel out the ship's magnetic field. Degaussing equipment was installed in the hull of Navy ships and could be turned on whenever the ship was in waters that might contain magnetic mines, usually shallow waters in combat areas. It could be said that degaussing, correctly done, makes a ship "invisible" to the sensors of magnetic mines, but the ship remains visible to the human eye, radar, and underwater listening devices. (24)

Just to confuse things, however, the Navy offers yet another theory to explain the effects on the crew:

43

Another likely genesis of the bizarre stories about levitation, teleportation and effects on human crewmembers might be attributed to experiments with the generating plant of a destroyer, the *USS Timmerman*. In the 1950's this ship was part of an experiment to test the effects of a small, high frequency generator providing 1000 hz. instead of the standard 400hz. The higher frequency generator produced corona discharges, and other well-known phenomena associated with high frequency generators. None of the crew suffered effects from the experiment. (25)

Nevertheless, these explanations did not sway the believers, who continue to allege that the *Eldridge* was directly involved in a super-secret experiment that resulted in the ship becoming invisible. For its part, the Navy maintains that it has fully reviewed all of the available files on the *Eldridge*, and unswervingly asserts that those same files contain nothing to confirm those allegations. On this matter, the Navy says:

Records in the Operational Archives Branch of the Naval Historical Center have been repeatedly searched, but no documents have been located which confirm the event, or any interest by the Navy in attempting such an achievement.

The ship involved in the experiment was supposedly the *USS Eldridge*. Operational Archives has reviewed the deck log and war diary from *Eldridge's* commissioning on 27 August 1943 at the New York Navy Yard through December 1943. The following description of *Eldridge's* activities are summarized from the ship's war diary.

After commissioning, *Eldridge* remained in New York and in the Long Island Sound until 16 September when it sailed to Bermuda. From 18 September, the ship was in the vicinity of Bermuda undergoing training and sea trials until 15 October when *Eldridge* left in a convoy for New York where the convoy entered on 18 October. *Eldridge* remained in New York harbor until 1 November when it was part of the escort for Convoy UGS-23 (New York Section).

On 2 November the convoy entered Naval Operating Base, Norfolk. On 3 November, *Eldridge* and Convoy UGS-23 left for Casablanca where it arrived on 22 November. On 29 November,

Eldridge left as one of escorts for Convoy GUS-22 and arrived with the convoy on 17 December at New York harbor. *Eldridge* remained in New York on availability training and in Block Island Sound until 31 December when it steamed to Norfolk with four other ships. During this time frame, *Eldridge* was never in Philadelphia. (26)

And, with respect to the allegations that the *SS Andrew Furuseth* was somehow implicated in this distinctly strange affair, the Navy notes the following:

Supposedly, the crew of the civilian merchant ship *SS Andrew Furuseth* observed the arrival via teleportation of the *Eldridge* into the Norfolk area. *Andrew Furuseth's* movement report cards are in the Tenth Fleet records in the custody of the Modern Military Branch, National Archives and Records Administration, (8601 Adelphi Road, College Park, MD 20740-6001), which also has custody of the action reports, war diaries and deck logs of all World War II Navy ships, including *Eldridge*.

The movement report cards list the merchant ship's ports of call, the dates of the visit, and convoy designation, if any. The movement report card shows that *Andrew Furuseth* left Norfolk with Convoy UGS-15 on 16 August 1943 and arrived at Casablanca on 2 September. The ship left Casablanca on 19 September and arrived off Cape Henry on 4 October. *Andrew Furuseth* left Norfolk with Convoy UGS-22 on 25 October and arrived at Oran on 12 November.

The ship remained in the Mediterranean until it returned with Convoy GUS-25 to Hampton Roads on 17 January 1944. The Archives has a letter from Lieutenant Junior Grade William S. Dodge, USNR, (Ret.), the Master of *Andrew Furuseth* in 1943, categorically denying that he or his crew observed any unusual event while in Norfolk. *Eldridge* and *Andrew Furuseth* were not even in Norfolk at the same time. (27)

And what of those allegations that Einstein was involved in Top Secret invisibility experiments? Again, the Navy has an answer for this controversial assertion as well:

The Office of Naval Research has stated that the use of force fields to make a ship and her crew invisible does not conform to known physical laws. ONR also claims that Dr. Albert Einstein's Unified Field Theory was never completed. During 1943-1944, Einstein was a part-time consultant with the Navy's Bureau of Ordnance, undertaking theoretical research on explosives and explosions. There is no indication that Einstein was involved in research relevant to invisibility or to teleportation. (28)

And on one final crucial point, the Office of Naval Research is adamant:

ONR has never conducted any investigations on invisibility, either in 1943 or at any other time (ONR was established in 1946.) In view of present scientific knowledge, ONR scientists do not believe that such an experiment could be possible except in the realm of science fiction. (29)

Not everyone agrees with the Navy's "realm of science fiction " assertions, however. Indeed, there is now a substantial body of evidence to show that there may well be far more to the Philadelphia Experiment than the mere ravings of a solitary lunatic. For example, interesting data suggests that attempts were made as far back as the 1930s to make a man invisible in a fashion very similar to that described by H.G. Wells in the pages of *The Invisible Man*.

Consider the following extract from an article that appeared in the May 1934, issue of *Popular Mechanics*. Titled "Photographs Show a Man Becoming Invisible," it states:

After years of research, a young British inventor claims to have produced an apparatus which can render a man invisible although he still stands before you in the flesh. Operation of the device, which is being used for exhibition purposes, is a closely guarded secret but the man who is to disappear is clothed in what is described as an 'electro-helmet' and a spectral mantle.

In this garb he looks like a deep-sea diver as he stands in

a cabinet, open at the front, on a brilliantly lighted stage. With both hands he touches contact gloves above his head and an electric current is switched on. As the current becomes stronger, it is claimed that the man seems to become transparent, then gradually vanishes, the feet disappearing first, followed by the rest of the body, and finally the head. (30)

Similar accounts abound. In the 1940s, Britain's BBC broadcast a radio series called *Brains Trust*. The December 21, 1943, edition highlighted a conversation between the English philosopher C.E.M. Joad, the writer Rupert T. Gould, and a navy official, one A.B. Campbell. The latter related the story of a sailor who allegedly was seen walking through a ship's bulkhead, before quite literally vanishing. Interestingly, Campbell's revelations surfaced less than two months after the alleged date of the Philadelphia Experiment–and, of course, long before the publication of the Jessup book and the surfacing of the admittedly odd ravings of Allende. (31)

And *Popular Mechanics* and *Brains Trust* are not the only sources of such material. Investigators Bill Moore and Charles Berlitz uncovered an intriguing clipping allegedly culled from a still-unidentified newspaper of the 1940s that appears to confirm one of the strangest aspects of Allende's account: that some of the sailors on-board the *Eldridge* during the fateful (and fatal) experiment later vanished into thin air during a barroom brawl near the Philadelphia harbour.

Titled "Strange Circumstances Surround Tavern Brawl," the clipping reveals the following:

Several city police officers responding to a call to aid members of the Navy Shore Patrol in breaking up a tavern brawl near the U.S. Navy docks here last night got something of a surprise when they arrived on the scene to find the place empty of customers. According to a pair of very nervous waitresses, the Shore Patrol had arrived first and cleared the place out–but not before two of the sailors involved allegedly did a disappearing act. "They just sort of vanished into thin air... right there," reported one of the frightened hostesses, "and I ain't been drinking either!" At that point, according to her account, the Shore Patrol proceeded to hustle everybody out of the place in short order.

A subsequent chat with the local police precinct left no doubts as to the fact that some sort of general brawl had indeed occurred in the vicinity of the dockyards at about eleven o'clock last night, but neither confirmation nor denial of the stranger aspects of the story could be immediately obtained. One reported witness succinctly summed up the affair by dismissing it as nothing more than "a lot of hooey from them daffy dames down there," who, he went on to say, were probably just looking for some free publicity. Damage to the tavern was estimated to be in the vicinity of six hundred dollars. (32)

Moore and Berlitz conclude that: "Little else can be said about the clipping itself. Anything approaching a proper analysis of the clipping is impossible, since the authors possess a photocopy only. Upon close examination, however, the possibly significant fact emerges that the column width is a bit greater than was used by any of the Philadelphia dailies in the 1940s. This suggests that the article may have originated in a local or regional newspaper in the Philadelphia area rather than in one of the metropolitan papers." (33)

In summing up, Moore and Berlitz state: "Until the article itself can be actually verified either by identifying the source of the photocopy or by discovering the name and date of the newspaper in which the article originally appeared, its existence will continue to remain a puzzle." (34)

While the origin and authenticity (or otherwise) of the elusive clipping remains a puzzle, the same cannot be said for every aspect of the story concerning the so-called "Bar-room Brawl." In February 1999, George Mayerchak, who served in the U.S. Navy from 1948 until 1952, revealed some startling data surrounding his own, personal knowledge of what prompted the aforementioned, curious newspaper report.

It was 1949, Mayerchak said, and at the time he was confined to the Philadelphia Navy Hospital for a month with a particularly bad bout of pneumonia. While he was there, however, Mayerchak began to hear whispered stories from both enlisted sailors and "some of the C.O.'s" concerning a strange event that had occurred at a local tavern near the Philadelphia Naval Yard in late 1943–an event that very closely fits the contents of the newspaper clipping described by Moore and Berlitz.

Mayerchak, however, disputed the claim that the sailors in question disappeared without a trace; rather, he maintained, it was his understanding that instead they had briefly "flickered on and off." As for the so-called "daffy dames" at the tavern, Mayerchak commented: "Oh, yeah, those gals were scared, because these guys walked into the bar and they seemed to almost disappear or something." From Mayerchak's own perspective, however, the most important aspect of his recollections is that he heard these accounts no later than 1949 – a full seven years before Carlos Allende told his story to Morris Jessup. (35)

Bill Moore also cites the testimony of one Harry Euton, who was reportedly involved in a top-secret wartime experiment to test a new concept of camouflage for ships against enemy radar:

Euton went on to relate that during the experiment something went wrong and the ship literally "vanished" from the second anti-aircraft mount to the rear of the vessel. Suddenly the ship had no bottom and no stern. Euton described himself as standing, but with nothing beneath him to stand on. Several other people who had been near him at the time simply vanished with the ship. Other people forward of him were visible, but they did not look like they did normally–a point which Euton had steadfastly refused to clarify or even to discuss further. At the same time, Euton said that...his automatic reaction to "reach out and grab something to keep from falling" resulted in his grasping a cable or a pipe which he could feel but not see. (36)

Taken as a whole, one could argue that the Philadelphia Experiment may well have had at least some roots outside the world of fantasy. But even if there is some truth to the controversy, the full story seems to have vanished into the same swirling cauldron of invisibility that allegedly enveloped the *Eldridge* itself all those years ago.

■ ■ ■ | | | 6 | | ■ ■ ■

The Strange World of Kirk Allen

*"…I was taking part in cosmic adventures, sharing the exhilara-
tion of the sweeping extravaganza he had plotted."*

Today, in all probability, very few people have ever heard of a
strange, yet remarkably compelling book titled *The Fifty Minute Hour* that was written by a Dr. Robert Lindner in 1955
– that also turned out to be the year of the doctor's untimely,
early death. Born in New York City, Lindner had developed a
deep and long-lasting passion for science fiction as a child, and
received his Ph.D. in psychology from Cornell University in
1938. He went on to a short career as a psychoanalyst, his most
memorable work being this collection of five psychoanalytic
case studies. (1)

The fifth, and final, case study presented in his book was
titled "The Jet-Propelled Couch" and was certainly the most
significant chapter of all. It concerns the strange, and even eerie, story of a brilliant, yet deeply disturbed, physicist dubbed
by Lindner as one "Kirk Allen." Notably, Allen reportedly
worked at an ultra-secret government facility somewhere in
the southwest, possibly New Mexico, and maybe even at the
famous home of the atomic bomb: Los Alamos itself. (2)

According to Lindner, Allen's immediate supervisor had
telephoned Lindner one day, deeply concerned and worried
by the startling fact that Allen had been laboriously commit-
ting to paper reams and reams of strange, hieroglyphic-style
writing and seemed to be exhibiting distinct signs of extreme

The Los Alamos National Laboratory. From here "Kirk Allen" traveled to alien worlds. In his mind, at least...

mental-illness. Worse still, from the perspective of the supervisor, was the fact that when Allen was asked what he was doing, he matter-of-factly replied that he was a being from another world – and in a far-off solar system, no less. Somewhat amusingly, Allen then went on to deeply apologize to his boss for how much time he was allocating to his strange writings, and he promised that in future he would try and spend much more time on Earth. But there was a far more significant and serious issue, too: although Linder had been very careful to avoid providing a detailed description of where Allen worked, the rumor (which was never actually confirmed by Lindner) was that Allen was nothing less than a key figure in the development of the atomic bomb for the top-secret Manhattan Project during the Second World War. (3)

In August 1942, the Manhattan Engineer District was created by the government to meet the goal of producing an atomic weapon under the pressure of ongoing global war. Its central mission became known as the Manhattan Project. Under the direction of Brigadier General Leslie Groves of the Army Corps of Engineers, who had supervised the construction of the Pentagon, secret atomic energy communities were created almost overnight in Oak Ridge, Tennessee, at Los Alamos, New Mexico, and in Hanford, Washington, to house the workers and gigantic new machinery needed to produce the bomb. The weapon itself would be built at the Los Alamos laboratory, under the direction of physicist J. Robert Oppenheimer. (4)

Needless to say, if a scientist engaged on such a sensitive and secret project was indeed suffering from strange, alien-driven delusions, then not only was this a matter that should be rectified quickly, it was also one that – potentially, at least - had major national security implications.

Not surprisingly, officials duly dispatched Allen to Baltimore, which was where Lindner was based and had his office. Lindner described Allen, the son of a navy man, as being in his thirties with blonde hair and a love of seersucker suits and Panama hats. It seems that Allen's troubles had all begun in his youth when, after a traumatic sexual encounter with an older woman, he read a science fiction novel written by "a famous English author," in which the hero of the novel shared the same name as Allen and subsequently embarked upon an ever-escalating life of fantasy in an effort to subconsciously block out the earlier trauma.

Of course, Kirk Allen was merely a pseudonym created by Lindner to carefully protect the privacy of his deranged patient, but it has been suggested that the hero in question was John Carter of Edgar Rice Burroughs' Martian adventure novels. Whether or not there was a real John Carter, who was engaged on secret work for the Manhattan Project at Los Alamos, however, is something that is still unknown and an issue very much wide open to deep debate.

What is known for certain is that as Allen's strange mental condition progressed (if "progressed" is the correct term to use), he came to the startling conclusion that he was himself nothing less than an alien, firmly trapped inside the body of a human being. Somewhat astonishingly, Allen actually seemed to incorporate these odd beliefs quite comfortably into his everyday existence, though by the time he reached his thirties Allen had become a slave to his out-of-this-world delusions: they began to completely take over, and control, every aspect of his day-to-day existence—hence the concern shown by his "government" colleagues.

Indeed, in a complicated and somewhat convoluted fashion that saw him using the science fiction novels that he had read in his youth as a veritable springboard, Allen began to compile a truly huge amount of data in support of his bizarre delusions and beliefs. He would describe in truly excruciating detail the fantastic alien worlds he had traveled to, the nature of the incredible and bizarre life that existed on those planets, and their civilizations, histories, and politics.

It must be said that Lindner was truly shocked to the core when Allen finally showed him the mass of material that he had collated on his claimed journeys and adventures around the universe: a 12,000 page autobiography of his otherworldly exploits told in two hundred chapters, a further 2,000 pages of extensive notes and annotations, a 100-page-long glossary of alien names and terminology, 82 maps showing the continents and cities of the major worlds that Allen had "visited," as well as an abundance of drawings, tables, and charts. Even stranger was a two-hundred-page document that told the story of an alien "empire" that Allen himself ruled over (albeit in "astral" form, while his physical body remained on Earth, somewhat conveniently); as well as various memoranda on a variety of alien worlds, with titles such as *The Metabiology of the Valley Dwellers*, *The Transportation System of Seraneb*, *The Application of Unified Field Theory and the Mechanics of the Stardrive to Space Travel*, *Anthropological Studies on Srom Olma I*, and *Plant Biology and Genetic Science of Srom Olma I*.

At a personal level, Lindner was almost overwhelmed by the sheer volume of Allen's crazed delusions and his extraordinary written output–partly due to the fact that he had Allen submit to extensive and prolonged physical and neurological tests, all of which came back completely normal. This only deepened Lindner's interest and fascination in his number-one patient. Was it possible, therefore, that Allen was actually, and incredibly, speaking some semblance of truth? Was an employee of what was without any doubt the most sensitive and secret military project of the 20th century really an alien being in disguise? As a devoted fan of science fiction from a very young age, Lindner actually found himself beginning to muse upon the possibility that there might have been far more to Allen's claims than just the ravings of a mentally deranged but infinitely intelligent, individual, after all.

As prime evidence of this, Lindner recorded that: "At a startlingly rapid rate...larger and larger areas of my mind were being taken over by the fantasy...With Kirk's puzzled assistance I was taking part in cosmic adventures, sharing the exhilaration of the sweeping extravaganza he had plotted."

Although Lindner did not know it at the time, Allen had finally come to the realization, after many lengthy therapy sessions, that he was simply delusional after all, and that his alien excursions had no basis in reality outside of his own fantastic imagination. But truly ironic and even weirder is the fact that as Allen came to accept his delusion state, Lindner was actually beginning to believe Allen's tales of visiting far-off alien worlds, and Allen decided to continue the cosmic charade out of concern for the well-being of his friendly, devoted therapist! (5)

The renowned Carl Sagan, who studied the Kirk Allen saga, asked some provocative questions: "What if the physicist hadn't confessed? Might Lindner have convinced himself, beyond a reasonable doubt that it really was possible to slip into a more romantic era? Would he have said he started out as a skeptic, but was convinced by the sheer weight of the evidence? After a few similar cases, would Lindner have impatiently resisted all arguments of the 'Be reasonable, Bob' variety, and deduced he was penetrating some new level of reality?" (6)

But a far more important question remains: who really was Kirk Allen? Was he actually a senior physicist with the secret Manhattan Project? Or did he hold a position of responsibility and sensitivity in another top-secret arm of government or the military?

A persistent rumor within science fiction circles suggests that Allen was, in reality, Dr. Paul Myron Anthony Linebarger, who wrote science fiction stories under the pen name of Cordwainer Smith. Even outside of the world of literary fantasy, Linebarger was a notable figure in his very own right. As the godson to Dr. Sun Yat Sen, the father of the Chinese Republic, he grew up in Asia and received his Ph.D. in political science at the age of 23 from Johns Hopkins University, Baltimore (which was, perhaps not entirely coincidental, the state in which Dr. Robert Lindner had his office). During the Second World War, he served in China as an intelligence officer; and after the war penned a highly influential textbook, titled *Psychological Warfare*, and served as a colonel in U.S. Army Intelligence. Linebarger also advised the British Army during their suppression of Malayan nationalists and advised the American military on matters pertaining to psychological warfare. (7)

On the possibility that Allen was really Linebarger, Alan

C. Elms, a researcher and writer who has dug very deeply into the Kirk Allen controversy, states: "That identification of Kirk Allen was first published in Brian Aldiss's 1973 history of [sci-fi], *Billion Year Spree*. But Aldiss didn't take credit for the idea. As he said in a footnote, 'I am indebted to Dr. Leon Stover for evidence that 'Kirk' is, in fact, the pseudonym for...Cordwainer Smith.' And who is Leon Stover? He's an anthropologist, a China expert, a science fiction scholar, an occasional collaborator with Harry Harrison." (8)

After contacting Stover, Elms received a rather mysterious reply. Stover, writes Elms, said that "his remark to Aldiss about the Lindner-Linebarger connection had been intended as a private confidence, and he sternly ordered me not to mention his name 'at all' in my research. He implied that I was reaching for secret government stuff and had better back off." (9)

Was Kirk Allen really Paul Linebarger? Or was he someone else, whose real identity is now firmly and forever lost to the inevitable fog of time, and who worked on classified atomic research at Los Alamos? And what was it that prompted Leon Stover to advise Alan C. Elms to "back off" from his research? The answers to those questions are, in all likelihood, destined to remain just as enigmatic and as mysterious as the almost-other-worldly Kirk Allen himself.

■ ■ ■ ▌ ▐ ‖ 7 ‖ ▐ ■ ■ ■

The Dwarf, the Deros, and the Discs

*"I don't care much whether you believe or not,
I'm sick of the whole mess."*

The saga of the flying saucer began with the pilot Kenneth Arnold, whose June 24, 1947, encounter over the Cascade Mountains of Washington State kicked off the modern era of UFO sightings. At approximately three o'clock that afternoon, Arnold was searching for an aircraft that had reportedly crashed on the southwest side of Mt. Rainier. (1) At the time of its occurrence, Arnold's encounter with the flying disks attracted the keen interest of not just the public and the media, but also that of the all-powerful Federal Bureau of Investigation. The following is a verbatim statement made by Arnold, himself, and taken from previously Secret FBI records of 1947 that confirm their deep interest in his strange encounter:

I hadn't flown more than two or three minutes on my course when a bright flash reflected on my airplane. It startled me as I thought I was too close to some other aircraft. I looked every place in the sky and couldn't find where the reflection had come from until I looked to the left and the north of Mt. Rainier, where I observed a chain of nine peculiar looking aircraft flying from north to south at approximately 9,500 feet elevation and going, seemingly, in a definite direction of about 170 degrees.

I thought it was very peculiar that I couldn't find their tails but assumed they were some type of jet plane. The more I observed these objects, the more upset I became, as I am accustomed and familiar with most all objects flying whether I am close to the ground or at higher altitudes. The chain of these saucer-like objects [was] at least five miles long. I felt confident after I would land there would be some explanation of what I saw. (2)

No conclusive explanation for Arnold's sighting ever surfaced, and the mystery regarding what he did or did not see on that day has now raged for more than sixty years. Three days before Arnold's encounter, however, another UFO incident is alleged to have occurred – at Maury Island, Tacoma, Washington. This strange story concerns key personalities involved in the formative years of pulp science fiction magazines, crashed flying saucers, government agents, Men in Black, Kenneth Arnold himself, and the highly suspicious deaths of key figures in this episode. And it all began with a hunchbacked dwarf named Raymond Arthur Palmer, who had a deep fascination with sci-fi.

Born in 1910, Ray Palmer had a difficult childhood: at the age of seven, he was hit by a truck, which shattered his spine. Worse still, surgery on Palmer's spinal column only aggravated the situation and severely stunted his growth, hence his dwarfish frame. As a youngster the solitary Palmer immersed himself in the science fiction publications of the day, which he eagerly and regularly devoured. Realizing that he had stumbled upon his true calling in life, Palmer became ever more fascinated by – and obsessed with – the world of fantasy and science fiction and established, in 1930, what is widely recognized today as the first science fiction fanzine: *The Comet*. But Palmer's big breakthrough came in 1938. (2)

That was the year in which Ziff-Davis, the publisher of the influential science fiction magazine *Amazing Stories*, transferred production from New York to Chicago, and promptly fired the then editor, T. O'Connor-Sloane. As Palmer lived nearby, in Milwaukee, the company inquired of Palmer if he would be at all interested in becoming the new editor of the

Office Men,candum • UNITED ,OTES GOVERNMENT

TO   : D. M. LADD   DATE: August 6, 1947

FROM   : ████████████

SUBJECT: FLYING SAUCERS

Special Agent ████████████ of the Liaison Section contacted Lieutenant Colonel ████████ Army Air Forces Intelligence, inquiring about an article which appeared in the West Coast newspapers recently stating in substance that an airplane carrying recovered flying saucers, crashed in route from Portland, Oregon, to Los Angeles, California.

████████████ advised ████████ that the only information that has been received by Headquarters of the Army Air Forces is that a CIC Agent of the 4th Air Force Headquarters, Hamilton Field, San Francisco, was killed in an airplane crash. The Headquarters of the Air Forces have been advised that he was on a top secret mission. ████████ indicated that he was under the impression that the CIC Agent was either on route to or from an interview with ████████ who is one of the individuals who first saw one of the flying saucers.

RECORDED
████████████ stated that the Air Forces have no additional information and will receive none until the report is received from the 4th Air Force. ████████ suggested that the San Francisco Field Office contact Colonel ████████ Headquarters 4th Air Force, Hamilton Field, San Francisco, who undoubtedly would be able to furnish the details regarding this matter which are at this time unknown by the Headquarters of the Air Forces. ████████ pointed out to ████████, however, that it was his belief that no flying saucers have been recovered but that it was merely an attempt to reinterview an individual who previously had reported seeing one of the flying saucers.

A previously-classified FBI report on the "Maury Island UFO" caper of 1947 in the state of Washington.

publication. For Palmer, of course, this was an absolute dream come true, and he readily, and heartily, accepted the cosmic challenge. Not everyone was happy with the new editor, however, as poorly written, fast-paced adventures replaced what had previously been provoking science fiction. (3)

"Hard-core SF fans were disappointed by the new *Amazing*," notes writer Bruce Lanier-Wright, "and most of its prose was fairly dire even by pulp standards, but it was lively and well-received by the casual newsstand readership, the one yardstick that interested its owners." (4)

Nevertheless, Palmer did have at least two claims to fame: during his time with *Amazing Stories* he purchased Isaac

Asimov's first professional story, "Marooned off Vesta," and he became a big champion of something that went on to become known as the Shaver Mystery. (5)

This mystery all began in 1943 when a man named Richard Shaver wrote a very strange letter to *Amazing Stories*. Shaver stated that he had uncovered the secrets of an ancient race of people who, thousands of years ago, had abandoned their lifestyle of highly advanced surface-dwellers and elected instead to build huge, underground cities where they lived for millennia before finally leaving the Earth altogether for a new world in a star system far away. Not only that, but Shaver had succeeded in deciphering the secret and archaic language of the ancients, which was apparently known as Mantong.

And how, precisely, had Shaver uncovered these stunning facts? Was he an "Indiana Jones" traveling to exotic locales in search of adventure and intrigue? Not exactly. In 1932, Shaver said, he was working in a automobile factory as a welder, when, one day, his welding gun began telepathically transmitting to him the thoughts of his work colleagues. But of greater concern to Shaver was the fact that his wondrous gun was also able to pick up the thoughts of an untold number of people who were being imprisoned and tortured deep underground.

An enthusiastic and excited Palmer quickly wrote back to Shaver asking for more details. The welding-weirdo responded with a fantastic, 10,000-word account in which he explained that after this prehistoric race had exited the Earth for pastures new millennia ago, they left behind them all of their diseased offspring who, over time, had devolved into a race of mentally deranged sadists known as the Deros–or Detrimental Robots. Most alarming, the Deros were routinely kidnapping human beings at a truly alarming rate and were taking them to their underground caverns and caves where they were used as food for the utterly insane Deros. Shaver claimed to know this because he himself had been held prisoner by the dastardly creatures for a considerable period of time.

Recognizing that, regardless of whether or not there was any literal truth to Shaver's outrageous, rambling report, it was still a monumentally entertaining story, Palmer duly and laboriously reworked it, ultimately publishing it under the title of "I Remember Lemuria" in the March 1945 issue of *Amazing Stories*. The issue became an instant bestseller, and Palmer claimed that over the next few years the magazine's offices received literally tens of thousands of letters on the subject from fans all eager to learn more about the strange world of the Deros, or to provide details of their own encounters with the creatures of the underworld. (6) Among the latter group was a highly enigmatic character named Fred Crisman.

In the May 1947 issue of *Amazing Stories,* a letter written by Crisman was published that detailed one such encounter. Crisman's main reason for writing was actually to highlight and critique an article that had appeared in the September 1946 issue of *Harper's Magazine*, in which writer William S. Baring-Gould expressed his deep criticism of Palmer's audience.

Quoting a New York fanzine, *Fantasy Commentator*, Baring-Gould wrote that the readers of *Amazing Stories* "are not interested in learning anything which would change their beliefs...they can learn more from their inner consciousness than from without; and some have gone so far as to state that they abhor mathematics and allied modern sciences because they disprove their beliefs. [Palmer's publications] propitiate these crackpots' views in fictional guise." (7)

This totally outraged Crisman and, taking issue with Baring-Gould's words, he wrote to Palmer:

I have just finished reading the September issue of *Harper's Magazine,* and I noted where William S. Baring-Gould had selected my letter to you last winter as an example of crackpot letters. I bitterly resent this. It is all well and good to sit in a comfortable office or home and look upon far places and strange things as through a veil of unbelief; however, when you are there and death looks you right in the eye, you feel a little different and the safe, comfortable U.S.A. becomes the world of never-was and "does it really exist?" I felt that you, too, Mr. Palmer had given me up for a jerk who was only trying to pull your leg. Well, you see how it is. Dick and I have made our Alaska journey and we failed, we lost and we lost a lot, Dick lost his life. The details I don't suppose you are interested in; however, Shaver would get a kick out of a journey to the Alaska cave. It seems strange to read AS and see the "little" people still wondering and still "investigating" their claims of caves. Go and take a look for yourself, I say. Sure, it takes money and guts. I know; I have spent all I have of both. It sickens me when I read an article like Gould's. So smug and sure. After all, Dick is dead, and that meant a lot to me. I don't care much whether you believe or not, I'm sick of the whole mess. I don't even want to think of last year, and of Alaska least of all. Just wanted to go on record as being further sickened by Gould's article. (8)

Palmer printed his own response to Crisman's letter in the same issue of *Amazing Stories*: "…we are interested in the details of your little journey, and we offer herewith to publish your story of that Alaska cave complete. Our readers want proof. We want proof. If you've got any at all, we want it." (9)

Crisman failed to respond. But it hardly mattered, as only a month later Kenneth Arnold's historic UFO encounter over the Cascade Mountains eclipsed the Dero controversy, and the media and the science fiction magazines of the day were full of talk about flying saucers as well as theories concerning their possible origins and motives. Indeed, Palmer played an integral role in the Arnold saga himself. Although many UFO researchers and writers are keen to distance their subject from the world of sci-fi, it is an often-neglected fact that Arnold's 1952 book on his experience, *The Coming of the Saucers: A Documentary Report on Sky Objects That Have Mystified the World*, was co-written with Palmer and was even published by Palmer's own company. Arnold had also written articles in 1948 in the spring and summer issues of *Fate* magazine (that Palmer himself founded) titled "I Did See Flying Saucers" and "Are Space Visitors Here?" (10)

It is worth noting, too, that in the build up to the flying saucer craze of the summer of 1947, *Amazing Stories* had been publishing imagery that was astonishingly saucer-like in nature. As evidence of this, in the September 1946 issue of the magazine, Palmer printed a letter from a U.S. Army lieutenant named Ellis L. Lyon, who was concerned by the potential psychological impact of the Shaver Mystery and wrote:

What I am worried about is that there are a few, and perhaps quite large number of readers, who may accept this Shaver Mystery as being founded on fact, even as Orson Welles put across his invasion from Mars, via radio some years ago. It is of course, impossible for the reader to sift out in your "Discussions" and "Reader Comment" features, which are actually letters from readers and which are credited to an *Amazing Stories* staff writer, whipped up to keep alive interest in your fictional theories. However, if the letters are generally the work of readers, it is distressing to see the reaction you have caused in their muddled brains. I refer to the letters from people who have "seen" the exhaust trails of rocket ships or "felt" the influence of radiations from underground sources. (11)

John Keel – the author of the classic book *The Mothman Prophecies* – specifically commenting on *Amazing Stories'* letter-writers like Lyon, said:

Palmer assigned artists to make sketches of objects described by readers and disc-shaped flying machines appeared on the covers of his magazine long before June 1947. So we can note that a considerable number of people–millions–were exposed to the flying saucer concept before the national news media was even aware of it. Anyone who glanced at the magazines on a newsstand and caught a glimpse of the saucers-adorned

Amazing Stories cover had the image implanted in his subconscious. In the course of the two years between March 1945 and June 1947, millions of Americans had seen at least one issue of *Amazing Stories* and were aware of the Shaver Mystery with all of its bewildering implications. Many of these people were out studying the empty skies in the hopes that they, like other *Amazing Stories* readers, might glimpse something wondrous. World War II was over and some new excitement was needed. Raymond Palmer was supplying it. (12)

Perhaps not surprising, therefore (taking into consideration his deep association with *Amazing Stories*), is the fact that less than a month after Kenneth Arnold's UFO encounter, none other than Fred Crisman wrote to Palmer, asserting that three days before Arnold's sighting, he had been implicated in a far more sensational UFO encounter at a place called Maury Island, which was situated in Tacoma, Washington State. Moreover, Crisman claimed to have in his possession fragments from the UFO, which had spectacularly malfunctioned and exploded over the Puget Sound harbor. Realizing that Crisman was already claiming to be deeply implicated in the Shaver Mystery, Palmer unsurprisingly found these new revelations about a flying saucer link to Crisman to be highly suspicious and hired Kenneth Arnold to travel to Tacoma and investigate Crisman's claims for himself – which Arnold did.

The story is that on June 21 a lumber salvager named Harold Dahl, his son, and two still-unidentified individuals witnessed six, disc-shaped aircraft – one in the middle, wobbling in a strange fashion while the remaining objects surrounded it – maneuvering in formation over Puget Sound, Tacoma, at a height of around 2,000 feet. Dahl described the objects as being "shaped like doughnuts," with "five portholes on their sides." Suddenly, the central disk began to wobble even more and dropped to a height of no more than 700 feet. The remaining discs then broke formation, with one of them descending to the same height as the apparently malfunctioning disc, and which then proceeded to "touch it."

Without warning, the malfunctioning disc then began to "spew forth" what appeared to be two different substances: one was a white-colored material that Dahl described as a thin, white "newspaper-like" metal that floated down to the bay; and the other was a black substance, that also hit the water and was reportedly hot enough to "cause steam to rise." Sections of the black substance allegedly hit both Dahl's son and his pet dog, both on the boat, and reportedly killed the unfortunate animal outright.

According to the story, Dahl reported the events in question to his superior, who happened to be none other than Fred Crisman and who was described as being "a harbor patrol officer." Dahl duly convinced Crisman to go to the Maury Island shore and take a look at the strange evidence himself. He did, and claimed that he saw on the shore an "enormous amount" of both the black and the white material and quickly recovered some of it for his own careful safekeeping. Bizarrely, in the immediate aftermath of the affair, Dahl alleged that he was visited by a proto-Man in Black, who warned him never to discuss with anyone what had occurred at Maury Island.

For his part, Kenneth Arnold delved deeply into the story while spending time in town at Palmer's not-inconsiderable expense. He was later joined by two Air Force investigators, a Captain William Lee Davidson and a First Lieutenant Frank Mercer Brown, who were working under General Nathan Twining to collect information on the then-current wave of UFO encounters that was being widely reported across the United States.

Crisman turned over samples of the mysterious debris collected at Puget Sound to the Air Force investigators, who intended to fly the material to its final destination: Wright Field, Ohio. Fate had other, and far deadlier, plans in store for the pair, however. Shortly after Brown and Davidson departed from Washington State, their plane caught fire in mid-air, crashed, and killed both men. A team was dispatched to clean up the site. Reportedly, however, the strange debris had completely vanished.

Many students of the Maury Island story have concluded that the entire event was nothing more than an unfortunate hoax borne out of the science fiction oriented imagination of Crisman – a hoax with a bitterly tragic outcome for Brown and Davidson. The intense and dedicated research of investigative-author Kenn Thomas, however, has shown that the affair might not be as black-and-white as has previously been assumed. Crisman, it seems, moved in highly intriguing and powerful secret circles. (13)

An article that appeared in the May 10, 1946, edition of the *Tacoma News Tribune* described Crisman as being a "special investigator for the State Department of Veteran Affairs," who served in the military during the Second World War, specifically spending 22 months "in the China-Burma-India and Central Pacific theaters as a fighter pilot with the second air commando group." Furthermore, the same news article referred to Crisman as having worked with the Office of Strategic Services–a secret, wartime precursor to today's CIA. Moreover, in the direct wake of the Maury Island caper, Crisman applied for a job with the ultra-secret Atomic Energy Commission that he ultimately declined to take. (14)

Even more startling is the fact that in 1968 Crisman was subpoenaed by New Orleans District Attorney Jim Garrison, as part of Garrison's investigation into the assassination of President John F. Kennedy on November 22, 1963. In a well-known report titled *The Torbitt Document*, Crisman is named as one of three hoboes picked up in the rail-yard directly behind the infamous Grassy Knoll at Dealey Plaza, Dallas, where, some maintain, a second gunman was located during the still-controversial killing of Kennedy. (15)

The passage of time has effectively resulted in many aspects of the Maury Island case remaining utterly unresolved. For some researchers, the case is still nothing more than a hoax from the science fiction fantasies of Fred Crisman and channeled to a gullible and wide-eyed Ray Palmer who was on the hunt for hot tales for *Amazing Stories*. For others, however, it is one of the most important cases of all, involving the actual recovery of debris from a malfunctioning UFO. The involvement of shadowy players on the periphery of the intelligence community, the possibility of the deliberate murder by persons unknown of Air Force personnel in possession of the strange materials recovered at Maury Island, and the indirect links to the JFK assassination, all serve to ensure that the controversy surrounding the Maury Island affair continues, however.

As evidence of this ever-continuing controversy, writer and researcher John Keel strongly suspected that the incident, although a hoax, was employed by the U.S. Government to carefully draw public attention away from controversial claims that hazardous, radioactive waste from a breeder-reactor located in nearby Hanford was being secretly and unlawfully dumped upon Maury Island. (16)

On the other hand, there is the testimony of one Michael Riconosciuto, who was a key player in a saga that investigative journalist Danny Casolaro was pursuing for his proposed book *The Octopus*, the subject matter of which was a shadowy, powerful group of people within the military, government, and intelligence community. The Octopus of the book's title was deeply involved in a host of issues, including UFOs and biological warfare. Casolaro was found dead under very dubious circumstances in a hotel room on August 10, 1991.

Riconosciuto worked with people tied to the shadowy Octopus – a group that also had links to Iran-Contra; the Lockerbie, Scotland, Boeing 747 crash in 1988; gunrunning; and the so-called October Surprise. Michael's father, Marshall, was a close business associate of Fred Crisman. The younger Riconosciuto claims to know the true story behind Maury Island. When interviewed by Kenn Thomas, he offered the possibility that the Maury Island UFOs were some sort of "advanced radar platform" secretly flown by the military, that they were either nuclear-powered or had nuclear materials on board, and that Fred Crisman clandestinely participated in the dissemination of a spurious UFO incident to hide the real story. (17)

Today, all of the key players in the saga are long gone. Shaver continued to tell his stories of the Dero world until the 1970s, although his time in the spotlight was largely over by then. In 1965, somewhat to his consternation, Palmer learned that "Shaver had spent eight years not in the Cavern World, but in a mental institution." (18)

Nevertheless, Palmer was still willing to give Shaver the benefit of doubt and concluded that the Dero-hunter had been speaking truthfully, initially at least; he didn't retreat into an imaginary world, believed Palmer. Rather, Shaver entered a very real world, or "what the psychics say is astral." (19) Palmer died in 1977, still a firm and faithful believer in the unique messages that had issued forth so many years before from Shaver's fantastic welding gun. (20) Crisman had already passed away, in 1975, at the young age of 56 (21), and Kenneth Arnold shuffled off this mortal coil in 1984. (22)

Was Fred Crisman really a deep-cover intelligence agent, hired to officially manipulate Palmer, Arnold, and *Amazing Stories* and to obfuscate the truth behind the UFO mystery in general and the events at Maury Island in particular? Was his involvement designed to hide the fact that the strange things being seen in our skies were, in reality, secret military aircraft of a type that Michael Riconosciuto alluded to? Or was he possibly being completely truthful about the nature of the Maury Island affair? And, if so, did Crisman have in his possession actual fragments of an exploded, alien spacecraft?

Interestingly, researcher Gary Leslie, in an effort to try and resolve the complexities of the Maury Island story once and for all, corresponded with Harold Dahl in the 1960s. And although Dahl stated somewhat enigmatically that he could say very little without Crisman's personal approval, he spoke "glowingly" of Crisman and compared him to the character David Vincent, portrayed by the actor Roy Thinnes in the 1960s science fiction television series *The Invaders*, whose mission and obsession in life it was to hunt down and expose the hostile aliens who have secretly infiltrated human society. (23)

With regard to *The Invaders,* author Otto Binder stated that: "According to *Saucer News* the show was not dropped due to poor ratings but because of the impending resignation of Roy Thinnes, the star. Thinnes was supposedly threatened on various occasions when the show dealt with topics 'too hot to handle.' When Thinnes himself was asked for a comment on the show's demise, he said: 'I have no comment other than the fact that there is more truth behind the TV plots than most people realize.'" (24)

And perhaps there was more truth to Maury Island than people realized, too.

■■▮▮| | 8 | |▮■▮■

Roswell and Crashed UFOs

"If a special type of balloon or drone…had been flown over New Mexico, such a device might well have been brought down during a thunderstorm."

In the summer of 1947, something crashed to earth in the blisteringly hot and barren deserts of New Mexico. The event in question has been the subject of dozens of books, official investigations undertaken by elements of both the government and the U.S. Air Force, numerous television documentaries, a science fiction movie starring Martin Sheen, and intense media coverage and speculation, leaving in its wake a legacy of controversy and a web of intrigue that continue to reverberate more than sixty years later. That event has come to be known infamously as The Roswell Incident.

It is a matter of recorded fact that in early July 1947, the then-Army Air Force announced that it had recovered the remains of a "flying disc" that had been found on a ranch not too far from the town of Roswell, New Mexico. Not surprisingly, intense media frenzy followed in the wake of the announcement and was only brought to a swift and conclusive halt when the AAF hastily retracted its statement: the flying disc story was a huge mistake and nothing more unusual than a weather balloon was retrieved. Today, the Air Force tells a different story: that the debris found at Roswell came not from a weather device but from a top secret balloon-based operation designed to monitor Soviet nuclear tests, and that claims

Welcome to Roswell - the UFO capital of the world.

of unusual-looking or "alien" bodies found at the site were, in reality, based upon witnesses seeing "crash-test dummies" utilized in parachute experiments.

Meanwhile, those who champion the idea that something truly anomalous occurred at Roswell scoff at the ever-mutating assertions of the Pentagon, and maintain that a conspiracy of truly cosmic proportions exists at the highest levels to hide the out-of-this-world truth of the affair and its alien origins.

But what if there was another, distinctly darker explanation behind the Roswell legend – one that summarily dismissed the balloon and crash-test dummy claims but that also laid to rest the theories that extraterrestrials met their deaths in New Mexico? From 1996 to 2004, I spoke with a number of military and intelligence whistleblowers, all of who related to me the details of a series of shocking, alleged, post-Second World War experiments undertaken on American soil. That collective – and admittedly controversial – body of data and testimony formed the crux of my 2005 book *Body Snatchers in the Desert: The Horrible Truth at the Heart of the Roswell Story*, which demonstrated that the Roswell event almost certainly had more to do with classified experimentation undertaken on captured Japanese prisoners of war, who were utilized in secret balloon-based tests in New Mexico to determine the effects of, among other things, high altitude exposure on the human body, than it did with anything of a truly out-of-this-world nature.

In an effort to try and hide the dark and disturbing truth, however, American authorities decided to ingeniously take advantage of the flying saucer craze that existed at the time, and began to carefully spread bogus tales that aliens had crashed at Roswell as a convenient way to bury the much darker truth, just in case the media and the Soviets came looking.

And, it would appear to be the case that someone within the science fiction world seemed to know an awful lot about this very subject as far back as the late 1940s. (1)

Bernard Newman's science fiction novel of 1948, *The Flying Saucer*, was the first in the world to deal with the emotive topic of crashed flying saucers. A prolific author, Newman wrote more than a hundred books on subjects ranging from real-life espionage to global politics and current affairs. It was his brief foray into science fiction and crashed UFOs that was perhaps most notable, however. Published only eleven months after the alleged recovery by the military of a flying saucer at Roswell, New Mexico in July of 1947, *The Flying Saucer* tells the *X-Files*-like tale of an elite group of scientists who decide to secretly stage a series of fake UFO crashes with the express purpose of attempting to unite the world against a deadly alien foe who, in reality, does not even exist.

It appears that Newman's novel was prompted by a speech made by former British Prime Minister Sir Anthony Eden, who in 1947 said: "It seems to be an unfortunate fact that the nations of the world were only really united when they were facing a common menace. What we really needed was an attack from Mars."

Cue Newman's novel.

The Flying Saucer tells of the secret construction of a number of UFO-type craft by human scientists, who then deliberately crash them in specific locations: England, New Mexico, and Russia. The crash sites are carefully chosen by the scientists and involve the three major powers that emerged out of the carnage of the Second World War. But the work of the scientists is only just beginning. Not content with creating its bogus crashed UFOs, the team decides to take things one step further and constructs a faked alien body (created from the remains of a variety of exotic animals) that is pulverized in one of the crashes and is then presented to the world's scientific community as evidence of the alien origin of the creatures that pilot the craft. As a result of these carefully and rapidly stage-managed and manipulated events, the many and varied differences between the governments of the Earth dissolve under the "Martian" threat, and the final chapter of Newman's book sees practically every international political problem hastily resolved.

That the U.S. Government was faking crashed UFO stories at the same time that Bernard Newman was presenting an extremely similar scenario within the pages of his science fiction novel is significant indeed. And there is more.

Researcher Philip Taylor makes some interesting observations: "In his unrevealing autobiography *Speaking From Memory,* [Newman] describes how from 1919 onwards he was apparently employed in an undemanding Civil Service job in the Ministry of Works. Somehow he seemed able to take extremely long and, for those days, exceedingly adventurous holidays, including lengthy stays in Eastern Europe and Russia. His destinations invariably seemed to include areas of particular political interest: for example several extended holidays to Germany in the 1930's."

Taylor also notes that Newman claimed to have prepared a report on the German rocket-site at Peenemunde in 1938, which he duly sent to the British Government's Foreign Office. And adding yet more mystery to the story is an article that was published in *The New York Times* in 1945 that describes Newman as having spent most of the First World War acting as a double agent in the German Intelligence Service. While Newman was indeed fluent in German, the very idea of a then-eighteen-year old "boy-spy" operating deep within the heart of German forces and successfully influencing senior officers stretches credulity to its absolute finest line, states Taylor, adding that: "an addendum to Newman's obituary in the *Times* [in 1968] contains a reference to the alleged episode that relegates it to the realm of fiction." It does seem highly unlikely that Bernard Newman really could have been operating on mainland Europe as a "double agent" in German Intelligence, and yet, the ever-present rumors that Newman had high-level links with the British Government should not be ignored or dismissed.

That may be the case, but it is notable that what we have here, albeit in a specifically science fiction format, is a Top Secret project that utilizes the crashed UFO scenario as a cover story for very different purposes. Did Newman learn of the secret plans to make use of the crashed UFO subject as a tool of psychological warfare? And, if so, did he subsequently weave his own science fiction story around this planned operation? Or, incredibly, did Newman's story actually galvanize American intelligence into following a similar path?

More than sixty years on, there seems to be no real clear answer. But of one thing we can be absolutely certain: less than one year after the events at Roswell occurred, an author who had numerous, high-level, official connections and who had written extensively on espionage issues, wrote a science fiction novel that specifically linked the worlds of crashed UFOs, faked alien autopsies, and bogus flying saucer tales promoted by military officials. That the U.S. Government was doing something practically identical, and at the same time, no less, makes the story far more intriguing.

But Newman was not the only person to carefully and expertly blend the world of science fiction with Cold War era secret tales of crashed UFOs, that some believed to be real. (2) In August 1980, Playboy Press Paperbacks published a little-known book titled *The Ogden Enigma*. Written by novelist Gene Snyder, the book tells the story of an unidentified object that crashes in the vicinity of Ogden, Utah, in 1950, and that is promptly spirited away by the military to a "sealed airplane hangar" for thirty years.

Is the object, as some believe it to be, a Russian secret weapon or, incredibly, is it the remains of a vehicle from another world? These and many other questions are asked and ultimately answered in what is a highly entertaining piece of sci-fi. However, according to the author, *The Ogden Enigma* was based upon secret facts. Snyder states that, in 1977, he had occasion to meet a man that he referred to as "Charlie," who related a remarkable account. "He told me of something secreted in the Utah desert for nearly three decades," said Snyder, who then added:

He said the secret was housed in an airplane hangar at a U.S. Army supply base, near Ogden, Utah. He claimed that on a June night in 1950, five air force personnel had driven a flatbed truck onto the base in the middle of the night. The truck's cargo was covered with a tarpaulin that had been carefully lashed down. He went on to say that after driving the truck into the hangar, the five men hurriedly closed the doors and bent the bolt locks.

In the days that followed, a huge security screen was erected around the hangar. It included electrified fences, guard dogs, and a restricted air traffic space above the building. An Air Force Security Service detachment, he maintained, still guarded the hangar, despite the fact that such a detachment would be unusual on an Army base.

The strangest part of the story, according to Snyder, was still to come. "Charlie" asserted that within twelve months of the event all five of the men involved in the delivery of the unknown object to the base were dead. "On this note," recalled Snyder, "he left, with a vague half commitment to return and tell me more. He never did. I tried to reach him in the wake of the story. I never succeeded. I have not seen 'Charlie' since." (3)

In 1989, best-selling horror novelist Whitley Strieber (the author of the 1987 book *Communion* that was an examination of his own, intensely personal involvement in the so-called "alien abduction" mystery) wrote a science fiction novel on the Roswell crash titled *Majestic* that was also alleged to be based–in part–upon secret, insider knowledge. The jacket of the book revealed the premise of the story: "Strieber's gripping thriller opens in 1947, when an unusual aircraft crashes in the desert of New Mexico, near the Roswell Army Air Field, scattering debris unlike anything previously found on this earth… Claiming it is a new kind of weather balloon, the government sends in a handful of experts to analyze the wreckage and camouflage the results–an operation code-named Majestic… In what is his most controversial book, Strieber takes the reader into the hidden world of what might have been, re-creating the crash landing that yielded three corpses…the secret 'shoot to kill' orders passed down from the president; the campaign to force civilian witnesses to recant their public testimonies; and the complete inferiority of the U.S. armed forces against the mind-boggling powers of the aliens."

More interesting is the fact that publisher specifically described *Majestic* as a blend of "fact and fiction." (4) But how much was fiction and how much was fact? Strieber's website revealed that: "When this book was published, the world was stunned at the detailed inner knowledge of the Roswell Incident that it apparently contained. Surely Whitley Strieber couldn't have invented all this detail. And indeed, he hadn't. He later admitted that his own uncle and his commanding officer were involved in the incident." (5)

Strieber himself would later elaborate: "In 1988, my uncle told me that he had personally been aware of and involved with the management of the debris that had been brought from Roswell to Wright Field in 1947. My uncle Edward Strieber was an honorable man, indeed, a very honorable man. He spent his career in the Air Force, mostly working in areas that were extremely classified. He was in a position to know what he was talking about, and, as I say, he was an honorable man.

"Not only that, he introduced me to his commanding officer and old friend, General Arthur Exon, who could not have been more frank. He stated, and this is a direct quote: 'Everyone from the White House on down knew that what we had found was not of this world within 24 hours of our finding it.'" (6)

The Roswell story also played a role in a 1998 science fiction novel titled *Alien Rapture–The Chosen*, co-written by Brad Steiger, a well-known author of books on unsolved mysteries, and Edgar Rothschild Fouche, who, in his own words, "was an Air Force expert with classified electronics countermeasures test equipment owned by the National Security Agency, and Automatic Test Equipment."

According to Fouche:

I worked with many of the leading military aircraft and electronics manufacturers in the U.S. I participated as a key member in design, development, production, and Flight-Operational-Test and Evaluation in classified Aircraft development programs, state-of-the-art avionics, including electronic countermeasures, satellite communications, cryptological and support equipment.

I wrote *Alien Rapture* in 1994 and '95, after my last trip to California, New Mexico, and Nevada. I undertook this trip to do research which included a meeting with five close friends who had agreed to release confidential information to me, and discuss their closely guarded personal experiences. I also interviewed other contacts who had worked classified programs or flown classified military aircraft to gather information about UFO sightings and contact.

The First friend, Jerald, was a former NSA or National Security Agency TREAT Team member. TREAT stands for Tactical Reconnaissance Engineering Assessment Team. He worked for the Department of Energy as a National Security Investigator. That was his cover, but he really worked for the NSA. His job required him to "watch employees" with Top Secret and "Q" clearances at the Nevada Test Site and the Nellis Range which includes Area 51. Area 51 is where the most classified aerospace testing in the world takes place...He was found dead of a heart attack a year after our last meeting.

The Second friend, Sal, was a person who had worked directly for the NSA with Electronic Intelligence and became a Defense Contractor after his retirement. The Third friend, Doc, was a former SR-71 spy plane pilot and a USAF test pilot at Edwards Air Force Base. The Fourth friend, Dale, and I were in the service together during the Vietnam conflict, and I've known him since the early 70s...The Fifth friend, Bud, was a DoD Contractor and Electronics Engineer. He had worked on Top Secret development programs dealing with Electronic Counter Measures, Radar Homing and Warning, ECM Jammers, and Infrared Receivers. He retired as a Program Manager and later died of a brain tumor within thirty days after his symptoms appeared.

Interestingly, Fouche, too, reported insider knowledge of the Roswell affair: "Has anyone ever heard of the super strong foil like material recovered after the Roswell crash?" he asked the audience at the 1998 Laughlin, Nevada UFO Congress. Answering the question himself, Fouche said:

> Another friend who worked for General Dynamics in Fort Worth, TX, described a program in which he worked with a plasma accelerator in the mid-sixties, researching gravity warping techniques. He is a physicist by education and work experience. This was his first Top Secret Program. He described a foil-like material, much like the material that was reported discovered after the Roswell Crash. He described the foil as twelve layers of material, less than ten thousandths of an inch thick. It was as flexible as a plastic trash bag, but virtually indestructible to piercing, burning or cutting. (7)

In January 2006, a French-language science fiction novel, titled *Stratageme*, written by renowned UFO researcher, author, and astronomer Jacques Vallee, was published and utilized in a distinctly fictional format exactly the same scenario for Roswell that I had developed within the pages of my *Body Snatchers in the Desert*. (8)

Vallee was born in France, where he received a B.S. in mathematics at the Sorbonne, and an M.S. in astrophysics at Lille University. In May 1955, Vallee had seen a flying saucer over his then Pontoise home and, six years later, while working on the staff of the French Space Committee, witnessed the destruction of tracking tapes that displayed unknown objects orbiting the earth. This understandably piqued his interest in the subject of UFOs.

Coming to the United States as an astronomer at the University of Texas, where he co-developed the first computer-based map of Mars for NASA, Vallee later moved to Northwestern University where he received his Ph.D. in computer science and went on to work at SRI International and the Institute for the Future, directing a project to build the world's first network-based conferencing system as a Principal Investigator on Arpanet, the prototype for the Internet. (9)

And although Vallee's own, first-hand experiences with the UFO phenomenon led him to believe that there was indeed a genuine mystery to be resolved, even he was not convinced that the events at Roswell, New Mexico in early July 1947 were a direct part of that particular mystery. In 1991, Vallee stated the following:

The material recovered in the [Roswell] crash itself, while it remains fascinating, was not necessarily beyond human technology in the late Forties. Aluminized Saran, also known as Silvered Saran, came from technology already available for laboratory work in 1948. It was paper-thin, was not dented by a hammer blow, and was restored to a smooth finish after crushing.

Roswell was the site for the very first air base equipped with atomic bombs. If a special type of balloon or drone, designed to monitor atmospheric radioactivity in the area, had been flown over New Mexico, such a device might well have been brought down during a thunderstorm. Given the extremely high sensitivity of anything related to the bomb or radioactivity at the time, it would have been a high priority, top secret task to recover any lost device of that type and to explain it away at all costs: as a weather balloon, as a radar test instrument, as a probe, or even as a crashed flying saucer. (10)

We may never know for certain what really happened in the desert near Roswell, New Mexico, on that now-famous day, but, having reviewed the stories of Bernard Newman, Whitley Strieber, Ed Fouche, and Jacques Vallee, it seems that the secret world of Roswell and that of science fiction are hardly what we might call strangers.

And on the subject of UFOs (crashed or otherwise) in fact and fiction, John Harney commented in 2000, in the *Magonia* monthly supplement: "[A] number of writers, notably Martin Kottmeyer, have shown how many of the motifs found in UFO reports...have been derived from science fiction books and films. Even some of the believers have had to concede that science fiction has colored the accounts given by many witnesses. However, this leads to the question of how the science fiction writers got their ideas." (11)

Harney further noted that in *Hollywood Vs. the Aliens: The Motion Picture Industry's Participation in UFO Disinformation*, a 1997 book by Bruce Rux, the author "developed the idea that the process is really the other way around; science fiction writers get their ideas from genuine UFO reports." (12)

Harney concluded: "Perhaps it would be more reasonable to consider the possibility of a two-way traffic between ufology and science fiction ." (13) Indeed.

■ ■ ■ I I 9 I I ■ ■ ■

THE UFO THAT NEVER WAS

"I have scenes of the saucer landing, taking off, flying and doing tricks. The saucer is not created in miniature or by trick photography."

Born in Columbus, Ohio on July 30, 1919, Mikel Conrad began to carve out a career for himself in Hollywood's movie world when he secured a small role in the 1947 production *Untamed Fury*, in which he played the memorably named Gator-Bait Blair. No less than 23 other movies followed, including 1948's *The Man from Colorado* that saw Conrad acting alongside leading actors of the day, William Holden and Glenn Ford. Twelve months later, Conrad made an on-screen appearance in *Abbott and Costello Meet the Killer: Boris Karloff*. He also starred with Tony Curtis in *Francis*, a 1950 comedy about a talking mule. But it was the science fiction movie, *The Flying Saucer*, also released in 1950, that was Conrad's crowning glory, for the prime reason that it attracted the Top Secret attention of none other than the United States Air Force.

The storyline of *The Flying Saucer* that Conrad starred in, produced, directed, and co-wrote with Howard Irving Young, is a highly intriguing one: American intelligence officials learn that Soviet spies have apparently begun secretly exploring a remote region of the Alaskan Territory in search of answers to the worldwide reports of flying saucers. American authorities duly convince a wealthy playboy named Mike Trent, played by Conrad himself, who was raised in the particular part of Alaska

Copy

5D-OSI/JCS/emb

5D-24-21DD

27 September 1949

SUBJECT: FLYING DISCS - Alleged observation
of flying discs by MIKEL CONRAD
during winter of 1948/49 in
Territory of Alaska.

TO: Acting District Commander
       18th OSI District (IG)
       822nd USAF Specialized Depot
       P. O. Box 310
       Maywood, California

1. Transmitted herewith for your information, facsimile of newspaper clipping extracted from 14 September 1949 issue of the "Journal-
Herald" published in Dayton, Ohio, wherein, under-by-line of ALINE
MOSBY, Hollywood, dated 13 September 1949, it is alleged that one,
_____ did, during the winter of 1948/49 in Alaska, observe so-
called "flying saucers", located one of same and took motion pictures
of cited saucers in various flight stages and maneuvers.

2. Request appropriate investigation be conducted by your district
in accordance with provisions of AFCSI Letter No. 85, dated 12 August
1949.

3. For the purpose of this investigation, it is requested that the
title to be used in the preparation of Report of Investigation be as
indicated above.

4. Request Report of Investigation be submitted this office,
in six copies, so that this office may comply with Paragraph 3e(1),(2),
(4), of cited AFCSI Letter.

5. In the event investigation has already been initiated, by your
office, covering incident referred to in title, it is requested instructions
contained in above paragraphs be ignored and six copies of investigation
furnished this district.

Incl: JAMES F. X. O'CONNELL
Facsimile of newspaper   Lt Colonel, USAF
clipping extracted from   District Commander
14 Sep 49 issue of
"Journal-Herald" (in trip)

Copy

*A letter from the USAF's secret file on science fiction film-maker
Mikel Conrad.*

where all of the action is taking place, to assist a United States Secret Service agent in exploring the area on behalf of the U.S. intelligence community, and as part of a concerted effort to determine why the Soviets are so intensely interested in flying saucers.

To Trent's surprise and delight, he learns that the Secret Service agent is a beautiful woman, Vee Langley, portrayed by actress Pat Garrison, and they set off together in hot pursuit of the truth, with Conrad's character posing as someone suffering from a nervous breakdown, and Langley pretending to be his nurse. The pair subsequently make their way to Trent's cabin in the Alaskan wilderness, where a caretaker named Hans, who has a distinct foreign accent that sounds suspiciously Russian, meets and greets the pair.

Trent is overwhelmingly skeptical of the entire UFO issue—until he spots just such a craft soaring across the skies near the cabin. The story then takes an intriguing turn when Hans is shown to be an undercover Soviet intelligence agent, and the UFO is revealed to be not an alien spacecraft after all but the product of an American scientist who has sold the secrets of his revolutionary aerial invention to his secret masters at the Kremlin. Eventually, Trent and Langley bring the spies to justice, locate the Soviets' hiding place of the flying saucer, and finally watch as it less-than-spectacularly explodes in mid-air, and as a Russian spy attempts to escape with the vehicle – the result of a bomb placed aboard it by the now-repentant American scientist. (1)

It must be said that *The Flying Saucer* was hardly a classic, the special-effects leave a lot to be desired, and the movie vanished into obscurity shortly after its release, which surely begs the question: why would the United States' military take such an interest in Conrad's far from impressive foray into the world of sci-fi? The answer is quite simple: when *The Flying Saucer* was still at production stage, Conrad began spreading rumors in Hollywood, and with several media outlets in his home state of Ohio, to the effect that the movie would contain not special-effects footage of a UFO, but genuine, and highly spectacular, film of a real flying saucer in aerial action.

At the time, the Air Force was deeply involved in trying to determine the truth that lay at the heart of the UFO mystery. Between 1948 (the year that saw the creation of the Air Force's first UFO program, Project Sign, which was shortly afterwards replaced by another operation known as Project Grudge) and 1969, the year in which its final study, Project Blue Book, was closed down, the Air Force officially investigated 12,618 reported UFO sightings, of which 701 remained unexplained. And so, given that Conrad was making controversial claims to the effect that he was in possession of stunning footage of real UFOs in flight, it is of little surprise that the Air Force secretly began looking into Conrad's activities and his claims.

The saga all began on September 14, 1949, when journalist Aline Mosby wrote an article titled "Film Actor Finds Flying Disc, But Press Agent Doubts Tale" that appeared in the Dayton, Ohio *Journal Herald* newspaper. Mosby's article told a story that, if true, was startling, to say the very least.

The article began: "Having taken care of rocket ships, atomic bombs and Superman, Hollywood now is starring a flying saucer in a movie. The Army's latest decision was there isn't any such thing, but this has not dampened the spirit of actor Mikel Conrad. He is acting in, producing, directing and writing 'The Secret of the Flying Saucers.' The star, he insists, is a whirling disc, or reasonable facsimile thereof. The movie is a spy mystery which also features a blond heroine, a handsome hero and Russians as the villains."

Mosby then turned her attention to the most significant aspect of the story: the apparent acquisition by Conrad of real footage of flying saucers that he was going to reveal to the world in his science fiction movie: "The actor got this colossal idea, he says, while on location in Alaska last winter for a Universal-International movie, *Arctic Manhunt*. 'I heard about flying saucers there so I went back last summer with a camera crew from Whitehorse (Canada) and two players, Pat Garrison and Hans von Teuffen,' he says. 'I found a saucer, I'm not telling how,' a claim not believed even by one of his press agents."

The article went on to quote Conrad as stating: "I have scenes of the saucer landing, taking off, flying and doing tricks. The saucer is not created in miniature or by trick photography. It is a mechanical, man-made object."

Mosby continued: "Whether it is a dishpan sailing across the camera or some garage-made contraption, he won't say. Conrad and crew shot silent footage for three months. He'll begin shooting interior scenes and dubbing in sound Sept. 26, he says." Then, Mosby added: "His press agents have seen part of the film. They report it has some nice avalanches. They did not see any flying saucers."

Why? According to Mosby's feature, Conrad said: "The saucer footage is locked in a bank vault. I'm not showing it to anyone yet." Mosby followed with a brief account of the movie's plot that was somewhat different to the final, filmed version: "The plot concerns a playboy, Michael Trent (Conrad), who steels his weak chin and goes saucer-hunting in Alaska for the government. To throw Russian spies off his track, he cleverly disguises himself as a drunkard seeking the cure. Trent is accompanied by an FBI agent, who turns out to be a beautiful blond (Miss Garrison), cleverly disguised as his nurse."

Conrad told Mosby: "We get snowbound in a remote cabin and romance finds a way." Mosby seemed less than impressed by Conrad, his claims, and his then-forthcoming movie, as her closing words noted: "Will Michael and Violet get out of the cabin before they're trapped by snow? Or the Russians? Or the Saucers? Will they capture the saucer? Will they drop dead before the end of the movie? Will you?" (2)

Two days later, staff at the Air Technical Intelligence Center (ATIC) at Wright-Patterson Air Force Base, which was deeply involved in the investigation of UFO sightings at the time, recorded in an internal memo that details of Aline Mosby's article had been brought to their attention. Interestingly, and somewhat mysteriously, however, ATIC officials noted that Conrad was claiming that his forthcoming movie was being made "with the permission of authorities." The Mosby article makes no such claim, however, which suggests that only 48 hours after the article in the *Journal Herald* appeared the Air Force was pursuing and had uncovered still further data on Conrad, his claims, and his activities.

As a result of the growing official interest in Conrad's movie, in September 1949, Lt. Colonel James F. X. O'Connell, District Commander with the Air Force Office of Special Investigations, prepared a confidential memorandum for the attention of the Acting District Commander of the 18th OSI District, 822nd USAF Specialized Dept, at Maywood, California. Titled "FLYING DISCS – Alleged observation of flying discs by MIKEL CONRAD during winter if 1948/49 in Territory of Alaska," it read:

1. Transmitted herewith for your information, facsimile of newspaper clipping extracted from 14 September 1949 issue of the "Journal-Herald" published in Dayton, Ohio, wherein, under byline of ALINE MOSBY, Hollywood, dated 13 September 1949, it is alleged that one, Mikel Conrad did, during the winter of 1948.49 in Alaska, observe so-called "flying saucers", located one of same and took motion pictures of cited saucers in various flight stages and maneuvers.

2. Request appropriate investigation be conducted by your district.

3. For the purpose of this investigation, it is requested that the title to be used in the preparation of Report of Investigation be as indicated above.

4. Request Report of Investigation be submitted to this office, in six copies.

5. In the event investigation has already been initiated, by your office, covering incident referred to in title; it is requested instructions contained in above paragraphs be ignored and six copies of investigation furnished this district.

Clearly, the matter was being taken seriously at an official level. Indeed, for the next two months various elements of the Air Force investigated Conrad's claims and *The Flying Saucer*. A November 12, 1949, confidential Air Force report summarizes the facts and conclusions pertaining to this strange affair. The first paragraph of the document reveals that the Air Force had heard additional rumors to the effect that not only was Conrad in possession of film footage of UFOs, but that he actually had nothing less than an honest-to-goodness flying saucer "in his possession."

On 20 September 1949, the 5th OSI District Office, Wright-Patterson AFB, was requested by Lt. Col. A.J. HEMSTREET, JR., Acting Chief, Analysis Division, Intelligence Department, Hq., AMC [Air Materiel Command], to initiate an investigation for the purpose of confirming or denying the allegations made by one MIKEL CONRAD, wherein he claimed to have in his possession a "flying saucer," as well as various scenes showing the alleged saucers landing and taking off. As a result of this request the 5th OSI District Office prepared a letter to the 18th OSI District Office, Maywood, California, requesting that appropriate investigation of this matter be conducted in the Hollywood area.

On 17 October 1949, 5th District was informed by Lt Col H.W. POTE, Deputy Chief, Public Information Office, Hq. AMC, Wright-Patterson AFB, that he had received a telephone call from Lt. J.G. MORRIS, Public Relations Office, Hq. USAF, Washington, D.C., advising that his (MORRIS) office was in receipt of a telephone call from [Deleted] the Editor of "Film Daily" and that he had received a press release from one MIKEL CONRAD to the effect that he CONRAD had in his possession 900 feet of film about "flying saucers" in Alaska; that [Deleted] requested any information available as to the authenticity of CONRAD'S material and whether an investigation had been conducted of subject matter. Lt MORRIS asked Colonel POTE whether Wright Field investigated the subject matter and for any information available concerning CONRAD.

Air Force documentation shows that Pote then contacted Lt. H.W. Smith, the Project Officer with Project Grudge, at the Air Technical Intelligence Center at Wright-Patterson Air Force Base, and Smith advised Pote that he was personally unaware of such an investigation. Smith was careful to add, however, that if Wright-Patterson was involved, then it was likely that its Office of Special Investigations (OSI) would have been the specific office on the case, and that he, Smith, would have been kept out of the loop with respect to any such secret inquiries.

The Freedom of Information Act has shown that an extensive investigation of Mikel Conrad and his fantastic claims did proceed, and that it was conducted by elements of the 18th OSI District. Evidence of this can be found in a report dated November 22, 1949:

A report subsequently submitted by the 18th OSI DO [District Office] dated 3 November 1949 stated that after some investigation in an effort to locate MIKEL CONRAD, it was determined that he was presently an actor-producer-writer in Los Angeles, California. When contacted CONRAD informed OSI Agent SHILEY that his picture "The Flying Saucer" was to be previewed by the censors of the [Deleted] office in Hollywood, and invited Agent SHILEY to attend the showing after which, he suggested, the Agent could question him concerning the "saucer."

As the following, final extract from the document indicates, Conrad decided to come clean to Agent Shiley and admitted that his story about having filmed real flying saucers was nothing more than a fabrication that had been designed purely as a means to generate much-welcome publicity for his movie. Possibly, with the Air Force now asking questions, Conrad was concerned that legal action might follow, and this was an attempt on his part to appease the military and prevent matters from escalating to a potentially far more serious level. The report states:

Agent SHILEY attended the preview of CONRAD'S movie on 26 October 1949, and after the showing CONRAD indicated that the "flying saucer was a figment of his imagination," and stated that he had released the story in order to advertise his picture. He admitted that the alleged observation, location, and the motion picture of the "flying saucer" in various flight stages and maneuvers was not a reality.

CONRAD apologized to Agent SHILEY for the story which appeared in the press and said he was sorry that he had misled the USAF, and admitted that the article was purely for enhancing interest in his coming picture. He requested that the USAF not furnish any newspaper correspondent or other persons making inquiries with the fact that the "saucer is a hoax." CONRAD was advised that OSI would not because OSI had no interest in his picture, since he had not actually sighted any unconventional object in the sky.

And, thus, one of the stranger episodes in the early years of the Air Force's UFO investigations was brought to a close. But an intriguing question remains: why was the Air Force so keen to determine the truth behind Conrad's claims that he had genuine footage of UFOs in flight in his possession? If the Air Force thought that UFOs were not worthy of investigation, it would surely have avoided expending both valuable manpower and money on investigating Conrad's story. Yet investigate it, the Air Force certainly did, even to the extent of ensuring that an agent of the OSI was in place at the first, private viewing of *The Flying Saucer*.

Perhaps we should consider the possibility that the seriousness and diligence shown by the Air Force in investigating Conrad and his science fiction movie stemmed from the possibility that the military, itself, knew that UFOs existed because that same military was already in possession of Top Secret films of a similar nature to those that Conrad had asserted he possessed. It would be ironic if Conrad's lies had actually touched upon a very real, and highly classified, official story concerning genuine footage of flying saucers in the skies of Alaska.

And, incredibly, that may be precisely what happened.

Formerly classified FBI files tell of startling UFO encounters in Alaska in the period 1947-1950—and it is not at all out of the question that at least some of the 1947 cases, in particular, may have been the ones that Conrad claimed knowledge of to journalist Aline Mosby in 1949. More interesting is the fact that another flurry of UFO activity kicked off in Alaska in January 1950—only three months after AFOSI agent Shiley got to see an advance-screening of *The Flying Saucer* and just before the movie hit the big-screen.

It was in August 1947 that a highly impressive account of a UFO incident involving two serving members of the military was supplied to the FBI at Anchorage. The report read: "This is to advise that two army officers reported to the Office of the Director of Intelligence Headquarters Alaskan Department, at Fort Richardson, Alaska, that they had witnesses an object passing through the air at a tremendous rate of speed which could not be judged as to miles per hour."

According to the official report, the UFO was initially sighted by only one of the two officers, but he soon alerted his colleague to the strange sight. "The object appeared to be shaped like a sphere and did not give the impression of being saucer-like or comparable to a disk. The first officer stated that it would be impossible to give minute details concerning the object, but that it appeared to be approximately two or three feet in diameter and did not leave any vapor trail in the sky."

Experienced officer that he was, in his first attempt to gauge the altitude of the object, and, from a comparison with cloud formations in the area, he determined that whatever the nature of the mystery sphere, it was cruising at a height of more than ten thousand feet. And it should be noted that to be at such a height and still be visible, in all probability the UFO must have exceeded by a wide margin the initial size estimate of "two or three feet."

When questioned, the second officer gave a substantially similar account, the only marked difference being that, in his opinion, he considered the object to have been approximately ten feet in diameter, and compared it to "half the size of a full moon on an ordinary night." This discrepancy in size was apparently due to the fact that the second officer believed the UFO was more likely to have been at a height of three-to-four thousand feet, rather than at an altitude of ten thousand feet as had been suggested by his colleague.

The difference of opinion over the altitude and size of the object may or may not have been significant; the important factor, however, was that both officers agreed that some type of anomalous object had most definitely been seen. And as the report concluded: "...the second officer pointed out that one of the remarkable features of this report was that it was definitely traveling against the wind."

Shortly afterwards, the FBI Office at Anchorage reported to Bureau Director J. Edgar Hoover that: "...we have been able to locate a flyer [who] observed some flying object near Bethel, Alaska in July 1947."

The report to Hoover continued:

[The pilot] related that the occasion of seeing the flying object near Bethel was on a July day when the sky was completely clear of clouds, and it being during the early part, it is daylight the entire night. The time of his sighting [of] this flying object was about 10 PM and the sun had just dropped beyond the horizon. Flying weather was extremely good and he was coming into the Bethel Airport with a DC-3.

On approaching the airport the pilot was amazed to see to his left an unidentified craft "the size of a C-54 without any fuselage," which seemed to resemble a "flying wing." As a result of its unique shape, the pilot was initially unable to determine whether the object was heading towards his aircraft or away from it, and elected to make a 45-degree turn in an attempt to diffuse any possible chance of collision. The FBI noted that the pilot was certain that the craft was free of any external power source, such as a propeller-driven engine, and exhibited no exhaust as it flew by. The document added:

> He called on his radio to the Civil Aeronautics Administration station at Bethel, asking what aircraft was in the vicinity and they had no reports of any aircraft. The object he sighted was some five or ten miles from the airport before his arrival and [he] stated that the path did not go directly across the airport. He, of course, could not tell whether the object was making any noise and stated that it was flying at a thousand foot altitude and estimated travel at 300 miles per hour. It was traveling in the direction from Bethel to Nome, which is in a northwesterly direction. He noted no radio interference and is unable to describe the color other than it appeared dark but of definite shape and did not blend into the sky but had a definite, concise outline. [He] clearly observed the object at this time.

As the 1940s drew to a close and a new decade dawned, the FBI continued to receive and log high-quality UFO reports on a regular basis. Of those, one of the more credible related to a noteworthy series of encounters that occurred in Alaskan airspace over the course of two days in early 1950.

Forwarded to the FBI by an official U.S. Navy source, the confidential three-page intelligence report paints a startling picture of multiple UFO encounters involving the military. Titled "Unidentified Phenomena in Vicinity of Kodiak, Alaska," it concerns "a report of sightings of unidentified airborne objects, by various naval personnel, on 22 and 23 January 1950."

...at 220240W January Lt. Smith, USN, patrol plane commander of P2V3 No. 4 of Patrol Squadron One reported an unidentified radar contact 20 miles north of the Naval Air Station, Kodiak, Alaska. When this contact was first made, Lt. Smith was flying the Kodiak Security Patrol. At 0243W, 8 minutes later a radar contact was made on an object 10 miles southeast of NAS Kodiak. Lt. Smith checked with the control tower to determine known traffic in the area, and was informed that there was none. During this period, the radar operator, Gaskey, ALC, USN, reported intermittent radar interference of a type never before experienced. Contact was lost at this time, but intermittent interference continued.

Smith and Gaskey were not the only two to report that unidentified vehicles had intruded into Alaskan airspace. At the time of these encounters, the *USS Tilbrook* was anchored in the vicinity of "buoy 19" in the nearby man ship channel. On board the *Tilbrook* was a seaman named Morgan (first name unknown) who was standing watch. At some point between 0200 and 0300 hours, Morgan reported that a "very fast moving red light, which appeared to be of exhaust nature seemed to come from the southeast, moved clockwise in a large circle in the direction of, and around Kodiak and returned out in a generally southeast direction."

Perhaps not quite believing what he was seeing, Morgan alerted one of his shipmates, Carver, to the strange spectacle, and both watched as the UFO made a "return flight." According to the testimony of Morgan and Carver: "The object was in sight for an estimated 30 seconds. No odor or sound was detected, and the object was described to have the appearance of a ball of fire about one foot in diameter."

The report then records yet another encounter with the mystery visitor: "At 220440W, conducting routine Kodiak security patrol, Lt. Smith reported a visual sighting of an unidentified airborne object at a range of 5 miles, on the starboard bow. This object showed indications of great speed on the radar scope. The trailing edge of the blip gave a tail like indication."

Lieutenant Smith quickly advised the rest of the crew of the PV23 No. 24 that the UFO was in sight, and all watched fascinated as the strange vehicle soared overhead at a speed estimated to have been around 1,800 mph. Smith climbed to intercept the UFO and vainly tried to circle it. Needless to say, its high speed and remarkable maneuverability ensured that Smith's actions was futile. However, neither Lieutenant Smith nor his crew was quite prepared for what happened next. "Subsequently the object seemed to be opening the range," the official report reads, "and Smith attempted to close the range. The UFO was observed to open out somewhat, then to turn to the left and come up on Smith's quarter. Smith considered this to be a highly threatening gesture and turned out all lights in the aircraft. Four minutes later the object disappeared from view in a southeasterly direction."

At 0435 hours on the following day, Lieutenants Barco and Causer of Patrol Squadron One were conducting the Kodiak Security Patrol when they, too, sighted an unidentified aerial vehicle. At the time of their encounter the aircraft in which the officers were flying was approximately 62 miles south of Kodiak. For ten minutes, Barco and Causer, along with the pilot, Captain Paulson, watched stunned as the mysterious object twisted and turned in the Alaskan sky. An assessment of these reports read thus:

1. To Lt. Smith and crew it appeared as two orange lights rotating about a common center, "like two jet aircraft making slow rolls in

tight formation." It had a wide speed range.
2. To Morgan and Carver, it appeared as a reddish orange ball of fire about one foot in diameter, traveling at a high rate of speed.
3. To Causer, Barco and Paulson, it appeared to be a pulsating orange yellow projectile shaped flame, with regular periods of pulsation on 3 to 5 seconds. Later, as the object increased the range, the pulsations appeared to increase to on 7 or 8 seconds and off 7 to 8 seconds.

The final comment on the encounters reads: "In view of the fact that no weather balloons were known to have been released within a reasonable time before the sightings, it appears that the object or objects were not balloons. If not balloons the objects must be regarded as phenomena (possibly metcorites), the exact nature of which could not be determined by this office."

. The "meteorite" theory for this series of encounters is particularly puzzling. It goes without saying that meteorites do not stay in sight for "an estimated 30 seconds," meteorites do not close in on military aircraft in what is deemed to be a "highly threatening gesture," and they do not appear as "two orange lights rotating about a common center." In other words, it seems safe to conclude that genuinely anomalous phenomena were indeed witnessed by experienced military personnel at Kodiak, Alaska in January 1950.

And there is still more to the story. In his 1997 book *Remote Viewing*, Jim Schnabel recounts the story of the U.S. Intelligence community's involvement in the controversial issue of psychic spying that largely began in the early-to-mid 1970s. Commenting on the skills of a talented remote-viewer, Pat Price, Schnabel noted Price was of the opinion that "Alaska's Mount Hayes, the jewel of a glacial range northeast of Anchorage, housed one of the aliens' largest bases." According to Price, the aliens that lived deep inside Mount Hayes were very human looking, differing only in their heart, lungs, blood, and eyes. Ominously, he added that the aliens use "thought transfer for motor control of us."

"The site has also been responsible for strange activity and malfunction of U.S. and Soviet space objects," added Price.

We may never know for sure if it was these, and perhaps other, official UFO reports from Alaska that prompted the Air Force to take so much interest in the activities and spurious claims of Mikel Conrad, but of one thing we *can* be certain: the military's secret surveillance of Conrad, as he sought to bring *The Flying Saucer* to life, was certainly the highlight of his career. Several more movie roles followed: a low-budget science fiction picture of 1952 called *Untamed Women*, which (believe me) is far less exciting than its title suggests, and a 1956 production of *Godzilla, King of the Monsters*. After that, Conrad largely vanished into obscurity. Long forgotten, just like his masterpiece *The Flying Saucer*, Conrad died in poverty in Los Angeles on September 11, 1982.

SCI-FI, SCIENTOLOGY, AND THE FBI

"He has been described as having 'delusions of grandeur,' and one newspaper item of divorce action quoted his wife as saying he was hopelessly 'insane.'"

L. Ron Hubbard, the founder of the Church of Scientology that Hollywood stars John Travolta, Kirstie Alley, and Tom Cruise, among others, are so enamored with, was born in Nebraska in 1911. While in his early twenties, Hubbard began to seriously pursue his passion for writing, ultimately publishing many stories in a variety of pulp science fiction magazines and going on to become one of the best-known celebrity authors of the day in the genre of fantasy fiction. His celebrated horror story "Fear" (a memorable tale of witches, spirits, and demons) was published as a novella in the July 1940 issue of *Unknown Fantasy Fiction*, a pulp fantasy magazine edited by John W. Campbell, which ran from 1939 to 1943. Closely associated with *Astounding Science fiction*, which was also edited by Campbell at the time, the magazine helped make Hubbard's name well-known within the genre. (1)

Hubbard's 1980 novel *Battlefield Earth* was seen by his followers as a triumphant return to the genre after he had spent years immersing himself with Scientology, and the book was ultimately turned into a mega-bucks Hollywood movie of the same name that starred John Travolta. However, the cinematic version of *Battlefield Earth* was almost unanimously, and quite justifiably, savaged by critics worldwide upon its release. But more intriguing is Hubbard's introduction to the world of science fiction and his subsequent establishment of the Church of Scientology – both of which are filled to the brim with official secrets, personal secrets, and intense FBI surveillance. (2)

In August 1945, while on leave from his career with the United States Navy, Hubbard was introduced to a man named Jack Parsons. As Parsons' biographer John Carter notes:

In his short 37 years, John Whiteside "Jack" Parsons filled at least several different roles in one tormented but glorious life. By day, Parsons' unorthodox genius created an explosive rocket that helped the Allies win the war and NASA send spacecraft to the moon. The Aerojet Corporation – which Parsons personally founded–even today produces solid-fuel rocket boosters for the Space Shuttle based on his innovations. A large crater on the dark side of the moon was named after him. Every year, on Halloween, NASA's Jet Propulsion Laboratory holds an open house memorial, complete with mannequins of Jack Parsons and cohorts for what JPL calls "Nativity Day." In the aerospace community, there is a joke that JPL actually stands for "Jack Parsons" Laboratory' or even "Jack Parsons Lives." Though honored on "Nativity Day," Jack Parsons called himself the Antichrist at night when he practiced Aleister Crowley's Thelemic Rituals to create a new sort of human being that would finally destroy Christianity. In his Pasadena mansion (called "The Parsonage"), the dark, handsome Parsons hosted soirees for science fiction , visited by writers such as Robert Heinlein, Jack Williamson, Anthony Boucher, Ray Bradbury, and none other than L. Ron Hubbard. In front of Hubbard, Parsons enacted his dark "Babalon" rituals. (3)

And as writer George Pendle states with respect to the early world of sci-fi:

Inspired by these futuristic stories, amateur rocketeers formed space travel clubs and intended to develop rockets not for entertainment nor for weapons, but for the cause of space exploration. Holding up the science-fiction magazines as their scriptures, enthusiasts from all walks of life constructed small, primitive rockets, fated to blow up on take-off or explode in mid-air, in the hopes of progressing towards their far-off goal...Jack Parsons was just such a figure, living on the cusp between an old world in which the very idea of space travel was a scientific absurdity and a new world in which it would become scientific fact. (4)

Parsons was highly impressed by Hubbard's enthusiasm for the teachings of Aleister Crowley and said so in corespondence to Crowley: "I deduced that he is in direct touch with some higher intelligence. He is the most Thelemic person I have ever met and is in complete accord with our own principles."

As a result, Hubbard moved in with Parsons, was initiated into Crowley's Ordo Templi Orientis and immediately had his sights set on Parsons' girlfriend: Sara Northrup.

Beginning in 1946, Parsons and Hubbard embarked upon a lengthy magical ritual known as the Babalon Working, the purpose of which was to try and manifest an elemental entity. Parsons instantly became convinced that the lengthy invocation had succeeded when, two weeks later, a beautiful woman named Marjorie Elizabeth Cameron entered his life. As John Carter states, Cameron was "sprung from Parsons' head like Sophia from the Godhead or Pallas Athena from Zeus."

On February 26, Parsons wrote to Crowley: "I have my elemental!" Two months later, Parsons, Cameron and Hubbard embarked upon the next stage of the Babalon Working – the purpose of which was to invoke a "moonchild" in the exact fashion portrayed within the pages of Crowley's novel of the same name. Things did not quite go according to plan, however. Northrup, growing tired of Parsons' fascination with Cameron, left him for Hubbard, and the two promptly vanished with no less than $10,000 of Parsons' money. Notable is the fact that Parsons finally found the pair out at sea and quickly cast a dark spell upon them. In the wake of Parsons' dark incantation, Hubbard and Northrup almost drowned in an immense storm that surfaced out of nowhere.

It has been said that Hubbard's real motivation for getting to know Parsons was that he, Hubbard, was engaged in a classified mission for the U.S. Government, one that was designed to end Parsons' magical activities and to rescue Northrup from the dark clutches of Crowley's disciple. Crowley, however, considered Hubbard to be nothing more than a "stupid lout" who stole Parsons' money and his girlfriend in what he merely described as an "ordinary confidence trick." (5)

And with respect to Hubbard's credibility, or lack of it, Nieson Himmel, who was a young journalist in the 1940s and who had a passion for sci-fi, has made some highly enlightening comments. Himmel had met Parsons after the War and was subsequently introduced to Hubbard. He is therefore in a prime position to comment on the formative years of Hubbard's life and work when he reveals that: "I was not one of his favorite people – I didn't believe what he said and I wouldn't lend him any money. He was a real conman.... But he was not a dummy. He could charm the shit out of anybody and had tremendous personality." (6)

In May 1950, Hubbard unveiled to the world what he called Dianetics, or, as Hubbard himself explained it, "The modern science of mental health," that could allegedly eliminate emotional problems, cure bodily ailments, and vastly increase a person's intelligence. Hubbard was certainly not shy in his promotion of Dianetics when he outrageously described it as "a milestone for man comparable to his discovery of fire and superior to his inventions of the wheel and arch." (7)

When mainstream publishers dismissed Hubbard's book manuscript on the subject, he approached science fiction editor John W. Campbell, who had published Hubbard's novella

"Fear" in the pages of *Astounding Science fiction* magazine. Many of Hubbard's fellow science fiction authors were hardly impressed with the premise, however. Isaac Asimov, of *I, Robot* fame, criticized its unscientific aspects, while Jack Williamson came straight to the point, describing Dianetics as "a lunatic revision of Freudian psychology" that "had the look of a wonderfully rewarding scam." (8)

Nevertheless, Hubbard's self published book of the same name, *Dianetics*, became a huge success: no less than 150,000 copies were sold within the first twelve months. Following publication, the Hubbard Dianetic Research Foundation was unveiled in Elizabeth, New Jersey, with branch offices surfacing in a number of other American cities before the end of 1950. (9)

While the book was certainly highly successful and very influential in terms of bringing Dianetics to the masses, many professionals were not at all enamored by its contents, including the American Psychological Association, which was quoted by *The New York Times* in September 1950, as stating that, "the association calls attention to the fact that these claims are not supported by empirical evidence." (10)

In 1952, Hubbard modified Dianetics into a philosophy that he termed Scientology, and, in December 1953, he grandly proclaimed that Scientology was nothing less than a full blown religion. As a result, the First Church of Scientology was founded at Camden, New Jersey. Today, the Church of Scientology continues to have numerous followers all across the world. (11)

In-depth study of the formerly classified files of the FBI – which was also looking into the world of Jack Parsons at the time, as a result of unfounded rumors that (a) he was engaged in espionage activities for Israel, and that (b) he was a communist – shows that far more can be learned about L. Ron Hubbard, science fiction author extraordinaire and guru to the rich and the famous of Hollywood. An FBI document detailing certain events of 1951 makes Hubbard look downright weird, to say the very least:

In one lengthy letter in May, 1951, it is perhaps noteworthy that Hubbard stated that while he was in his apartment on February 23, 1951, about two or three o'clock in the morning his apartment was entered. He was knocked out. A needle was thrust into his heart to produce a coronary thrombosis and he was given an electric shock. He said his recollection of this incident was now very blurred, that he had no witnesses and that the only other person who had a key to the apartment was his wife... It is further reported that he has been previously committed to a mental hospital.

Of equal controversy, but for entirely different reasons, was the following note in the FBI's documents:

During March, 1951, the Board of Medical Examiners, State of New Jersey, had a case against the HDRF [Hubbard Dianetics Research Foundation] scheduled for trial on the grounds that the organization was conducting a school, teaching a branch of medicine and surgery, without a license. In 1951 the HDRF established national headquarters at Wichita, Kansas, and sponsored the Allied Scientists of the World, which organization has as its avowed purpose "to construct and stock a library... in an atomic proof area where the culture and technology of the United States could be stored in a state of use by science and preserve it in case of attack."

And the FBI was careful to note what Hubbard's enraged and by-then-estranged wife, Sara Northrup, had recently blabbed about him, too: "The April 24, 1951, issue of the *Times Herald,* Washington, D.C., revealed that Hubbard's wife charged in a divorce suit that 'competent medical advisers recommended that Hubbard be committed to a private sanitarium for psychiatric observation and treatment of a mental ailment known as paranoid schizophrenia.'"

The FBI continued to record controversial data on Hubbard in the early 1950s:

He has been described as having "delusions of grandeur," and one newspaper item of divorce action quoted his wife as saying he was hopelessly "insane." Allegations have been made that organizations he was affiliated with were of particular interest to perverts, hypochondriacs and curiosity seekers. In 1951 the State of New Jersey reported it had a case against him for teaching medicine without a license and in 1952 the Post Office was investigating him for mail fraud.

Somewhat humorously, on May 22, 1953, the FBI reported on Hubbard and the work of his group: "People who were bothered with mental problems were being treated by this organization with the use of an apparatus involving two beer cans which were attached to an electric meter somewhat resembling a lie detector machine."

The FBI continued to collect data on Hubbard and his work in the field of Scientology into the 1960s. A document dated February 15, 1963, stated that the Bureau possessed, "considerable information concerning [Hubbard] and his various business enterprises."

An April 14, 1967, memo titled "Review of Bankruptcy Docket, U.S. District Court, Eastern District of Pennsylvania, reflected the Hubbard Dianetic Foundation, Inc., filed for bankruptcy on December 16, 1952," detailed an illuminating, fifteen-year-old fact:

A perusal of the bankruptcy file...revealed that a warrant was issued on December 16, 1952, for L. RON HUBBARD to bring him forthwith before the court for examination in Ancillary Proceedings in Bankruptcy. The warrant was signed by Judge ALLAN

K. GRIM, executed by the U.S. Marshal and bail was allowed in $1,000. HUBBARD, who is Chairman of the Board of Directors of Hubbard Dianetics of Kansas, wrongfully withdrew $9286.99 from his bankrupt corporation. On December 17 and 19, 1952, he was examined before the bankrupt court and agreed with the Ancillary Receiver to make restitution. Judge GRIM then discharged HUBBARD. After the Kansas Corporation went bankrupt, he opened the "Hubbard College" in Wichita, Kan., and when creditors began claiming against this establishment, he moved to Phoenix, Arizona. The file when on to say that it appears HUBBARD displays a fine talent for profiting personally although his firms generally fail.

In 1966, Hubbard headed to Rhodesia, where he offered to invest a considerable amount of money into the economy of the country. Twelve months later, Hubbard resigned as executive director of the church and became the self-appointed "commodore" of a flotilla of Scientologist-crewed ships that sailed the high seas of the Mediterranean for the next eight years. Hubbard finally returned to the United States in the 1970s, but his dealings with the FBI were far from over. (12)

Hubbard retired to a ranch in Creston, California, where he died on January 24, 1986, reportedly from a stroke. He was 74 years old. His organization, its attendant controversy, and its endorsement and support by numerous Hollywood personalities, however, all continue to survive and thrive. (13)

It is perhaps apt to close this strange saga with the words of writer Michael Crowley:

There's a deep chasm between the erudite, noble Hubbard of Scientology myth and the true identity of the church's wacky founder. To those not in his thrall, Hubbard might be better described as a pulp science-fiction writer who combined delusions of grandeur with a cynical hucksterism. Yet he turned an oddball theory about human consciousness — which originally appeared in a 25-cent science fiction magazine — into a far-reaching and powerful multimillion-dollar empire. (14)

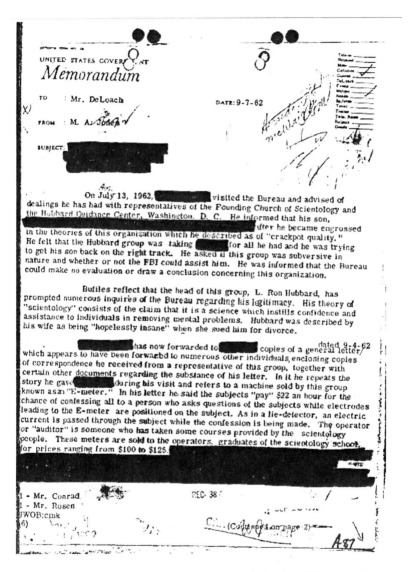

On July 13, 1962, ▮▮▮▮▮ visited the Bureau and advised of dealings he has had with representatives of the Founding Church of Scientology and the Hubbard Guidance Center, Washington, D. C. He informed that his son, ▮▮▮▮▮ after he became engrossed in the theories of this organization which he described as of "crackpot quality." He felt that the Hubbard group was taking ▮▮▮▮▮ for all he had and he was trying to get his son back on the right track. He asked if this group was subversive in nature and whether or not the FBI could assist him. He was informed that the Bureau could make no evaluation or draw a conclusion concerning this organization.

Bufiles reflect that the head of this group, L. Ron Hubbard, has prompted numerous inquiries of the Bureau regarding his legitimacy. His theory of "scientology" consists of the claim that it is a science which instills confidence and assistance to individuals in removing mental problems. Hubbard was described by his wife as being "hopelessly insane" when she sued him for divorce.

▮▮▮▮▮ has now forwarded to ▮▮▮▮▮ copies of a general letter dated 9-4-62 which appears to have been forwarded to numerous other individuals, enclosing copies of correspondence he received from a representative of this group, together with certain other documents regarding the substance of his letter. In it he repeats the story he gave ▮▮▮▮▮ during his visit and refers to a machine sold by this group known as an "E-meter." In his letter he said the subjects "pay" $22 an hour for the chance of confessing all to a person who asks questions of the subjects while electrodes leading to the E-meter are positioned on the subject. As in a lie-detector, an electric current is passed through the subject while the confession is being made. The operator or "auditor" is someone who has taken some courses provided by the scientology people. These meters are sold to the operators, graduates of the scientology school, for prices ranging from $100 to $125.

1 - Mr. Conrad
1 - Mr. Rosen
JWOB:cmk
(6)

(Continued on page 2)

An FBI report on Church of Scientology brainchild and science fiction writer L. Ron Hubbard.

■■■|| II |||■■

Weapons of Mass Destruction

"Dr. Longoria turned the ray on rabbits, dogs and cats. They fell over, instantly killed, their blood turned to water."

On the silver screen, and in the printed pages, it has felled death-dealing aliens and marauding robots, and has even destroyed worlds and entire galaxies. It is easily the most awesome weapon of mass destruction and is one of the most recognizable motifs within the annals of sci-fi. It is the death ray.

One of the earliest examples of the usage of such a weapon, in the form of what was described as a "Heat-Ray" device, appeared in H.G. Wells' novel of Martian invasion, *The War of the Worlds*. As a result of the overwhelming popularity and success of Wells' novel, many early science fiction authors picked up on his highly original premise; the deadly ray technology was often graphically shown in pulp magazines of the 1940s and 1950s, usually accompanied by giant electric arcs, lightning-style flashes, and thunder-like crashes and roars. (1)

With the advent of the laser in 1960 and its accompanying famous pencil-thin red light, however, the death ray was quickly modified within science fiction (partly as a result of the memorable use of just such a device in the 1960s movie version of Ian Fleming's James Bond story *Goldfinger*) (2) and gained a new and more popular relation, the ray gun, which was perhaps most universally recognized in the form of the Phaser from *Star Trek*. (3) Indeed, the *American Heritage Dictionary* defines a ray gun as "A gun that fires a ray of energy, especially

as depicted as a destructive weapon in science fiction." (4)
There are countless examples of the utilization of such technology in science fiction circles. In the movie *Aliens*, Rambo-like soldiers are seen fighting off vicious, extraterrestrial hordes with a shoulder-carried weapon known as the Plasma Gun. (5) In *Babylon 5*, the similarly named Phased Plasma Gun appeared regularly. (6) *Resident Evil 3: Nemesis*, a spin-off of the science fiction / horror computer-game of the same name, features a device called the Paracelsus Sword, which is essentially a huge cannon that fires an all-destructive energy beam. (7) And, of course, in *Star Wars*, Darth Vader and Luke Skywalker possessed trusty light-sabers. (8)

According to some, however, the classic death ray of science fiction is not merely, or specifically, a tool of fantasy writers. Rather, it is a very real, and very deadly, technology that has attracted the attention of the highest echelons of government agencies, the military, and the scientific community, all of whom have attempted to valiantly harness such deadly devices for reasons that are Top Secret.

Born on July 9, 1856, (at the witching-hour, according to legend) in what is today Croatia, Nikola Tesla was without doubt a scientific genius and, arguably, definitively ushered in the modern-age of electrical power. Tesla completed his elementary education in Croatia, continuing his schooling in the Polytechnic School in Graz, and finishing at the University of Prague. He worked as an electrical engineer in Germany, Hungary, and France before immigrating to the United States in 1884.

Arriving in New York City with, quite literally, nothing but four cents in his pockets, Tesla soon found employment in New Jersey with none other than Thomas Edison. Differences over money and wages between the two men soon lead to their separation, however. Undaunted, Tesla established a laboratory in New York City in 1887, where experiments ranging from the exploration of electrical resonance to studies of lighting systems were routinely undertaken. Four years later, Tesla developed the induction motor, new types of generators and transformers, a system of alternating-current power transmission, fluorescent lights, and a new form of steam turbine. He also became highly intrigued with the transmission of power via wireless. But it was his foray into the world of the death ray that is certainly the most intriguing.

The mechanism behind Tesla's death ray is not well understood at all. It was apparently some sort of particle accelerator that Tesla said was an outgrowth of his magnifying transformer, which focused its energy output into a thin beam so concentrated it would not scatter, even over huge distances. He promoted the device as a purely defensive weapon, intended to knock down incoming attacks–not unlike the latter day Strategic Defense Initiative, SDI, in fact. No one is entirely sure if Tesla ever utilized the power of the weapon he claimed to have created. However, for years an intriguing rumor has circulated to the effect that Tesla's device was somehow linked with the devastation that occurred at Tunguska, Russia in 1908.

That year, Robert Peary, a well-known explorer, was attempting to reach the North Pole. Somewhat cryptically, according to rumor, legend, and a little bit of verifiable fact, Tesla advised Peary that he would try and establish contact with him. Tesla further advised Peary that he should be on the lookout for anything "unusual." On June 30, at Wardenclyffe Tower, Tesla, along with an associate and friend named George Scherff, supposedly fired his death-ray to a spot that he determined was to the west of Peary. Tesla switched on the device. Legend states that, at first at least, it was difficult to know if the experiment had proven successful, as the extremity of the device emitted a light that was barely visible. However, again according to legend, an unfortunate owl that happened to be in the area at the absolute worst time flew from the branch of a tree towards the tower and was instantly disintegrated as it crossed the beam's destructive path.

Less concerned about the bird, however, Tesla's main interest was in trying to determine if Peary had indeed seen anything "unusual" in the area. Only silence followed, however, until the news came in of the strange devastation at Tunguska–also on June 30. Tesla concluded that his death ray had missed its planned target and, as a result, had unfortunately flattened Tunguska. Perhaps with some justification, and not altogether surprisingly, Tesla quickly dismantled his death ray, deeming it far too dangerous to remain in existence. But others would follow in his footsteps. (9)

British inventor and definitive eccentric Harry Grindell-Matthews made similar assertions. Born in 1880 at Winterbourne, England, he was schooled at the Merchant Venturer's School in Bristol and went on to become an electronic engineer. In 1923, Grindell-Matthews asserted he had created "an electric ray" that could disable engines, aircraft, and even soldiers – all from a considerable and safe distance.

A highly intrigued British War Office contacted Grindell-Matthews and asked for a demonstration of his device. He failed to reply but instead gave a demonstration for journalists, allegedly confirming his claims that the device could remotely ignite gunpowder. Grindell-Matthews then announced that he had an offer to develop his device in France, as *The New York Times* noted on May 21, 1924:

Paris, May 20 - If confidence of Grindell Mathews, inventor of the so-called 'diabolical ray,' in his discovery is justified, it may become possible to put the whole of an enemy army out of action, destroy any force of airplanes attacking a city or paralyze any fleet venturing within a certain distance of the coast by invisible rays. Grindell-Matthews stated that his destructive rays would operate over a distance of four miles and that the maximum distance for this type of weapon would be seven or eight miles. Tests have been reported where the ray has been used to stop the operation of automobiles by arresting the action of the magnetos, and an quantity of gunpowder is said to have been exploded by playing the beams on it from a distance of thirty-six feet. Grindell-Matthews was able, also, to electrocute mice, shrivel plants, and light the wick of an oil lamp from the same distance away.

Interestingly, *The New York Times* learned that other rumors were surfacing about death rays in the same period, including one from the Soviet Union that the newspaper highlighted on May 28: "News has leaked out from the Communist circles in Moscow that behind Trotsky's recent war-like utterance lies an electromagnetic invention, by a Russian engineer named Grammachikoff for destroying airplanes."

For its part, the British Government was initially, but privately, very interested in the claims of Grindell-Matthews but was equally highly cautious of being potentially deceived by what it feared might simply be a crackpot inventor looking for unlimited money to promote and further his strange and futuristic pursuits. Indeed, when Grindell-Matthews finally allowed the British Air Ministry to sit in on one of his tests–that saw his device apparently switch on a light bulb and disable an electric motor–officials suspected that nothing more mysterious than rank fakery was in evidence.

On May 28, questions were raised at an official level in the British Government's House of Commons with regard to what steps would be taken to prevent the inventor from marketing his death ray to potentially hostile, overseas nations. The Under-Secretary for Air replied that Grindell-Matthews had not been willing to let them investigate the ray to their satisfaction and added that one brave (or very stupid) Ministry employee had actually stood in front of the ray and lived to tell the tale–completely intact, too. And so, therefore, what further action could the Government reasonably take?

And so, a compromise was finally reached. The Government stated that if Grindell-Matthews proved to its satisfaction that his death ray could render a petrol-drive motorcycle useless, he would receive a generous four-figure grant to allow for further funding to commence. But from his new location in France, Grindell-Matthews flatly declined the offer. In fact, he continued to decline offers from other potential investors, including Sir Samuel Instone and his brother, Theodore, who offered the inventor (or "mad professor") a truly huge salary to work for them. The proof that Grindell-Matthews' death ray actually worked continued to remain overwhelmingly elusive.

In July 1924, Grindell-Matthews embarked upon a trip to the United States in an attempt to secure financing for his potentially deadly invention. But having been offered the impressive sum of $25,000 to demonstrate the powers of his device to one and all at the Radio World Fair at Madison Square Garden, he again declined, giving the somewhat lame excuse that usage of the device outside of the confines of the British Isles was wholly unacceptable.

By 1930, Grindell-Matthews was once again back in his home-country of England with yet another ingenious creation—one designed to project images onto thick clouds. Success continued to elude him, however, and it wasn't long at all before bankruptcy came calling. Grindell-Matthews died of a heart attack on September 11, 1941, completely forgotten by the British Government. But strange activity suggestive of death rays would continue in the British Isles during the 1940s. (10)

It is a verifiable, historical fact that the British Air Ministry had been working on a number of secret radar-related projects as far back as the 1930s, and on January 28, 1935, the Tizard

Committee, established under the directorship of Sir Henry Tizard, convened its first meeting that eventually led to the development of a workable radar system of the type employed during the Second World War. Much of that research was conducted at a place called Bawdsey Manor on the Deben Estuary, just north of the town of Felixstowe, an area that, at the time and in years since, had a rich history replete with mysterious car-engine failures not unlike those that Harry Grindell-Matthews had claimed his death-ray could successfully accomplish. (11)

UFO researchers Jenny Randles, Dot Street, and Brenda Butler noted the following:

Local inhabitants were not so impressed by the goings on at Bawdsey Manor. They often complained that vehicles approaching the village suffered engine failure due to "invisible rays," which interfered with their electrical circuits. Others even said that aircraft had fallen out of the sky like stones, when over flying the radar station. Officially, there was no justification for these views. Experimental radar should not have created these drastic effects, but the rumors took hold that secret and more deadly experimentation was being conducted. Some people knew of the experiments that the radio genius Marconi was supposed to have worked on in Italy. He was said to have developed a "death-ray" when trying to perfect radar, and its side-effects were very like those claimed by the Bawdsey residents. (12)

The theory that secret research along these lines was being undertaken at Bawdsey Manor, and elsewhere, is something that was addressed by the renowned R. V. Jone, a man who played an integral role in British scientific intelligence between 1939 and 1945. Moreover, Jones was in charge of coordinating British intelligence with respect to the German V-1 and V-2 rockets at the time. Jones, therefore, cannot be dismissed when he stated: "At the outset, Tizard and his Committee had a tremendous stroke of luck, for on 18th January 1935 Wimperis [H.E. Wimperis, the Director of Scientific Research in the Air Ministry at the time] saw R.A. Watson-Watt of the Radio Research Station at Slough, and asked him to advise on the practicability of proposals of the type colloquially called 'death-ray.'"

In addition, Jones maintained that one weapon that would have surely served the British military very well during the war and that "must be considered seriously" was an "engine-stopping ray"–very much like the one Harry Grindell-Matthews claimed to have created. (13)

Further evidence that research into so-called death ray-type devices was being undertaken in both the immediate pre-war era, as well as during the conflict itself, comes via a series of noteworthy newspapers and magazines. The first, a United Press Release of June 6, 1934, states:

A death-ray machine was conspicuously absent today from the exhibition room of the National Inventors Congress, presumably at the request of the Federal Government. Its death-dealing potentialities were described to the congress last night by President A.G. Burns of Oakland, California. The machine, invention of Dr. Antonio Longoria of Cleveland, resembles a motion picture projector, Burns said.

"I witnessed a demonstration of the machine in Cleveland last October," Burns said. "Several Government scientists were there. Dr. Longoria turned the ray on rabbits, dogs and cats. They fell over, instantly killed, their blood turned to water. The same thing happened to pigeons. They fluttered to the ground and were dead when picked up."

Because of the ray's death-dealing possibilities, Burns said that Dr. Longoria readily agreed with Government scientists that the machine will be suppressed. (14)

On the same day, the following article appeared in various newspapers in Cleveland, Ohio:

An electric ray, whose death-dealing potentialities are said to be almost unlimited, will be suppressed until such time as it is needed for American defense, its inventor indicated today. Dr. Antonio Longoria, Cleveland physician and electrical engineer, informed that a report of his death-ray had been made to the Congress at Omaha, said details of the machine would remain a secret until a foreign invader entered the United States. Dr. Longoria, who perfected an inexpensive violet-ray machine and the first electrical device to measure the speed of an airplane, declined to comment on reports that his ray had been suppressed by governmental request. (15)

Whether or not Dr. Longoria did indeed hand over the designs for his weapon to the government of the United States is debatable. But according to *Popular Science* of February 1940, the doctor had decided that humankind would be far better off without the benefit of such a weapon:

Pigeons on the wing killed by death-rays from a machine from four miles away– that is the feat reputedly accomplished by a deadly apparatus developed by Dr. Antonio Longoria, of Cleveland, Ohio, who recently announced that he had deliberately destroyed the lethal machine for the good of humanity. The Cleveland inventor declared that he had stumbled upon the deadly rays while experimenting on the treatment of cancer with high-frequency radiations. The actions of the fatal rays, he declared, is [sic] painless and they work by changing the blood into a useless substance, much as light transforms silver salts in the photographic process. Before a group of scientists, it is reported, he once demonstrated that the radiations would kill rats, mice and rabbits, even when they were encased in a thick walled metal chamber. The rays, Dr. Longoria believes, could kill human beings just as easily. (16)

Perhaps Nazi Germany was engaged in something similar, too, at the time. Nigel Pennick, who has made a study of advanced German technology, has made a noteworthy contribution with specific regard to Adolf Hitler's interest and involvement in high-energy research:

> In connection with this high-energy research, various mysterious "transmitters" were erected at several "key points" in the Reich. In 1938, the Brocken, a celebrated peak in the Harz Mountains, was the site of feverish construction work...This "transmitter" was a strange contraption, a tower surrounded by an array of posts with pear-shaped knobs on top. At the same time, a similar system was erected on the peak of the Feldberg near Frankfurt. When it began operation, there were soon reports of strange phenomena in the vicinity of the Brocken tower. Cars traveling along the mountain roads would suddenly have engine failure. (17)

Possibly of equal relevance is the following, February 15, 1957, extract from the FBI's extensive file on none other than Albert Einstein:

> In May, 1948, [Einstein] and "10 former Nazi research brain trusters" held a secret meeting to observe a new beam of light secret weapon which could be operated from planes to destroy cities, according to the "Arlington Daily," Arlington, Virginia, May 21, 1948. The Intelligence Division of the Army subsequently advised the Bureau that this information could have no foundation in fact and that no machine could be devised which would be effective outside the range of a few feet.

To what extent the Army was being entirely truthful with the FBI is debatable, primarily due to the fact that research into such technology has undoubtedly continued unabated for decades–and apparently continues, too.

In a January 3, 2006 article titled "America's New Ray Guns," writer Taylor Dinerman noted that: "...such weapons are on the verge of being deployed (or, according to some sources, already have been.) Some of the better-known weapons include the Air Force's Airborne Laser (ABL), an anti-missile laser mounted inside a Boeing 747 and designed to shoot down medium range ballistic missiles in the boost phase of their flight. Another even more controversial system is the Active Denial System (ADS), a non-lethal crowd control weapon that uses high-powered microwaves to inflict serious, but temporary pain, on anyone affected by the beam." (18)

Another peak into the super secret world of "death ray" research appears in a 2009 book, *Connecting the Dots*, by Robert Howard, who was a major player in the development of numerous technologies, including cable television and the dot matrix printer. Howard reveals how, at the dawn of the 21st century, he undertook classified research for the military to build a workable death ray of the type that Nikola Tesla had envisaged.

Based out of Tucson, Arizona, Howard's company, Ionatron, created "…what we called a Laser Induced Plasma Channel (LIPC), which is a straight-line conductive channel that could carry very high-voltage electrical energy and be used as a destructive force weapon. In short, a death ray."

It seems that least some in the military were very impressed with the device: "When retired U.S. Navy Rear Admiral Thomas W. Steffens first saw a demonstration of this technology in 2002, he commented: 'This will change the nature of warfare and the battlefield long into the future.'" (19)

Bureaucratic infighting and red tape forced a change in the company name (to Applied Energetics, Inc.), but their work on developing directed-energy weapons continues to this day.

CI _____ (s) (b)(1)   SECRET

Also, the Soviet Union has allegedly had access
to some of Tesla's papers, possibly in Belgrade and/or
else where, which influenced their early research into directed
energy weapons, and _____ feels access to much of Tesla's
papers on lightning, beam weapons and/or "death rays" would
give him more insight into the Soviet beam weapons program.
This is Butler's area of expertise and responsibility. He
has been unable to locate any Tesla papers or copies of same
in the classified or unclassified libraries at WPAFB. However,
there are reports that some portions of them were shipped by
the Custodian of Alien Property Office in Washington, D.C. to
a technical research lab at WPAFB, possibly the "Equipment
Lab", now closed for some years or reorganized into another
organization.

_____ and _____ are both desirous of learning
the locations of such papers of Tesla as now exist in the U.S.,
for both intelligence and research purposes. Therefore, _____
would like to examine FBI files relating to Nikola Tesla and
possibly any on Sava Kosanovic, his nephew who received the
bulk of his papers after Tesla's death, and may possibly
have been the subject of FBI investigation.

_____ travels to the Washington, D.C. area on
FTD business periodically and can review FBI files at FBIHQ
relating to Tesla and Kosanovic.

REQUEST OF THE BUREAU

The Bureau is requested to conduct full indices checks
on both Nikola Tesla and Sava Kosanovic.

Should there be such files at FBIHQ, as well as at
New York, it is requested that Bureau consider granting the
above _____ of FTD, official access to same, in the
interest of national security.

LEADS

NEW YORK

AT NEW YORK, NEW YORK

Will conduct same indices check as requested of
Bureau and advise the Bureau and Cincinnati of results and
confirm such files and references still exist there.
                        -3-   SECRET

*A U.S. Government document on Nikola Tesla and his ominous
"Death Ray."*

■ ■ ■ ■ | | 12 | | ■ ■ ■ ■

Lightning Conspiracies

"There have been reports by observers of 'ball-lightning' to the effect that the phenomenon appeared to float through a room or other space for a brief interval of time without making contact with or being attracted by objects."

Ball lightning is a very poorly understood electrical, atmospheric phenomenon that almost exclusively manifests in the form of an airborne spherical object that varies in size from that of a tennis-ball to several meters. And it is a subject that has cropped up on more than a few occasions within the world of sci-fi.

One particularly early account of ball lightning surfaced in a children's book titled *On the Banks of Plum Creek*. Written by Laura Ingalls Wilder, the book was presented as historical fiction, but the author maintained that its content was based upon actual events that had really occurred in her life. In Wilder's version of events, one night, at the height of a winter storm, three balls of lightning appear near a cast-iron stove in the family's kitchen. They first manifest near the stovepipe and then roll across the floor, finally to vanish as the mother-character frantically pursues them with a willow-branch broom. (1)

In Dean Koontz's novel, *Dark Rivers of the Heart*, the protagonist encounters ball lightning while traveling through the Mojave Desert. (2) Similarly, within the pages of Eric Frank Russell's novel *Sinister Barrier*, ball lightning is explained as spheres of energy that dine upon human emotion. (3) But perhaps the most famous mention appears in Jules Verne's classic novel, *Journey to the Center of the Earth,* which tells of the chief characters' encounter with ball lightning while negotiating a vast underground ocean. (4)

So much for sci-fi, but what of the real–and highly-secret– military world's interest in ball lightning?

U.S. military files demonstrate that only two years after pilot Kenneth Arnold's now-legendary sighting of nine UFOs over the Cascade Mountains, Washington State on June 24, 1947, the military started to secretly study potential ways to exploit such phenomena for its own defensive and offensive needs. While the Air Force was attempting to determine if the saucers were extraterrestrial vehicles, Soviet inventions, or the brainchild of some deeply hidden branch of the U.S. military, the Department of Commerce (DoC) was following a far stranger path. In its own search for the answers, the DoC decided to focus its attention on ball lightning.

A technical report that was prepared on behalf of the Air Force's UFO research body, Project Grudge, in 1949, detailed the findings of the DoC's Weather Bureau in relation to ball lightning. The phenomenon, the DoC said, was

...spherical, roughly globular, egg-shaped, or pear-shaped; many times with projecting streamers; or flame-like irregular "masses of light." Luminous in appearance, described in individual cases by different colors but mostly reported as deep red and often as glaring white. Some of the cases of "ball-lightning" observed have displayed excrescences of the appearance of little flames emanating from the main body of the luminous mass, or luminous streamers have developed from it and propagated slantwise toward the ground.

In rare instances, it has been reported that the luminous body may break up into a number of smaller balls which may appear to fall towards the earth like a rain of sparks. It has even been reported that the ball has suddenly ejected a whole bundle of many luminous, radiating streamers toward the earth, and then disappeared. There have been reports by observers of "ball-lightning" to the effect that the phenomenon appeared to float through a room or other space for a brief interval of time without making contact with or being attracted by objects. (5)

Moreover, documentation released into the public domain under the provisions of the Freedom of Information Act in 2008 has disclosed the identity of a hitherto-unknown project based at the Edgewood Arsenal, Maryland, known as Harness-Cavalier, the specific goal of which was to try and understand ball lightning, control it, and ultimately turn it into an all-powerful weapon of warfare.

Nearly 130 separate documents have now surfaced from the archives of the project, including "Theory of the Lightning Ball and its Application to the Atmospheric Phenomenon Called 'Flying Saucers,'" written by Carl Benadicks in 1954; "Ball-lightning: A Survey," prepared by one J.R. McNally for the Oak Ridge National Laboratory, Tennessee (year unknown); D.V. Ritchie's "Reds May Use Lightning as a Weapon," which appeared in *Missiles and Rockets* in August 1959; and "An Experimental and Theoretical Program to Investigate the Feasibility of Confining Plasma in Free Space by Radar Beams," which was written by C.M. Haaland in 1960 for the Armor Research Foundation, Illinois Institute of Technology.

But, more significantly, as files generated via the Harness-Cavalier project demonstrate, staff attached to the program also held copies of two early science fiction novels: Bernard Newman's *The Flying Saucer*, and Gerald Heard's *Is Another World Watching?* Precisely why the employees of a clandestine project with distinct UFO overtones should have been studying science fiction stories on UFOs and aliens is worth pondering. And there is more still.

The most detailed evidence that completely confirms Edgewood Arsenal's fascination with trying to make use of ball lightning in a hostile environment can be read in a December 1965 report entitled "Survey of Kugelblitz Theories for Electromagnetic Incendiaries." Penned by W.B. Lyttle and C.E. Wilson, it was contracted by the Army's New Concepts Division/Special Projects at Edgewood.

The report states:

The purpose of this study was to review the theory and experimental data on ball-lightning, to compare the existing theory and experimental data to determine whether ball-lightning is a high or low energy phenomenon, and if it is a high-energy phenomenon, define an effective theoretical and experimental program to develop a potential incendiary weapon.

The authors added:

Three major categories were established for the purpose of grouping the numerous theories on the subject. These categories are the classical plasma theories, the quantum plasma theories, and the non-plasma theories. A theoretical and experimental Kugelblitz program is recommended by which the most promising high energy theories could be developed so that a weapons application could be realized.

The authors addressed the possibility that ball lightning might be explained as (A) a "plasma created by a lightning strike and maintained by electromagnetic standing waves," (B) a "non-plasma phenomenon...in the form of a highly ionised gas," and (C) the "nuclear theory," which was "based on the assumption that the content of the ball is radioactive carbon-14 created from atmospheric nitrogen by the action of thermal neutrons liberated by a lightning strike."

Most of the theories demanded additional investigation

but the team of Lyttle and Wilson did conclude that "since the high energy Kugelblitz is clearly the only type weapon of importance, we believe that the major effort should be expended along these lines."

One avenue the pair studied was the means by which ball lightning could conceivably be harnessed in the skies and "aimed" at a particular target on the battlefield:

If Kugelblitz is to be developed as a distinctive weapon, a means of guiding the energy concentration toward a potential target must be achieved. Some preliminary considerations on this subject have resulted in the idea of applying laser beams to such a task.

The pair added that "modulation of the vertical component of laser incident" would without doubt allow for "control of the Kugelblitz" and added that "forces necessary for guidance only will depend on local charges, as well as the net Kugelblitz charge and wind forces." In fact, Lyttle and Wilson believed that it was possible to mutate ball lightning into a laser-driven tool of warfare, noting:

The problem is a difficult one, but some light is beginning to appear on the subject. A concentrated analytical and experimental effort should be made soon as the implications of successful work could be far reaching. Only an adequately planned programme, utilizing a full time, competent staff with adequate equipment, can hope to succeed within a reasonable time period.

Needless to say, this all raises a variety of pertinent matters. The investigations at Edgewood were reportedly initiated in the formative months of 1950, but the "Survey of Kugelblitz Theories for Electromagnetic Incendiaries" paper that was prepared in 1965 indicates that the subject was still wholly theoretical. In view of this, it might be reasonable to state

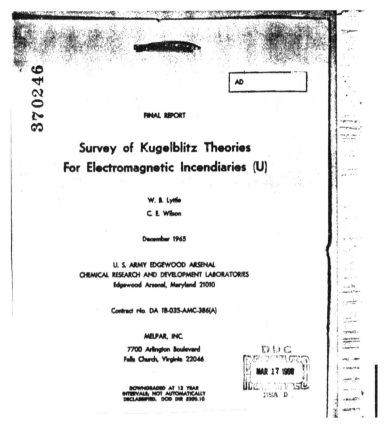

Has the military clandestinely turned ball lightning into a weapon?

that little headway was made in this decade-and-a-half with respect to turning ball lightning into an offensive tool of the Army. Conversely, it could also be reasonably argued that the very fact that the secret studies were permitted to run for years and years may be an indication that the military at least saw potential merit in the overall project.

It should also not pass without comment that Lyttle and Wilson were only contracted to prepare a document on their own, personal conclusions on ball lightning and the idea of attempting to utilize it as a weapon of warfare. Moreover, there is no data to support the notion that Lyttle and Wilson were given access to any particular documentation on the very early years of interest in this area on the part of staff at the Edgewood Arsenal. (6)

But has the research into ball lightning secretly continued? If so, then that research may shed some much needed light on one of the most infamous UFO events in recorded history.

The distinctly odd and surreal events that reportedly took place at Suffolk, England's Rendlesham Forest in the latter part of December 1980 are perceived by countless UFO researchers as hard evidence that extraterrestrials exist and have paid visits to the Earth. Nevertheless, it is crucial to be aware of the fact that the whole area has been the site of military experimentation of a highly secret nature for decades.

As a perfect case-in-point, a coastal strip of land called Orford Ness, which is situated near Rendlesham Forest, was the site of Britain's early radar-based studies in the 1930s. And as full-scale war with Nazi Germany loomed, a great deal of the radar-experimentation work was moved to RAF Bawdsey, which is located just a few miles south of Orford Ness, but still on the edges of Rendlesham Forest. And secret operations continued to be undertaken in the area for decades, including one code-named "Cobra Mist," which was defined as an "over the horizon" radar system that was put in use in the latter part of the 1960s to offer some advance warning of any attempt by the Soviets to launch a cataclysmic nuclear attack on Britain. (7)

And perhaps much more of a secret scientific nature was afoot, too.

On January 13, 1981, Colonel Charles Halt of the U.S. Air Force, and a key player in the strange series of events, prepared a single-page memorandum for the attention of the British Ministry of Defense that carefully detailed a vast amount of *Close Encounters of the Third Kind*-style activity deep among the trees and high in the skies above them, too. As Halt wrote:

... a red sun-like light was seen through the trees. It moved about and pulsed. At one point it appeared to throw off glowing particles and then broke into five separate white objects and then disappeared. Immediately thereafter, three star-like objects were noticed in the sky...the object to the south was visible for two or three hours and beamed down a stream of light from time to time. (8)

Startling stories of beams of light – which were viewed alongside maneuvering lights from which glowing particles emanated – sound not unlike the work of some clandestine project putting into Top Secret practice the theories and ideas expressed within the pages of the "Survey of Kugelblitz Theories for Electromagnetic Incendiaries" paper: the harnessing and manipulation of ball lightning via the power of lasers.

Without any doubt, though with some hindsight, Colonel Halt's very own words, which described the object in the woods seeming to "throw off glowing particles," read very much like the terminology that the U.S. Weather Bureau had utilized in the late-1940s to describe ball lightning:

...it has been reported that the luminous body may break up into a number of smaller balls which may appear to fall towards the earth like a rain of sparks. It has even been reported that the ball has suddenly ejected a whole bundle of many luminous, radiating streamers toward the earth.

Could a highly secret test of the type referred to within the pages of the Edgewood Arsenal's documentation of 1965 have taken place deep within Rendlesham Forest in the final days of December 1980? It is worth pointing out that nearly everyone who was involved in the Rendlesham events was attached to the military of the United States. In light of this, it is not outside the realm of possibility that a select group of high-ranking officials was keenly interested in determining how the military might react, at a psychological level, to the presence of something perceived as extraterrestrial phenomena, but that in actuality had far closer-to-home origins.

And there is yet a further matter that may be integral to this particularly controversial saga: the Edgewood Arsenal's Bio-Medical Laboratory was, from the early part of the 1950s up until around the mid-1970s (if not, perhaps, longer), home to a highly controversial series of tests that were focused upon the lengthy and widespread testing of such hallucinogens as LSD, THC, and BZ, as well as a wide variety of both chemical and biological agents on U.S. military operatives. The fact that several of the Air Force personnel implicated in the Rendlesham Forest affair claimed they were drugged by sources unknown following the main wave of encounters in the woods might actually not be as outlandish as it seems at first glance. (9)

Needless to say, hallucinogenic drugs, advanced weapons and delivery-systems, an intriguingly-titled "New Concepts Division," and the possible harnessing and control of ball lightning – all linked to the Edgewood Arsenal – collectively paint a highly intriguing picture.

Finally, it is well worth noting that the late Ralph Noyes–who had a lengthy career with the British Ministry of Defense, officially investigated UFOs for the MoD, and even wrote a science fiction novel on the controversial events that occurred at Rendlesham Forest in 1980–had a deep and lasting interest in, yes, you guessed it, ball lightning. In an article titled "Like Ball Lightning: In Memory of Ralph Noyes," fortean writer Dennis Stacy said of his personal encounters with the somewhat-enigmatic Noyes:

I first came into contact with Noyes during the late 1980s, when he submitted an article (if memory serves) about ball lightning to the *MUFON UFO Journal*, of which I was then editor. I accepted it, a correspondence followed, and so did a handful of subsequent articles on the newest mystery of the time – crop circles. In July of 1990, I attended what I think was the first international conference on crop circles, Terence Meaden's Oxford conference, and then spent a day in the fields with Meaden and other atmospheric scientists, viewing a ringed quintuplet, numerous grapeshot, and several magnificent dumb-bells, although, as soon became clear, the circle-makers had barely gotten started in terms of size and complexity. I don't think Noyes was at that conference, but I'm almost certain that I visited him shortly afterwards in his London home...

Among the ashtrays was a computer he was learning. His fingers were never far from a cigarette and neither were mine in those days. As quickly became evident, we both shared a love of the pulped grape as well, a dark burgundy, preferably. We puffed and sipped, sipped and puffed, and of course conversed. What were these miraculous new crop circles? Did they bear an intimate relation to ball lightning and/or UFOs? Fine and well; now, what would either of those be? (10)

What indeed?

Perhaps, given his deep interest in ball-lightning and sci-fi–and not to forget his secret UFO work for the Ministry of Defense–we should carefully consider the notion that Ralph Noyes, who firmly believed in the existence of a real UFO puzzle but who generally dismissed the extraterrestrial hypothesis out-of-hand, knew far more about what really occurred at Rendlesham Forest than initially meets the eye?

■ ■ ■ ■ ‖ 13 ‖ ■ ■ ■

BIG BROTHER IS WATCHING

"…he had received several reports regarding the controversy at Forest Hills High School, which appeared to center around classroom use of the book, Brave New World *by Aldous Huxley…"*

There can be very little doubt at all that two of the most influential and groundbreaking science fiction driven novels of all time are Aldous Huxley's *Brave New World*, and *Nineteen Eighty-Four* by George Orwell.

Born in Britain in 1894, Aldous Leonard Huxley immigrated to the United States to live, and although widely published in numerous disciplines, he is forever recognized for *Brave New World. Men like Gods*, a utopian story written by science fiction author H.G. Wells, inspired Huxley's tale, and its title is taken from a quote in Shakespeare's *The Tempest. Brave New World* is set in London in the 26th century, which is free of hunger, and poverty, illness, racism, and warfare are completely unknown. And while such a situation sounds like the ultimate utopian paradise, it most assuredly is not. The future is purely hedonistic and the "paradise" has been achieved only by the complete elimination of those aspects of civilization that are integral to many of us today: family, cultural diversity, art, literature, philosophy, and religion. (1)

Nineteen Eighty-Four is a satirical, political novel by George Orwell, who was born Eric Arthur Blair in 1903, and who authored another, truly enlightening and chilling book on tyranny: *Animal Farm. Nineteen Eighty-Four* takes place in

a nightmarish society where the State enforces perfect confor-
mity among members of a totalitarian Party through indoctrination, propaganda, fear, and ruthless punishment. The novel
introduced the concepts of the ever-present, all-seeing Big
Brother, Room 101, the Thought Police, and the bureaucrats'
and politicians' language of control: Newspeak.

A key difference between *Nineteen Eighty-Four* and *Brave
New World* is that while in the former the populace is firmly kept away from knowledge perceived to be subversive by
means of continual mass surveillance, censorship, and punishment, in the latter the characters do not care in the slightest
about dangerous knowledge in the first place. (2)

Social Critic Neil Postman contrasted the worlds of *1984*
and *Brave New World* in his 1986 book *Amusing Ourselves to
Death*: "What Orwell feared were those who would ban books.
What Huxley feared was that there would be no reason to ban
a book, for there would be no-one who wanted to read one."
(3)

But truly ironic is the fact that both Huxley and Orwell—
whose books graphically described the disastrous effects of
state-controlled society and surveillance, but in very different
ways—were watched closely by elements of the U.S. Government.

In 2000, the London *Times* newspaper reported that:

Many people remember reading George Orwell's *Animal Farm* in
high school or college, with its chilling finale in which the farm
animals looked back and forth at the tyrannical pigs and the ex-
ploitative human farmers but found it impossible to say which
was which. That ending was altered in the 1955 animated version, which removed the humans, leaving only the nasty pigs.
Another example of Hollywood butchering great literature? Yes,
but in this case the film's secret producer was the Central Intelligence Agency.
The CIA, it seems, was worried that the public might be

too influenced by Orwell's pox-on-both-their-houses critique of the capitalist humans and Communist pigs. So after his death in 1950, agents were dispatched (by none other than E. Howard Hunt, later of Watergate fame) to buy the film rights to *Animal Farm* from his widow to make its message more overtly anti-Communist. (4)

As for Aldous Huxley, he had the FBI to worry about after *Brave New World* began creating waves of trouble deep in the heart of Michigan. It was March 14, 1962, when a special agent from the FBI's head office in Michigan informed Bureau Director, J. Edgar Hoover, under cover of a document titled "Activities in Educational Institutions," of the fuss that Huxley's book was causing:

On March 9, 1962 [Deleted of] Michigan, advised she has children attending Forest Hills High school, 5091 Hall SE, Ada, Michigan, near Grand Rapids. She said she and other parents of children at the above school are concerned about the conduct of certain of the teachers there, and particularly the use of a book, "Brave New World", by Huxley, which is a subject of study at the school. [Deleted] said she had heard through sources that a history teacher at Forest Hills, had displayed a Russian flag in his classroom during the visit of Soviet Premier Kruschev to the United States, explaining that he did so in honor of a visiting head of state. She said she heard he had not displayed flags of other nations when their heads of state visited the United States.

[Deleted] said [a] recent graduate of Dartmouth College, who is an English teacher at Forest Hills, is using the novel "Brave New World" by Huxley, as a text for classroom study. She said she heard [Deleted] had a picture of a Russian flag on the blackboard or bulletin board in his classroom.

[Deleted] advised he had received several reports regarding the controversy at Forest Hills High School, which appeared to center around classroom use of the book, "Brave New World" by Aldous Huxley. The Forest Hills School Board had apparently ordered this book banned from use at the school, but a review of this decision was ordered when faculty members showed that only three of the seven members of the School Board had read the book. [Deleted] said he had no indication that any subversive activity was involved in the above controversy.

It seems that Big Brother really was watching, after all.

▪▪▎▊▏▏ 14 ▏▏▊▪▪▪

Secrets of The War Game

"The aim of the Government would be to avoid giving such a pessimistic picture that the public would feel 'what is the use of doing anything?'"

Seldom are the on-screen worlds of science fiction and reality blended so successfully as to attract the attention and concern of the highest echelons of government. But such a scenario is by no means unknown. A perfect example was a British TV production called *The War Game*. Produced in 1965 by Peter Watkins for the British Broadcasting Corporation (BBC), *The War Game* painted a horrific, futuristic picture of what life would be like in Britain in the event of a global, thermonuclear war: atomic devastation, death on a truly massive scale, widespread radiation poisoning, disease, starvation, mercy killings of irradiated members of the public at the hands of the military, firing squads for looters – presuming, of course, that anyone in an official position would be left alive to order the firing squads, to prevent the total breakdown of society, and to oversee the subsequent development of a somewhat *Mad Max*-style future. (1)

Whereas Hollywood's 1983 science fiction drama on nuclear war, *The Day After*, produced lasting images of hope for the masses, to the effect that humanity would ultimately surface from the ashes and all would one day be well again, *The War Game* gave precisely the opposite image. (2) Its bleak–yet far more realistic–message was that following a complete nuclear

Why was the BBC's futuristic drama The War Game, about a devastating nuclear attack on the British Isles, not shown for 20 years?

exchange between the super-powers of the Cold War, those who survived the initial holocaust and the inevitable complete and utter breakdown of society and civilization that is sure to follow would be faced with a future so terrible, and from which widespread recovery would be an impossibility for centuries, that instant death in the atomic inferno would seem like a veritable blessing.

Today, more than forty years after it was made, *The War Game* has lost none of its stark and powerful impact. Despite the fact that the show was produced in 1965, it was never shown on British television until 1985–the same year that the BBC broadcast an even more unsettling and graphic science fiction drama on nuclear war titled *Threads*. (3)

But why, for decades, would the BBC ban a drama that combined in such a unique fashion science-fact and sci-fi? Was it simply a unilateral decision of the BBC to spare the population at large the horrific reality of a nuclear war that might never happen, anyway? To answer those questions, it becomes necessary to examine a formerly classified British Government file that has remained classified for decades.

It was in 1963 that Peter Watkins first put forward a proposal to the BBC for *The War Game*–a proposal that would graphically, and specifically, illustrate the effects of a nuclear attack on the British county of Kent. Despite the controversial nature of Watkins' idea, it *was* accepted by the BBC that stated: "So long as there is no security risk, and the facts are authentic, the people should be trusted with the truth." Nevertheless, "the people" were not given the facts. (4)

In November 1965, with the production of *The War Game* complete, the then-Director-General of the BBC, Hugh Greene, arrogantly announced that the program would not be broadcast: "This is the BBC's own decision. It has been taken after a good deal of thought and discussion but not as a result of outside pressure of any kind." A condescending Greene stated that *The War Game* was "too horrifying for the medium of broadcasting." (5)

As a result, for two decades both the film and its apocalyptic message lay buried deep in the darkened vaults of the BBC. While it is true that the ultimate decision not to broadcast Peter Watkins' show was the BBC's, as Duncan Campbell noted in his chilling book *War Plan UK*, "outside pressure" had indeed been brought to bear on the BBC. As Campbell stated: "Late in September [1965] a party of Whitehall's highest visited the Television Center, unannounced." (6)

That party, Campbell added, consisted of the British Government's Cabinet Secretary, Sir Burke Trend; Home Office Permanent Under-Secretary, Sir Charles Cunningham; officials from the Ministry of Defense; and the Defense Chiefs of Staff. The Government was unanimous: it was not, in what was patronizingly termed, the "public interest" for *The War Game* to be broadcast, and a blanket ban at the hands of the BBC was the order of the day. (7)

Now declassified, official files reveal, however, that the seeds of the Government's decision to bring pressure to bear on the BBC to ensure that the film was not shown to the masses had, in fact, been sown at least as far back as 1954. "I am informed that the BBC are proposing to broadcast in the New Year a program on the Hydrogen bomb," wrote British Prime Minister Winston Churchill in a personal minute to the minister responsible for the BBC, Earl De La Warr, on December 17, 1954. Churchill continued: "I doubt whether it is wise that they should do this. And I am sure that Ministers should see the script in advance, in order to satisfy themselves that it contains nothing which is contrary to the public interest."

As a result of Churchill's desire to try and influence the BBC, immediate steps were taken on the part of the Government to determine the extent of the BBC's proposed plans. Within 24 hours the BBC faced a battery of questions: What did the Corporation intend to broadcast? What information on thermonuclear weapons would be contained in the program? And would such a production be in the public interest? The Government demanded answers.

For its part, the BBC flatly denied that it had any firm plans for such a program, but did admit that ideas had been mooted by "one of our producers." Despite the BBC's assurances that at that stage nothing concrete had been decided, behind the closed doors official concern was mounting fast. An extract from a four-page report of January 7, 1955, stamped "Highly Confidential" and titled "Government 'Interference' with BBC Program" stated: "It would be quite wrong to have programs on this subject which tended to persuade the public in the U.K. that there was no point in trying to defend themselves against such an all-destructive weapon."

Additional documentation contained within the file reiterates this point and makes it very clear that the Government's prime concern was not so much the fact that the BBC was contemplating the broadcast of a program on the hydrogen bomb per se. Rather, the major area of worry was whether or not any proposed show would reveal the true, devastating effects that a nuclear attack would have on the population of Great Britain. For example, a Secret memo of February 15, 1955, contained within the file, which dealt with official nuclear policy, stated: "The aim of the Government would be to avoid giving such a pessimistic picture that the public would feel 'what is the use of doing anything?'"

Perhaps most astonishing of all, however, is an entry in the document collection that refers, in apparent seriousness, to the Government's sincere hope that in the event of a nuclear war—with an official forecast of tens of millions likely to be killed in Britain alone in the initial bombing, and millions more dying in the immediate aftermath from the effects of radiation, burns, starvation, disease, and bomb-blast—there would be a "resolute determination" on the part of the population to "see the thing through whatever befall." Needless to say, such comments defy belief.

It is also interesting to note that the British were very possibly following a lead set down by their American cousins. A Secret report contained in the file reveals:

Up to the present the United States Government were compelled by their existing law to be very secretive about thermonuclear bombs and they had given us little or no information on the effects produced by the bomb. It was only recently that we were able to get such information from our own experiments. Nevertheless, we had been in the closest touch with the United States Government as to how the matter should be presented to the public. (8)

It is not surprising that British authorities did not wish to see the effects of a nuclear attack made available to the public by the BBC. In the same year that Prime Minister Winston Churchill expressed concern over the BBC's proposals, President Dwight D. Eisenhower's Technological Capabilities Panel of the Scientific Advisory Committee published a report titled "Meeting the Threat of Surprise Attack" that outlined one particularly bleak scenario that would follow a major nuclear strike by the Soviet Union on the continental United States. In part, the document stated:

A surface blast 10 Megaton bomb can result in covering an area of 2500-5000 square miles with sufficient activity that a person in the open for one day immediately following detonation will receive a dose large enough to cause radiation sickness; an area of 700 to 1400 square miles would receive sufficient activity to cause death to most people who are similarly exposed. (9)

Doubtless, some of this information would have filtered back to Winston Churchill, hence his Government's policy of keeping the BBC and the public ignorant and away from the controversy surrounding nuclear war. Meanwhile, another entry in the file makes much the same point:

The Government's main anxiety was that they should retain control over the manner in which the effects of nuclear weapons were made known to the public. Great care would be needed in striking the right note, so that the public were made aware of the full power of these weapons without being led thereby to adopt an attitude either of despair or of indifference to the need for effective measures of defense.

Notably, a memo dated February 16, 1955, asserted that the BBC had come to a decision by that date that: "It was unlikely that the BBC would wish to mount any feature program on 'fall out' or other effects of nuclear weapons but, if at any time they thought of doing so, they would certainly proceed in consultation with the Ministry of Defense."

It was this statement that led Churchill to maintain that the BBC had "willingly accepted" the Government's position, when in reality and behind closed doors, the BBC was vehemently against any such form of Government censorship.

Nevertheless, thus was laid down the unofficial and uneasy policy between the BBC and the Government that ultimately relegated *The War Game* to its twenty-year burial behind the closed-doors of the BBC. Indeed, it was this same policy that gave the Government of the day a profound sense of relief. For example, extracts from the file show that to some officials, the idea of officially banning the BBC from producing a TV drama on nuclear war was perceived as a highly fraught move. One unnamed official said: "The Government must have the right to indicate to the BBC where it felt the Corporation might be stepping beyond the bounds of international safety, yet the independence of the BBC from Government control was a vital matter." (10)

In an age that has seen the fall of the Berlin Wall and the collapse of the Soviet Union, it might seem irrelevant to be discussing decades-old official documents on a futuristic television drama about nuclear war. However, both *The War Game* and the papers in question address much bigger issues in our lives: they deal with the public's right to know; the ability of the media to freely—and without government interference and surveillance–inform the public on matters of critical concern; and the fine line that exists between what should remain withheld in the interests of national security and that which some dark-suited official figure has loftily and outrageously deemed is not in the "public interest."

■ ■ ■ ■ ‖ 15 ‖ ■ ■ ■ ■

Alien Invaders and Iron Mountain

"Experiments have been proposed to test the credibility of an out-of-our-world invasion threat; it is possible that a few of the more difficult-to-explain 'flying saucer' incidents of recent years were in fact early experiments of this kind."

"Mercury Theatre on the Air" performed Orson Welles' radio adaptation of H.G. Wells' classic science fiction book *War of the Worlds* on October 30, 1938, specifically as a Halloween special. The program was broadcast from the 20th floor of 485 Madison Avenue, and was ingeniously presented in the form of a regular show that was repeatedly interrupted by a series of disturbing and escalating news stories detailing gigantic explosions on the planet Mars that were rapidly followed by frantic reports of the landing of an alien spacecraft near the town of Grover's Mill, New Jersey.

As the broadcast progresses, more Martian war-machines land and proceed to wreak havoc throughout the continental United States. The Secretary of the Interior informs the pain-stricken populace of the grave nature of the ever-growing conflict, and the military launches a desperate counterattack against the burgeoning Martian assault. Frantic reports describe thousands of people fleeing urban areas as the unstoppable Martians head towards New York City. "Isn't there anyone on the air?" pleads a desperate broadcaster in suitably dramatic and chilled tones.

Of course, Welles had merely intended the show to be an

entertaining radio rendition of *War of the Worlds* and nothing more. However, those listeners who were unfortunate enough to have missed the beginning of the production–in which Welles was very careful to say that the broadcast was simply a piece of fictional entertainment and absolutely nothing else– really did believe that a Martian attack on the Earth had begun, and that the end of civilization was possibly looming on the dark horizon. Indeed, newspapers of the day stated that large-scale panic followed in the wake of the show. And although later studies suggested the hysteria was actually far less widespread than newspaper accounts initially suggested, many people were indeed caught up in the initial cosmic confusion. (1)

The legend of what occurred on that fateful night left a deep impression on science fiction writers, too. The 1968 book *Sideslip*, written by Ted White and Dave Van Arnam, is an ingenious tale that takes place on an alternate Earth, where genuine Martians ruthlessly take advantage of the panic that follows Welles' broadcast and launch a real invasion of Earth. (2) The 1984 movie *The Adventures of Buckaroo Banzai Across the 8th Dimension* tells the tale of an extraterrestrial species known as the Lectroids, who take control of Welles's mind and force him to unknowingly present the show as merely a drama in order to hide the fact that the Martians really had invaded. (3) Even *The X-Files* got in on the act: the episode titled "War of the Coprophages" used the events of 1938 as the inspiration for a story that sees the fictional town of Miller's Grove overrun by an army of cyborg cockroaches. (4) And, in a skillfully developed plot in the *War of the Worlds* television series, Orson Welles is portrayed as a secret government asset whose show carefully masks the deeper truth of a small-scale penetration of the Earth by a race of Martians who subsequently embark on a successful, planetary-wide assault in the 1950s. (5)

It has also been suggested by conspiracy theorists, such as

the late William Cooper, that the *War of the Worlds* broadcast was actually a psychological warfare experiment secretly sponsored by elements of the U.S. Government to try and accurately determine how the population might react to the presence of a hostile alien menace, albeit an entirely false and officially manufactured one, rather like a "War on Terror" for the *X-Files* generation. (6)

Although the majority of those who have studied such claims have outright dismissed them, the scenario of Government officials conspiring to unite (or, perhaps, enslave) humankind under one banner, as a result of an intergalactic alien threat, was discussed extensively in a controversial publication titled *Report From Iron Mountain*.

Writer Philip Coppens states:

In 1967, a major publisher, The Dial Press, released *Report from Iron Mountain*. The book claimed to be a suppressed, secret government report, written by a commission of scholars, known as the "Special Study Group," set up in 1963, with the document itself leaked by one of its members. The Group met at an underground nuclear bunker called Iron Mountain and worked over a period of two and a half years, delivering the report in September 1966. The report was an investigation into the problems that the United States would need to face if and when 'world peace' should be established on a more or less permanent basis. (7)

And as the *Report*, itself, noted:

It is surely no exaggeration to say that a condition of general world peace would lead to changes in the social structures of the nations of the world of unparalleled and revolutionary magnitude. The economic impact of general disarmament, to name only the most obvious consequence of peace, would revise the production and distribution patterns of the globe to a degree that would make the changes of the past fifty years seem insignificant. Political, sociological, cultural, and ecological changes would be equally far-reaching. What has motivated our study of these contingencies has been the growing sense of thoughtful men in and out of government that the world is totally unprepared to meet the demands of such a situation. (8)

Upon its first appearance in 1967, *Report From Iron Mountain* ignited immediate and widespread debate among journalists and scholars with its disturbingly convincing conclusion: namely, that a condition of "permanent peace" at the end of the Cold War would drastically threaten the United States' economic and social stability. Although subsequently identified as nothing more than an ingenious hoax written by Leonard Lewin, who had both conceived and launched the book with the help of a select body of players in the peace movement–including *Nation* editors Victor Navasky and Richard Lingeman, novelist E. L. Doctorow, and economist John Kenneth Galbraith–the controversy surrounding *Report From Iron Mountain* refuses to roll over and die. (9)

Long out of print, the *Report* suddenly began to reappear in bootlegged editions more than twenty years after its original publication, amid claims that its contents were all-too-real. Colonel Fletcher Prouty, a national security aide in the Kennedy Administration (and the model for Donald Sutherland' character, "X" in Oliver Stone's hit-movie *JFK*), continues to believe to this very day that the report is indeed authentic, and he specifically referred to it within the pages of his memoirs. Notably, in a 1992 Preface to Prouty's memoirs, no less a person than Oliver Stone himself cited the *Report From Iron Mountain* as specifically raising "the key questions of our time." (10)

After the book's initial publication, it was reported that then President Lyndon B. Johnson had deep suspicions that the late President John F. Kennedy had authorized the publication of the *Report*. Moreover, Johnson is famously alleged to have "hit the roof" upon learning of its publication. (11)

In 1992, *Iron Mountain* author Lewin filed a lawsuit for

copyright infringement against Willis Carto, a white suprem-
acist, for allegedly publishing the now-discontinued, bootleg
editions of the book. Interestingly, Mark Lane, an author who
has written extensively on the Kennedy assassination and who
served as Carto's lawyer, stated that *Report From Iron Mountain* may indeed have been a real government document and,
therefore, could not be seen to have any bearing upon current
United States copyright laws. (12)

Similarly, a May 1995, front-page article in the *Wall Street
Journal* reported that extreme-right fringe groups continued to
quote *Report From Iron Mountain* as "proof of a secret government plot to suppress personal liberties and usher in a New
World Order dominated by the U.N." (13)

The response of the media in 1967 to the initial publication of the *Report* was equally notable: "As I would put my
personal repute behind the authenticity of this document, so I
would testify to the validity of its conclusions. My reservations
relate only to the wisdom of releasing it to an obviously un-
conditioned public," said John Kenneth Galbraith in the Book
World supplement of the Sunday *Washington Post*. (14)

"It is, of course, a hoax–but what a hoax!–a parody so
elaborate and ingenious and, in fact, so substantively original,
acute, interesting and horrifying, that it will receive serious attention regardless of its origin," stated Eliot Fremont-Smith in
the pages of *The New York Times* in 1967. (15)

And in 1995, in the *New York Review of Books*, Garry Wills
wrote: "Fear of the Pentagon, fairly new on the right, is an old
companion of the left. A shrewd satire, *Report from Iron Mountain* was published in 1967 to mock delusions of 'wargamers.'
But people continue to copy and circulate it: if it is a government document, it is public property; and if it is copyrighted,
that just shows how the government uses its illegal power to
suppress information." (16)

But what of the scenario presented in the *Report* itself of Government officials secretly plotting to create a science fiction style, faked and potentially hostile, alien presence on the Earth that would be used as a tool of fear to unite–or, perhaps enslave–humankind and usher in a dark, cold dictatorship-style world? On this particularly controversial matter, the *Report* states:

Credibility, in fact, lies at the heart of the problem of developing a political substitute for war. This is where the space-race proposals, in many ways so well suited as economic substitutes for war, fall short. The most ambitious and unrealistic space project cannot of itself generate a believable external menace. It has been hotly argued that such a menace would offer the 'last, best hope of peace," etc., by uniting mankind against the danger of destruction by "creatures" from other planets or from outer space. Experiments have been proposed to test the credibility of an out-of-our-world invasion threat; it is possible that a few of the more difficult-to-explain "flying saucer" incidents of recent years were in fact early experiments of this kind. (17)

The *Report From Iron Mountain* was probably a work of fiction then–albeit a very thought-provoking one. And it was a brilliantly executed piece of fiction, too. Its contents, observations, and conclusions were, and still are, considered by many to be highly valid. And, of course, the *Report* still has its disciples who firmly believe it to be the absolute, real thing.

In view of that, if UFOs do one day attack, we would be very wise to consider the all-too-real possibility that they may not be manned by little green (or grey) men from Alpha Centauri, after all, but rather by large and burly men in standard-issue military flight suits, whose secret agenda it is to help usher in, in the minds of the world's population at least, the image of an overwhelming alien threat that has no more basis in reality than Iraq's forever-elusive weapons of mass destruction.

Keeping in mind the contents and the conclusions of the *Report From Iron Mountain*, perhaps we should be looking to the skies above us, not to the Middle East, for the next "threat" that will undoubtedly and shamefully impinge even further upon our rapidly eroding civil liberties.

■ ■ ■ ▮▮ 16 ▮▮■ ■ ■

THE ANDROMEDA STRAIN:
FACT OR FICTION?

*"The samples extracted from bodies found in New Mexico, have
yielded new strains of a retro-virus not totally understood, but,
give promise of the ultimate BW weapon."*

In 1929, Frederick County, Maryland, purchased ninety acres
of farmland for use as a municipal airport. Twelve months
later, this tract of land was leased to the Maryland National
Guard for use as a summer training camp for the 104th Observation Squadron, and ultimately became known as Detrick
Field. In 1941, President Roosevelt ordered the establishment
of the U.S. Biological Warfare program. As a result, in 1943,
Detrick Field was renamed Camp Detrick and was assigned to
the Army Chemical Warfare Service for the development of a
Biological Warfare Research Center. The original 90-acre tract,
plus an adjoining 53 acres, was purchased in 1944. By that time,
Camp Detrick was well established as the site for the research
and development of offensive and defensive biological warfare
techniques and agents.

The site received another name change in 1956 and was officially designated Fort Detrick. After official biological warfare
activities were discontinued on April 1, 1972, the control of Fort
Detrick was transferred from the U.S. Army Material Command to the Office of the Surgeon General, Department of the
Army, and further assigned as a subordinate installation of the
U.S. Army Medical Department. A year later, Fort Detrick was
reassigned from the U.S. Army Surgeon General to the newly

created U.S. Army Health Services Command (HSC). In 1995, HSC was itself reorganized into the U.S. Army Medical Command (MEDCOM). (1)

And while the majority of the work undertaken at Fort Detrick is of a wholly down-to-earth nature, there have been exceptions to the rule, according to Ralph Jameson, who undertook contract work there in the 1970s. Notably, one of those exceptions has a direct relationship to sci-fi, and specifically to author Michael Crichton's 1960s techno-thriller, *The Andromeda Strain*.

The Andromeda Strain of the book's title is a deadly extraterrestrial virus that is brought to Earth when an American space satellite crashes near a remote Arizona town. Within days the virus practically wipes out the entire local population. Four scientists, chosen specifically for their experimental and groundbreaking achievements in the fields of clinical microbiology, epidemiology, pathology, and electrolyte chemistry are summoned under conditions of total news blackout and utmost secrecy and urgency to the Wildfire secret laboratory that is situated deep below the Nevada desert where the contaminated individuals and bodies have been taken.

There, sealed off from the outside world, the scientists work against the threat of a worldwide epidemic, in an effort to find an antidote to the unknown microorganism. Step by step, they begin to unravel the puzzle of the Andromeda Strain, until, terrifyingly, the virus succeeds in rupturing the sterile environment of the laboratory and their already desperate search for a biomedical answer becomes a split-second race against time that results from the Government's decision to destroy the facility–and, hopefully, the virus–with an atomic weapon. (2)

And although *The Andromeda Strain* is merely an entertaining piece of sci-fi, it may have its real-life counterpart. Ralph Jameson states that, in 1972, while working and liais-

E. Nuclear Weapons Development

Miniturization of atomic bomb components is the goal of the AEC and the AFSWP. Studies at MIT indicate that such a technology is within reach before the decade is out. The apparent use of micro-circuitry found on the recovered planform indicates that miniturisation, low-power transmission, light conductor/sensitive components are required for interplanetary space travel. Atomic engines and nuclear propulsion technologies could be advanced based upon current use of hydrogen and electro-magnetic research and weapons components development in U.S. and U.K.

F. Biological Warfare Programs

BW programs in U.S. and U.K., are in field test stages. Discovery of new virus and bacteria agents so lethal, that serums derived by genetic research, can launch medical science into unheard of fields of biology. The samples extracted from bodies found in New Mexico, have yielded new strains of a retro-virus not totally understood, but, give promise of the ultimate BW weapon. The danger lies in the spread of airborne and bloodborne outbreaks of diseases in large populations, with no medical cures available.

G. Genetic and Pharmaceutical Development Programs

Current research in U.S. and U.K., can be accellerated when studies are complete. Understanding the human makeup through XXX research will bring a varied wealth of information in how cells replicate themselves and may help in developing new drugs and markets. Healthcare industries are considered the best source of R&D for DoD programs.

H. New Materials Development

Conclusions reached by the Air Materiel Command in 1948, upon the close examination of the material structure of the Corona and Oscura Peak, N.M. sites, compelled the Air Force to launch a new machinability research program. Samples tested and evaluated by the AMC, suggested that future materials would have to incorporate new alloys and composites, if space exploration and hypersonic dynamics are to be achieved. As a result, new machining techniques are underway for high-temperature alloys and titanium.

-5-

Is the subject of alien viruses a secret reality or science fiction?

ing with staff at Fort Detrick, he had the opportunity to read a document titled "The Andromeda Strain: Fact or Fiction?" Jameson is keen to stress that the document was not an officially sanctioned document. Instead, it had been researched and written by an employee of Fort Detrick in his free time. The man had reportedly submitted the document to his superiors in the event that it was deemed to be of interest to Fort Detrick employees, as well as for future research and consideration.

Jameson further elaborates that the report specifically addressed *The Andromeda Strain* scenario presented within the pages of Crichton's book and in the 1971 science fiction movie of the same name, and looked deeply into the issue of whether or not such a nightmare scenario could one day become a reality. The report ran to 194 pages and was concerned with two controversial issues (1) an alien virus finding its way to Earth, possibly on a meteorite, and (2) widespread contamination of the Earth by an alien virus as a direct result of astronauts bringing back samples from the Moon or, perhaps later, Mars.

The report allegedly dug deep into the way an out-of-control, extraterrestrial virus could spread wildly, how worldwide authorities might be forced to deal with it, what precautions would need to be taken if matters escalated, and how a viable vaccine might be created, if indeed such a vaccine could even be created. The report also discussed how, in a truly nightmarish scenario, a possible vaccine might remain completely elusive; if so, this real-life *Andromeda Strain* might lead to the eventual extinction of humankind. The report, Jameson says, was placed into Fort Detrick's document archive and was occasionally "pulled out" and read by interested parties employed there.

Jameson further maintains that although the original copy of the document never left Fort Detrick, on one occasion something distinctly strange occurred. One of the three copies of the document that had been made was subsequently forwarded to the CIA's Office of Science and Technology and remained with the "S&T people" for several months. Interestingly, when the document was returned to Fort Detrick, it quickly became clear that its contents had been closely scrutinized; various "red-pencil changes" had been made to the document. More significantly, says Jameson, certain sections had been underlined and commented upon by someone at the CIA who seemed to know a "hell of a lot" about real alien viruses. (3)

Jameson states that one person who "knew about the document at Detrick" was a Dr. Charles Rush Phillips, who"definitely read the original document, but outside of Fort Detrick." Dr. Phillips arrived at Camp Detrick in 1943 as a junior enlisted man and his work with gaseous sterilization and decontamination techniques ultimately revolutionized applied science. Fort Detrick authority Norman Covert wrote: "[Phillips'] work between 1943 and 1969 made it possible for scientists to have and maintain the tools they needed to develop medical knowledge about microorganisms. The result has been the development of vaccines for a variety of diseases and an understanding of how disease spreads at Fort Detrick" (4)

Jameson stresses that he can add nothing further to this story.

But there is a postscript to this story. In 1996, a UFO researcher and resident of Big Bear Lake, California named Timothy Cooper claimed to have received copies of a series of still-classified documents that had a bearing on the notorious "UFO crash" at Roswell, New Mexico in July 1947. These documents came from an elderly whistleblower who had worked in the U.S. intelligence community since the 1940s. One of those documents was allegedly prepared by a super-secret group comprised of scientists and military-officials in American intelligence known as Majestic 12. It was titled: the "1st Annual Report." Relevant is the fact that the "1st Annual Report" refers to a lethal alien virus present at the New Mexico crash site that supposedly killed a number of technicians involved in the recovery of the alien craft and its crew. The document also references Fort Detrick.

The relevant section of the "1st Annual Report" states:

BW [Biological Warfare] programs in U.S. and U.K. are in field test stages. Discovery of new virus and bacteria agents so lethal, that serums derived by genetic research, can launch medical science into unheard of fields of biology. The samples extracted from bodies found in New Mexico, have yielded new strains of a retro-virus not totally understood, but, give promise of the ultimate BW weapon. The danger lies in the spread of airborne and bloodborne [sic] outbreaks of diseases in large populations, with no medical cures available. (5)

The document continues:

The Panel was concerned over the contamination of several SED personnel upon coming in contact with debris near the power plant. One technician was overcome and collapsed when he attempted the removal of a body. Another medical technician went into a coma four hours after placing a body in a rubber body-bag. All four were rushed to Los Alamos for observation. All four later died of seizures and profuse bleeding. All four were wearing protective suits when they came into contact wit body fluids from the occupants.

Autopsies on the four dead SED technicians are not conclusive. It is believed that that four may have suffered from some form of toxin or a highly contagious disease. Tissue samples are currently being kept at Fort Detrick, Md. (6)

It must be stressed that the "1st Annual Report" has been denounced by many UFO researchers as nothing more than an ingenious and outrageous hoax designed to further cloud the already murky waters of whatever it was that did or did not occur at Roswell, New Mexico in the summer of 1947. And if the contents of the document and their links to Fort Detrick are disinformation, then we should perhaps look at the account of Ralph Jameson with somewhat cautious eyes, too. Alternatively, perhaps there really is a terrifying secret being kept from us, and perhaps it is one that offers the possibility that there is already a deadly, extraterrestrial biological threat among us. It is decidedly sobering to imagine that the scenario presented within the pages of Michael Crichton's *The Andromeda Strain* may not just be mere sci-fi, after all. And in a somewhat similar scenario, evidence exists that demonstrates the former Soviet Union's KGB studied science fiction to conjure up disinformation-driven stories about the U.S. Government conspiring to create one of the most lethal of all viruses.

It was in 1983 that one of the strangest episodes in the world of international espionage began. That year KGB operatives began spreading dark rumors to the effect that the HIV virus was a tool of biological warfare that had been secretly developed in U.S. military laboratories. There can be little doubt that this plan was quite successful. Even the very briefest of perusals of the internet reveals a veritable mountain of data concerning allegations that HIV is a manufactured virus, not a naturally occurring one. Regardless of the ultimate truth of this strange affair, background data on the KGB's involvement in spreading rumors to the effect that the United States Government deliberately engineered HIV as a weapon of biological warfare were addressed in a 2005 Department of State document.

Titled "AIDS as a Biological Weapon," the document states:

When the AIDS disease was first recognized in the early 1980s, its origins were a mystery. A deadly new disease had suddenly appeared, with no obvious explanation of what had caused it. In such a situation, false rumors and misinformation naturally arose, and Soviet disinformation specialists exploited this situation as well as the musings of conspiracy theorists to help shape their brief but highly effective disinformation campaign on this issue.

In March 1992, then-Russian intelligence chief and later Russian Prime Minister Yevgeni Primakov admitted that the disinformation service of the Soviet KGB had concocted the false story that the AIDS virus had been created in a US military laboratory as a biological weapon. The Russian newspaper *Izvestiya* reported on March 19, 1992:

"[Primakov] mentioned the well known articles printed a few years ago in our central newspapers about AIDS supposedly originating from secret Pentagon laboratories. According to Yevgeni Primakov, the articles exposing US scientists' 'crafty' plots were fabricated in KGB offices. The Soviets eventually abandoned the AIDS disinformation campaign under pressure from the U.S. Government in August 1987."

In a section of the document titled "The Real Origins of AIDS," the Department of State noted:

In the mid-1980s, there was still considerable confusion about how AIDS had developed, although scientists universally agreed that it was a naturally occurring disease, not one that was man-made. In the intervening years, science has done much to solve this mystery. There is now strong scientific evidence that the AIDS virus originated as a subspecies of a virus that commonly infects the western equatorial African chimpanzee, Pan troglodytes. An article in the February 4, 1999, issue of *Nature* magazine called "Origin of HIV-1 in the Chimpanzee Pan Troglodytes," explained how scientists used mitochondrial DNA analysis to determine that "all HIV-1 strains known to infect man" were closely related to a simian immunodeficiency virus (SIV) found in the Pan troglodytes chimpanzee. The article also notes that the natural range of Pan troglodytes chimpanzees "coincides precisely with the areas of HIV-1 group endemicity." The less common HIV-2, which also causes AIDS, had previously been determined to be related to a virus infecting another African primate, the Sooty Mangebey.

The Department of State elaborated:

Dr. Beatrice Hahn of the University of Alabama and her colleagues made this discovery after analyzing frozen blood and tissue samples from four chimpanzees, including a lab chimp

named Marilyn, which had died in 1985. Modern tests for HIV re-
activity were not available at that time, and Marilyn's tissue and
blood samples were rediscovered only in 1998, making the new
analysis possible.
Dr. Hahn and her colleagues estimate that SIV may have existed in Pan troglodytes chimpanzees for as long as several hundred thousand years. Although it cannot be known with certainty
how the virus gained a foothold in humans, hunting chimpanzees
for food, which is common in west equatorial Africa, could have
provided a source for transmission from chimpanzees to humans.
Other scientific discoveries place the oldest known human
case of HIV as occurring in 1959. A February 5, 1998, article in
Nature, "An African HIV-1 sequence from 1959 and implications
for the origin of the epidemic," reported that a plasma sample
obtained in early 1959 from an adult Bantu male living in what
is now Kinshasa, Democratic Republic of the Congo (DRC) had
tested positive for HIV-1.
In 2000, scientists at the Los Alamos National Laboratory
used their powerful supercomputers to analyze the relationships
among various strains of HIV-1. Their calculations showed that
the main HIV-1 virus probably established itself in humans in
about 1930, as explained in an article in the June 8, 2000, issue
of *Science* magazine called, "Timing the Ancestor of the HIV-1
Pandemic Strains."
Thus, although a simian immunodeficiency virus appears
to have existed for very long periods of time in Pan troglodytes
chimpanzees, it did not lead to a pandemic in humans before the
20th century. The beginnings of modernization and urbanization
in western equatorial Africa in the early 1900s may have contrib-
uted to the rise of the AIDS pandemic. Between 1900 and 1961,
the population of what is now Kinshasa, DRC increased approximately 100 times, from a few thousand in 1900 to 420,000 in 1961.
This exponential growth in urbanization and related dislocations
of traditional rural life may have led to conditions that were con-
ducive to the spread of AIDS. Such possibilities are explored
at greater length in an article "Origin of HIV Type 1 in Colonial
French Equatorial Africa?" published in the journal *AIDS Research and Human Retroviruses* (volume 16, number 1, 2000, pp.
5-8).

The Department of State document then concluded:

HIV-1, the virus that caused the AIDS pandemic, could not be man-made because direct evidence shows that AIDS has existed in humans at least since 1959 and scientific analysis shows that it was probably present some 75 years ago, which is long before humans had the means to genetically engineer microbes. HIV-1 is very closely related to a similar virus found in equatorial West African chimpanzees

The scientific evidence indicates that the HIV-1 virus resulted from cross-species transmission, which is known to occur in other human diseases, including influenza, plague, tuberculosis, and many other diseases, especially since this species of virus has a strong predilection for frequent mutation, making adoption to humans relatively easy. Social and economic conditions in western equatorial Africa changed dramatically in the 20th century, which could explain why the AIDS pandemic emerged at this time and not previously. (7)

V.L. Durov, formerly of the KGB, concurs with the State Department's stance that AIDS is not man-made and has stated unequivocally that the Soviet program of disinformation concerning the virus was "Distasteful, yes. But it did sow the seeds of suspicion, and that is what the game was about in the Eighties' time. But it was science-fiction; only science-fiction."

More significantly and highly relevant to the subject matter of this book, when questioned as to how the KGB had come up with the secret scenario, Durov replied: "From books – from science-fiction stories. The best place to look for science-fiction scenarios of plagues that we could use is in science-fiction books. It makes sense, right? Sometimes, the espionage game doesn't rely on large schemes. In this, we are just reading the books and conspired [sic] the idea from there." (8)

Certainly, when it came to the science fiction genre, the KGB had a wealth of material to choose from. Mary Wollstonecraft Shelley, who wrote the acclaimed novel *Frankenstein* in 1818, also wrote the less well-known story "The Last Man" eight years later that told the tale of a plague that wipes out all human life on Earth–other than one solitary individual. (9) Similarly, in 1933, in *The Shape of Things to Come*, H.G. Wells prophesized a devastating plague that would sweep the world and plunge the human race into a new dark-age. (10) Ray Bradbury's *The Martian Chronicles* and Richard B. Matheson's *I Am Legend* (which was made into a block-buster movie starring Will Smith in 2008) follow similar paths, as, of course, does Michael Crichton's *The Andromeda Strain*. (11)

And then there is 1979's *A Choice of Catastrophes* by acclaimed science fiction legend, Isaac Asimov. About the various scenarios that might lead to the destruction of our civilization, Asimov wrote: "It would seem that as long as our civilization survives and our medical technology is not shattered there is no longer any danger that infectious disease will produce catastrophe or even anything like the disasters of the Black Death and the Spanish Influenza." (12)

Within four years of making this statement, Asimov was himself HIV-positive.

In late March 2002, Prometheus Books published *It's Been a Good Life*, Asimov's autobiography, edited by his wife, Janet Jeppson Asimov. The book was actually compiled from selected extracts from three previous autobiographical volumes: *In Memory Yet Green*; *In Joy Still Felt*; and *I. Asimov: A Memoir*.

The book included an epilogue in which Janet Jeppson Asimov revealed, for the very first time, that Asimov's death in 1992 from heart and kidney failure was a direct consequence of the complications of AIDS that Asimov had contracted from a transfusion of tainted blood during a December 1983 triple-bypass operation. She explained how and when Asimov learned he had the disease, and why his doctors convinced him to keep it secret from the public. Notably, the epilogue also included a description of Asimov's final days, together with some very poignant passages that described his views on life and death. (13)

It is perhaps relevant here to call upon the words of the character Morpheus from the 1999 science fiction movie *The Matrix* that starred Keanu Reeves: "…fate, it seems, is not without a sense of irony." (14)

■ ■ ■ ┃ ┃┃ 17 ┃┃ ■ ■ ■

THE STRANGE TALE OF SOLARCON-6

"I heard only one code identification by this individual: Solar-con-6."

Born in Chicago in 1938, Philip K. Dick sold his first story in 1952, his first novel in 1955, and went on to become one of the most celebrated science fiction writers of the 20th century. He is perhaps best known for his novel *Do Androids Dream of Electric Sheep?* which was the basis for the 1982 worldwide hit movie *Blade Runner*, starring Hollywood crowd-puller Harrison Ford. (1)

On February 20, 1974, Dick was recovering at home from the effects of sodium pentothal, administered after the extraction of an impacted wisdom-tooth. Answering the door to receive a delivery of additional painkillers, he noticed that the delivery woman was wearing a pendant displaying what he later described as the "vesicle pisces." After her departure, Dick began experiencing strange visions of laser beams, geometric patterns, Jesus, and ancient Rome.

As the visions increased, Dick came to the remarkable conclusion that he was being contacted by some form of higher power that he referred to as Valis–an acronym for Vast Active Living Intelligence. Struggling to comprehend what was occurring, Dick kept an extensive journal, titled the *Exegesis*, which ultimately ran to 8,000 pages. (2)

Over time Dick's odd beliefs and worldview became increasingly paranoid. He believed that Valis had specifically contacted him as part of an attempt to have then President Richard M. Nixon impeached, and he believed that he was being persecuted by both the FBI and the KGB, the former Soviet Union's intelligence service.

And, as a result of seeing dark conspiracies practically here, there, and everywhere, Dick wrote to FBI Headquarters on August 15, 1975, requesting the declassification of his own FBI file, a file that throws a great deal of light on the man, his motivations, and his unusual beliefs. Dick knew that there had to be an FBI file on his activities because, as he told the Bureau in the letter requesting access to his file: "In the early 'fifties, two agents of the FBI, Mr. George Scruggs and Mr. George Smith approached me." (3)

Undoubtedly, one of the prime reasons why Dick attracted attention from the FBI was a series of bizarre letters he penned to the Bureau in the early 1970s, in which he described his personal knowledge of an alleged, underground Nazi cabal that was attempting to covertly manipulate science fiction writers to further advance its hidden cause. And the nature of that cause was even more bizarre: to initiate a Third World War by infecting the American population with syphilis. As evidence of his extreme theories, on October 28, 1972, Dick wrote to the FBI and outlined his distinctly odd beliefs:

I am a well-known author of science-fiction novels, one of which dealt with Nazi Germany (called MAN IN THE HIGH CASTLE, it described an "alternate world" in which the Germans and Japanese won World War Two and jointly occupied the United States). This novel, published in 1962 by Putnam & Co., won the Hugo Award for Best Novel of the Year and hence was widely read both here and abroad; for example, a Japanese edition printed in Tokyo ran into several editions. I bring this to your attention because several months ago I was approached by an individual who I have reason to believe belonged to a covert organization involved in politics, illegal weapons, etc., who put great pressure on me to place coded information in future novels "to be read by the right people here and there," as he phrased it. I refused to do this.

Dick then elaborated on his unusual theories:

The reason why I am contacting you about this now is that it now appears that other science fiction writers may have been so approached by other members of this obviously Anti-American organization and may have yielded to the threats and deceitful statements such as were used on me. Therefore I would like to give you any and all information and help I can regarding this, and I ask that your nearest office contact me as soon as possible. I stress the urgency of this because within the last three days I have come across a well-distributed science fiction novel which contains in essence the vital material which this individual confronted with me as the basis for encoding. That novel is CAMP CONCENTRATION by Thomas Disch, which was published by Doubleday & Co.

P.S. I would like to add: what alarms me the most is that this covert organization which approached me may be Neo-Nazi, although it did not identify itself as being such. My novels are extremely anti-Nazi. I heard only one code identification by this individual: Solarcon-6.

Were sinister, ultra-right-wing figures really attempting to infiltrate the world of science fiction as part of some greater, and highly sinister, conspiracy designed to bolster their political aims and ideologies? Dick appeared to be on a crusade as he sought to reveal his data to FBI agents. Moreover, declassified FBI records show that, only days later, Dick contacted an Inspector Shine in the Marin County Sheriff's Office, San Rafael, California, to whom he imparted further details of the alleged Nazi/science fiction plot:

As you may recall, on or about November 17, 1971, my house at 707 Hacienda Way, Santa Venetia, was extensively robbed. The last time I talked to you, during February of this year, you informed me that you had broken the case; a man named Wade

(Jerry Wade I believe) had been arrested with the Ruger .22 pistol of mine stolen during this robbery. I have been in Canada and now in Southern California and hence out of touch. Have any more of my possessions been recovered? Do you have anything more you can tell me at this date?

While I was in Canada evidently my house was robbed again, during March of this year. I did not know this until what remained of my things arrived down here; my realtor, Mrs. Annie Reagan, had stored them and at least one entire room of stuff is missing; the bedroom in which the control system of the burglar alarm was located, the one room not covered by the scanner. Obviously it was robbed by someone who intimately knew the layout of the alarm system and how to bypass it. I recall that Inspector Bridges thought that the November 17 robbery was an inside job, at least in part. I believe that this later robbery in March of this year proves it.

Dick had his theories about who was behind the robberies and what their motivations were:

Only two or three persons that I can recall knew the layout of the burglar alarm system. One was Harold Kinchen, who was under investigation by Air Force Intelligence at Hamilton Field at the time I left (Mr. Richard Bader was conducting the investigation; through Sergeant Keaton of Tiberon he asked me to come in and give testimony. It had to do with an attempt on the arsenal of the Air Force Intelligence people at Hamilton on I recall January first of this year). I have more reason to believe now than I did then that Kinchen and the secret extralegal to which he belonged were involved in both robberies of my house, although evidence seemed to point more toward Panthers such as Wade. I say this because this is Orange County where I live now, and I have come to know something about the rightwing paramilitary Minutemen illegal people here—they tell me confidentially that from my description of events surrounding the November robbery of my house, the methods used, the activities of Harry Kinchen in particular, it sounds to them like their counterparts up there, and possibly even a neo-Nazi group. Recently I've obtained, by accident, new information about Kinchen's associates, and the neo-Nazi organization theory does seem reinforced. In this case, the November robbery was political in nature and more than a robbery. I have thought this for some time, but until now had less reason to be sure.

As to the motive of the assault I'm not sure at all. Possibly it had to do with my published novels, one of which dealt with Nazi Germany–it was extremely anti-Nazi, and widely circulated. I know for a fact that Harry Kinchen and the Japanese relatives he had through his wife Susan had read it. Kinchen's Japanese-born mother-in-law, Mrs. Toni Adams, had read the novel in the Japanese edition. Beyond any doubt, Kinchen is an ardent Nazi trained in such skills as weapons-use, explosives, wire-tapping, chemistry, psychology, toxins and poisons, electronics, auto repair, sabotage, the manufacture of narcotics. Mr. Bader is of course aware of this. What I did not pass on to anyone, because I feared for my life, is the fact that Kinchen put coercive pressure, both physical and psychological, on me to put secret coded information into my future published writings, "to be read by the right people here and there," as he put it, meaning members of his subversive organization. As I told you last November, he accidentally responded to a phonecall [sic] from me with a code signal. Later he admitted to belonging to a secret "worldwide" organization and told me some details.

The coded information which Kinchen wished placed in my novels (I of course refused, and fled to Canada) had to do with an alleged new strain of syphilis sweeping the U.S., kept top secret by the U.S. authorities; it can't be cured, destroys the brain, and is swift-acting. The disease, Kinchen claimed, is being brought in deliberately from Asia by agents of the enemy (unspecified), and is in fact a weapon of World War Three, which has begun, being used against us.

In a recent confidential discussion I had with my Paris editor, a close friend of mine, this editor ratified my conviction that to allow this coded "information," undoubtedly spurious, to get into print, would be a disaster for this country. These neo-Nazis or whatever they are would "break" their own code and make public this phony information, this creating mass hysteria and panic. There is, of course, no such new untreatable paresis, despite rumors we have been hearing from Servicemen returning from Viet Nam. I have contacted the F.B.I. on the advice of my editor-publisher friend, but I felt I should contact you, too. You may wish to pass this information about the coded information in novels onto Mr. Bader.

P.S. Harold Kinchen introduced me to only one individual, who asked me to write for his underground pornographic publications; I refused. By accident I recently learned that this man, '"Doc" Stanley of Corte Madera, "was a student of the speeches of Hitler during his college days at the University of Chicago, advocating their doctrines and reading them to people." Neither Stanley or Kinchen mentioned this to me. (4)

Questioned years afterwards about the burglary, Dick admitted that "that whole thing is something that fills me with a great deal of anxiety. I try not to think about it." Nevertheless, Dick did later elaborate upon his relationship with the FBI and with agents Smith and Scruggs, referred to in Dick's August 15, 1975, Freedom of Information request to the Bureau. When asked to confirm some of the rumors that his science fiction stories of the 1950s were considered subversive and had created problems for him with the authorities, Dick stated: "They did more than that. They got me many friendly visits from Mr. Smith and Mr. Scruggs of the FBI...They came to my house every week for what seemed like ever and ever and ever...I honestly expected to be called before the House Un-American Activities Committee...Years later I wrote away for my FBI file under the Freedom of Information Act. Do you know what it had in it? Things like: 'has a long beard and frequented the University of Vancouver.' I delivered a lecture there. I was granted an honorary doctorate and was a guest of the faculty club. They made it sound like I hung out in the shadows selling dope." (5)

But what did government agents have to say about Dick's odd theories concerning a grand science fiction related conspiracy that implicated Nazi sympathizers in a plot to instigate a Third World War by infecting the population with syphilis? Were Dick's beliefs merely the result of too much LSD with

October 28, 1972

Federal Bureau of Investigation,
Washington, D.C.

Gentlemen:

    I am a well-known author of science fiction novels, one of which dealt with Nazi Germany (called MAN IN THE HIGH CASTLE, it described an "alternate world" in which the Germans and Japanese won World War Two and jointly occupied the United States). This novel, published in 1962 by Putnam & Co., won the Hugo Award for Best Novel of the Year and hence was widely read both here and abroad; for example, a Japanese edition printed in Tokio ran into several editions. I bring this to your attention because several months ago I was approached by an individual who I have reason to believe belonged to a covert organization involving politics, illegal weapons, etc., who put great pressure on me to place coded information in future novels "to be read by the right people here and there," as he phrased it. I refused to do this.

    The reason why I am contacting you about this now is that it now appears that other science fiction writers may have been so approached by other members of this obviously anti-American organization and may have yielded to the threats and deceitful statements such as were used on me. Therefore I would like to give you any and all information and help I can regarding this, and I ask that your nearest office contact me as soon as possible. I stress the urgency of this because within the last three days I have come across a well-distributed science fiction novel which contains in essence the vital material which this individual confronted me with as the basis for encoding. That novel is CAMP CONCENTRATION by Thomas Disch, which was published by Doubleday & Co.

                      Cordially,

Philip K. Dick
3028 Quartz Lane, Apt. #2
Fullerton,
Calif 92631.

P.S. I would like to add: what alarms me the most is that this covert organization which approached me may be Neo-Nazi, although it did not identify itself as being such. My novels are extremely anti-Nazi. I heard only one code identification by this individual: Solarcon-6.

To the FBI: The weird conspiracy theories of Philip K. Dick.

his beat-buddies? Or was there a grain of truth to the claims of the science fiction author? There is no doubt that official summaries of Dick's theories and bizarre beliefs were circulated within the FBI, as a memorandum of November 21, 1972, amply demonstrates:

DICK said KINCHEN telephoned him on one occasion. When DICK immediately redialed KINCHEN after terminating the phone call, DICK said he thought KINCHEN gave a code name of "Solarcon 6." He said he was not certain as to what was said and did not know why such a code name would be given. KINCHEN claimed he was a member of a "secret world health organization" which was tracking down paresis, an alleged new strain of syphilis sweeping the United States, which caused quick death. KINCHEN claimed paresis was the start of World War III, that DICK did not have long to live, and he wanted DICK to put science fiction code names in any of his new future science fiction novels. KINCHEN also told DICK that if DICK died, "they" would continue his novels and "they" would place code names in such novels. DICK said he did not know who KINCHEN was referring to as "they" or what the purpose of the code names was. He believed KINCHEN had probably read the science fiction novel, "Camp Concentration," which was a story regarding paresis. (6)

Additional FBI memoranda make it very clear, however, that after agents spoke with Dick, Bureau officials concluded that any deep investigation of his wild assertions was deemed as being wholly unwarranted: "The information reflected in those letters was presumption only on [Dick's] part regarding neo-nazism and Minutemen. He did not have any further business or substantiation, names of individuals, or additional information to which he had previously furnished." (7)

Dick's wife, Tessa, made a similar comment: "Phil told me he had only sent the first three or four letters, and he stopped mailing them because the FBI had lost interest in the case." (8)

Philip K. Dick died of a stroke in 1982 at the age of fifty-three.

■■■■||| 18 |||■■■

SCIENCE FICTION SECRETS
IN THE WHITE HOUSE

"…if the people of the world were to find out that there was some alien life form that was going to attack the Earth approaching on Halley's Comet, then that knowledge would unite all the peoples of the world."

On June 27, 1982, United States President Ronald Reagan is alleged to have made a startling and confidential comment to legendary film-director Steven Spielberg. On that day, a showing at the White House had been planned for the President, and his wife Nancy, of Spielberg's then-new movie, *E.T.: The Extraterrestrial* that was soon to be released throughout both the U.S. and the world. (1)

Declassified White House documents demonstrate that the Reagans were enthusiastic movie fans. During the course of his presidency, Reagan viewed no less than 377 movies in the White House Theater, including nearly all of the *Star Trek* movies and, two days before the screening of *E.T.*, Spielberg's *Poltergeist*. (2)

Of course, this is wholly understandable given the fact that Reagan had himself been a successful Hollywood actor. The screening of *E.T.*, however, was a particularly notable occasion. In addition to the Reagans and Spielberg, there were three-dozen guests. In other words, this wasn't just a film-showing, it was an *event*. And there can be absolutely no doubt that watching *E.T.* had a profound effect on both the President and his wife. Spielberg later said that "Nancy Reagan was crying towards the end, and the President looked like a ten-year-old-kid." (3)

What allegedly happened next, however, led to a long-standing and controversial allegation: namely, that *E.T.* had far less to do with science fiction and far more to do with real, high-level Government secrecy and conspiracies pertaining to genuine alien visitations of planet Earth. After the movie's credits rolled, President Reagan supposedly whispered sixteen unforgettable and earth-shattering words in Spielberg's ear: "You know: there aren't six people in this room who know how true this really is." (4)

Researcher Grant Cameron has said that Spielberg had written *E.T.* as sci-fi, but that he utilized the scenario presented in the movie from allegedly real accounts of encounters with extraterrestrials. Cameron adds that rumors were rife that the Government had provided Spielberg with "some input to *E.T.* such as how the alien was portrayed." (5)

Although Spielberg has never publicly discussed or confirmed the alleged conversation with Reagan, he is said to have admitted its reality in the 1980s to Hollywood television producer Jaime Shandera, who was involved at the time in the making of a documentary on Spielberg for Japanese television. (6)

In January 1988, Grant Cameron wrote to Spielberg in an attempt to resolve the matter, once and for all. His letter was answered by the director's publicity coordinator, Kris Kelley, who replied: "Unfortunately, Mr. Spielberg is currently away working on his next project and is unable to personally answer your question." (7)

Regardless of whether or not Reagan privately knew that *E.T.* was not science fiction but was telling a very real–if highly secret–story of a truly jaw-dropping nature, it is an undeniable fact that in the years that followed, and before his presidency ended in 1988, Reagan made a number of very intriguing public comments with respect to UFOs. The first came during the November 1985 Geneva Summit between Reagan and the Soviet Premier Mikhael Gorbachev, when the American president made a somewhat unusual comment that sounded like something straight out of a science fiction novel–linking hostile aliens with the looming arrival of Halley's Comet in the Earth's skies.

Declassified memoranda generated by the Department of State as a result of the Reagan-Gorbachev meeting states:

Reagan said that while the General Secretary was speaking, he had been thinking of various problems being discussed at the talks. He said that previous to the General Secretary's remarks, he had been telling Foreign Minister Shevardnadze (who was sitting to the President's right) that if the people of the world were to find out that there was some alien life form that was going to attack the Earth approaching on Halley's Comet, then that knowledge would unite all the peoples of the world.

Further, the President observed that General Secretary Gorbachev had cited a Biblical quotation, and the President is also alluding to the Bible, pointed out that Acts 16 refers to the fact that "we are all of one blood regardless of where we live on the Earth," and we should never forget that. (8)

One month later, on December 4, 1985, Reagan delivered a speech to an absolutely packed audience at Fallston High School, Harford County, Maryland. During the course of the speech Reagan discussed his now-historic meeting with Gorbachev, and surprisingly admitted that during the course of his meeting, the two leaders of the super-powers had privately discussed the UFO controversy. Indeed, as Reagan advised the Fallston High School audience:

I couldn't help but–when you stop to think that we're all God's children, wherever we live in the world–I couldn't help but say to him [Gorbachev] just how easy his task and mine might be if suddenly there was a threat to this world from some other species from another planet outside in the universe. We'd forget all the little local differences that we have between our countries and we would find out once and for all that we really are all human beings here on this Earth together. Well I guess we can wait for some alien race to come down and threaten us, but I think that between us we can bring about that realization. (9)

And there were still more alien-dominated comments to come. In a speech presented on February 16, 1987, at Moscow's Grand Kremlin Palace on the subject of the *Survival of Humanity*, Gorbachev confirmed the discussion with Reagan on all matters extraterrestrial:

At our meeting in Geneva, the U.S. President said that if the earth faced an invasion by extraterrestrials, the United States and the Soviet Union would join forces to repel such an invasion. I shall not dispute the hypothesis, although I think it's early yet to worry about such an intrusion. (10)

But it was Reagan's speech at the 42nd General Assembly of the United Nations on September 21, 1987, that, to this day, remains Reagan's most memorable alien-dominated speech. The President said:

In our obsession with antagonisms of the moment, we often forget how much unites all the members of humanity. Perhaps we need some outside, universal threat to make us recognize this common bond. I occasionally think how quickly our differences worldwide would vanish if we were facing an alien threat from outside this world. And yet, I ask you, is not an alien force already among us? What could be more alien to the universal aspirations of our peoples than war and the threat of war? (11)

We may never really know to what extent Steven Spielberg's science fiction movie *E.T.* had a bearing on Ronald Reagan's alien-driven statements at the height of his presidency, but there is one highly intriguing matter that has come to light and that is most definitely worthy of note.

On the morning after the screening of *E.T.*, Reagan; James Baker, who was the president's Chief of Staff; Michael K. Deaver, the Deputy Chief of Staff; and Counselor Edwin Meese, all convened in the White House Situation Room where the President was briefed on the then-current status of, and future plans for, the United States' space-program. Given the particular and specific nature of the briefing, and the fact that it was being delivered to the President of the United States of America, one would imagine that senior representatives from the National Aeronautics and Space Administration (NASA) would have been present. But they were not. Instead, the participants involved in the briefing were from the National Security Council (NSC). (12)

Is it only a coincidence that the President of the United States received a briefing on the U.S. space program from representatives of the ultra-secret NSC, only hours after watching one of the most famous science fiction movies of all time? Or did elements of the intelligence community provide a full and unexpurgated briefing to the President on the real story behind *E.T.*, of which Reagan quietly alluded to Spielberg he had at least some knowledge?

Reagan is now dead and Spielberg isn't talking. Will we ever really know what happened that day?

July 12, 1982

Dear Mr. Spielberg:

Nancy and I want you to know how much we enjoyed seeing "E.T." It is truly a film classic and you are to be congratulated for your splendid work. The quality and excitement of your films have helped to bring a much-needed boost to that industry and you should be proud of the mark you have made in movie history.

Again, we appreciate your sharing "E.T." with us. With our best wishes,

Sincerely,

RONALD REAGAN

X
Mr. Steven Spielberg
9125 Alto Cedro
Beverly Hills, California   90210

RR:AVH:KCS:pps

Reagan, Spielberg, and E.T.: A cosmic cover-up?

■■■║║ 19 ║║■■■

A False Prophet and
the Science Fiction Scientist

"In May 2000 there will be an atomic escalation which Scripture calls ARMAGEDDON. It will poison the earth's atmosphere for 5 years."

More than anyone else, the late Carl Sagan, whose television series *Cosmos* made him a celebrity all around the world, managed to successfully fuse mainstream science, sci-fi, and entertainment for the viewing masses. (1) Indeed, this was borne out most graphically in 1998 when his science fiction novel, *Contact*, was made into a blockbuster Hollywood movie of the same name that starred Jodie Foster and Matthew McConnaughey. (2)

Born on November 9, 1934, in Brooklyn, New York, Sagan received a Bachelor's degree in 1955 and a Master's degree in 1956, both in physics, and a Doctorate in astronomy and astrophysics in 1960, all from the University of Chicago. He played a major role in NASA's Mariner, Viking, Voyager, and Galileo spacecraft and received NASA medals for Exceptional Scientific Achievement and for Distinguished Public Service, as well as the NASA Apollo Achievement Award. He was the Chairman of the Division of Planetary Sciences of the American Astronomical Society, President of the Planetology Section of the American Geophysical Union, and Chairman of the Astronomy Section of the American Association for the Advancement of Science. (3)

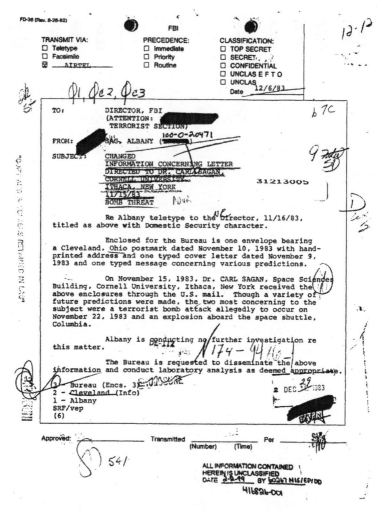

From the secret FBI files on Carl Sagan.

And, in the early 1980s, Sagan became the subject of a secret, 33-page FBI file after becoming involved in a very strange affair. On November 16, 1983, the FBI's Special-Agent-in-Charge at Cleveland, Ohio contacted the Washington, D.C.

offices to report a strange development in the life of Carl Sagan. The Cleveland Office recorded the following:

On November 15, 1983, Dr. Carl Sagan, Space Sciences Building, Cornell University, Ithaca, New York received a handwritten envelope postmarked Cleveland, Ohio, Nov 10 1983, containing a two page typewritten letter. Letter comprised of cover page dated November 9, 1983 stating it was an open letter directed to various news publishers and identifying Sagan as an influential person to convince others veracity [sic] of message. Both message and cover letter bear typed name of author as M. Springfield.

The letter to Sagan was, without doubt, a very unusual one. It read like something straight out of science fiction :

The message is so important that I want you to witness that you have received it before November 22 1983. You have been chosen because of your standing in the community. I believe you are a person of integrity with the ability to convince others that this message is true.
An Open Letter to All. Warning! Armageddon is Coming!
On Nov 22, 1983, there will be a terrorist bomb attack on a market or warehouse that is distributing free food to a crowd in San Salvadore [sic]. This will be a diversion for an attack on a fuel storage facility in the vicinity.
If [the space shuttle] COLUMBIA goes as scheduled there will be an explosion in the rocket due to a fuel leak. On May 7, 1985 a middle-east war will begin with Israel triumphant in the same year.
The American presidency will be Reagan-Bush–Bush and a democrat in 96 whose birthday is the same year as our first president. He will be our last. In 1990 Poland will be free.
On April 15, 1997 the earthquake of Revelation will strike America. New York is the image of Babylon that will sink into the sea. San Francisco shares the same fate.
In 1998 there will be a Third World War. An earthquake weakened America will be invaded.
In May 2000 there will be an atomic escalation which Scripture

calls ARMAGEDDON. It will poison the earth's atmosphere for 5 years. No life will survive that is not in the proper mode to survive. The full text of this work explains how these events are portended by the signs that Heaven has given us will be published soon. M. Springfield.

On receipt of the letter, Sagan immediately contacted the FBI, which duly swung into action, as a formerly Secret FBI document of November 18, 1983, noted:

A search of indices, State Law Enforcement Computer, and local directories, failed to locate a person identifiable with the author of captioned letter, described as "M. Springfield."

Cleveland telephone directory shows a listing for an "M. Springfield" which address is a large apartment complex. A suitable pretext telephone call to that address revealed that "M. Springfield" at that address died in 1972 and widow now resides there. She had no knowledge of a letter sent to a Dr. Sagan.

Additional FBI documentation demonstrates that the Bureau went to great lengths to try and identify the source of the letter. The original letter and envelope were sent to an FBI forensics laboratory for analysis, but in a report titled "Bomb Threat" it was revealed that unfortunately "no latent prints of value" could be found on the letter or the envelope, and that the scientific investigation was brought to a frustrating close without effecting an identification.

Interestingly, although Sagan was an entirely innocent party in this affair, detailed background checks on Sagan, his contacts, his associates, and his career were made with other, unnamed agencies to determine if there was any particular reason why he was personally singled out to receive the letter: "No derogatory information on Subject was found after consultation with [Deleted], [Deleted], [Deleted], and [Deleted]," was the official word on Sagan.

Needless to say, there was no terrorist attack, the space

shuttle *Columbia* was not destroyed (until February 1, 2003) there was no Third World War, the United States was not invaded (until 9-11) and New York did not "sink into the sea." The prophecies, like most prophecies, were not exactly true. The real identity of "M. Springfield" remains as mysterious today as it was in 1983.

In 2000, it was revealed that Carl Sagan had been secretly involved in another matter with distinctly science fiction overtones decades earlier. Few can forget the scenes in the 1998 science fiction thriller *Deep Impact*, in which astronauts are dispatched to try and alter the trajectory—via nuclear weapons—of a huge comet that is fast-approaching the Earth (4); or the similar portrayal in *Armageddon*, also in 1998, that saw Bruce Willis trying to prevent a giant asteroid from crashing into our planet—again through the use of nuclear explosives. (5)

But the scenario of launching fully armed, nuclear weapons into space was not one limited to science fiction. On May 14, 2000, the British-based *Observer* newspaper revealed the details of plans that the U.S. Air Force had secretly drawn up at the height of the Cold War to detonate a nuclear bomb on the surface of the Moon: Project A119. Dr. Leonard Reiffel, a physicist who fronted the project in the late 1950s at the military-sponsored Armor Research Foundation, revealed the details of the extraordinary plan:

"It was clear the main aim of the proposed detonation was a PR exercise and a show of one-upmanship. The Air Force wanted a mushroom cloud so large it would be visible on earth," said Reiffel, who added that: "The U.S. was lagging behind in the space race. The explosion would obviously be best on the dark side of the moon and the theory was that if the bomb exploded on the edge of the moon, the mushroom cloud would be illuminated by the sun."

Brief details of Project A119 had first emerged in 1999 within the pages of a biography of Carl Sagan. It transpires that at the height of Project A119 at the Armor Foundation in Chicago Reiffel had hired Sagan to mathematically model the expansion of an exploding dust cloud in the space around the moon. This was a key to calculating the visibility of such a cloud from the Earth. At the time, scientists still believed there might be microbial life on the moon, and Sagan had suggested a nuclear explosion might be used to detect such organisms. Despite the highly classified nature of the work, Sagan's biographer, Keay Davidson, discovered that Sagan had disclosed details of it when he, Sagan, applied for the prestigious Miller Institute graduate fellowship to Berkeley. Yet, until 2000, the full nature of Project A119 had not revealed to the public. (6)

Without doubt, Carl Sagan (who died from pneumonia on December 20, 1996, after a two-year battle against myelodysplasia, a pre-leukemia syndrome) was someone who moved effortlessly within the realms of science, sci-fi, and official secrecy.

20

Novel Secrets

"He sees speculative fiction as the ideal mode for grappling with these unusual areas of experience."

One of the most interesting aspects of the UFO puzzle is the way in which several former British military and Ministry of Defense officials have, on several occasions, written fantasy stories and science fiction novels on the subject–officials who have themselves experienced a degree of personal, official exposure to the mysteries of our world.

In 1915, for example, Lieutenant Colonel W.P. Drury, the Garrison Intelligence Officer of the British Admiralty at Plymouth, England, prepared an extraordinary document for his superiors titled "Report on the Dartmoor Floating (or Balloon) Light." The document detailed a series of early UFO-style encounters that had occurred in the wilds of the moorlands of Devonshire–the desolate and windswept setting for Sir Arthur Conan Doyle's classic Sherlock Holmes novel *The Hound of the Baskervilles*.

On numerous occasions throughout the month, strange, brightly lit aerial objects were seen to move silently across the moors late at night and seemed to exhibit definite signs of intelligent control. Despite the fact that there were numerous witnesses–including Drury himself–no definitive conclusion was ever reached and the affair was quietly filed away and classified as unexplained. But it was not Lt. Col. Drury's first brush with the unknown.

As far back as 1904, Drury had busily been writing adventure novels about a character he called "Mr. Pagett," the first being *The Peradventures of Private Pagett*. Described as a "one-time private in the Marines, and now hostelry landlord, parish councilor, and vicar's warden," Pagett's escapades all had a distinct tall-tale air to them. One such story, "Pagett Meets a Sailor on the Moor," sees our hero crossing paths with the ghost of Sir Francis Drake on the same moorland where Drury's own encounter with the unknown occurred in 1915. Coincidence, bizarre synchronicity, or was Drury possibly an early Fox Mulder type character, secretly undertaking investigations into the paranormal for his Government, and then presenting them under the guise of fictional stories? Drury is now long gone and can no longer provide an answer to that question. (1)

Dennis Yates Wheatley was born in South London on January 8, 1897, and joined the family wine business until the First World War intervened. Although only seventeen when the war broke out and twenty-one at its conclusion, he rose to the rank of 2nd Lieutenant in the Royal Field Artillery and, after several postings in the British Isles, saw service in Flanders on the Ypres Salient and in France at Cambrai and St. Quentin.

Wheatley's first book, *Three Inquisitive People*, was set aside by his publishers, Hutchinson, in favor of his next, *The Forbidden Territory*, which they published first in 1933. Although he retained an interest in the wine business for some years, he began to concentrate on his writing and used his innovative marketing skills to help promote a series of crime-based novels.

With the advent of the Second World War, Wheatley, by now a successful novelist, submitted a number of papers to the Joint Planning Staff of the British Government's War Cabinet, and was eventually asked to join them, subsequently becoming the only civilian ever to be given a commission in the Joint

Planning Staff with the rank of Wing Commander. Wheatley would continue his career as a writer after the war and ultimately penned 75 books, many on the occult, perhaps the best-known being *The Devil Rides Out*. (2)

But his 1952 science fiction novel, *Star of Ill-Omen*, is perhaps the most intriguing and relevant to the subject-matter of this book, although perhaps not his most memorable title. In the book, the hero, Ken Lincoln, a scientist named Escobar, and his wife, Carmen, are captured by giant Martians called the Bee-Beetles, who take the three in their stereotypical flying saucer to Mars. *Star of Ill-Omen* reveals that the Martian world is very much a dying one. As a direct consequence, the Bee-Beetles intend to take over the Earth–after they obliterate our civilization from the face of the planet, of course. The Martians proceed to show the trio a series of films, which chronicle a history of human civilization, and include many scenes of warfare and weaponry. Lincoln eventually realizes that the aliens wish to uncover the secrets of the atomic bomb–since, despite the fact that they have the technology to build spacecraft powerful enough and of sufficient size to reach the Earth, the power of the atom still eludes them.

The aliens are thwarted, however, and the story ends with Lincoln and Carmen fleeing Mars in a flying saucer that promptly, and spectacularly, crashes into the depths of London's River Thames. The pair subsequently ejects to safety in a capsule, but Government officials succeed in keeping the whole matter under wraps and away from the prying eyes of the media and the general public. (3)

At first glance, it would appear that Wheatley derived the entire plot of his novel from studying then-current UFO literature. For example, Gerald Heard's 1950 book *The Riddle of the Flying Saucers: Is Another World Watching?* hypothesized that intelligent insects piloted UFOs and probably came from Mars. So, given the fact that Wheatley's novel also focused upon intelligent, Martian insects, it seems safe to assume that this is where Wheatley got his scenario from. Or did he? (4)

On November 29, 1983, Dr. Robert Irving Sarbacher, of the Washington Institute of Technology Oceanographic and Physical Sciences, wrote to William Steinman, co-author with UFO researcher Wendelle Stevens of the book *UFO Crash at Aztec*:

Dear Mr. Steinman: Relating to my own experience regarding recovered flying saucers, I had no association with any of the people involved in the recovery and have no knowledge regarding the dates of the recoveries. If I had I would send it to you. Regarding verification that persons you list were involved, I can say only this: John von Neuman was definitely involved. Dr. Vannevar Bush was definitely involved, and I think Dr. Robert Oppenheimer also.

My association with the Research and Development Board under Doctor Compton during the Eisenhower administration was rather limited so that although I had been invited to participate in several discussions associated with the reported recoveries, I could not personally attend the meetings.

About the only thing I remember at this time is that certain materials reported to have come from flying saucer crashes were extremely light and very tough. I am sure our laboratories analyzed them very carefully.

There were reports that instruments or people operating these machines were also of very light weight, sufficient to withstand the tremendous deceleration and acceleration associated with their machinery. I remember in talking with some of the people at the office that I got the impression these "aliens" were constructed like certain insects we have observed on earth, wherein because of the low mass the inertial forces involved in operation of these instruments would be quite low.

I still do not know why the high order of classification has been given and why the denial of the existence of these devices.

Sincerely Yours,

Dr. Robert I. Sarbacher. (5)

Given the high level of secrecy that surrounded the work

of Dr. Sarbacher (who was attached the U.S. Government's Research and Development Board at the time that *Star of Ill-Omen* was published), it is highly illuminating to note that he, Gerald Heard, and Dennis Wheatley were all talking about insect-like aliens, and that both Wheatley and Sarbacher worked for the government.

And as noted, in Wheatley's novel, the aliens endlessly show the abducted Lincoln, Escobar, and Carmen imagery of terrestrial warfare, as part of their efforts to uncover the secrets of the atomic bomb. This eerily parallels the experiences of today's so-called alien abductees who routinely report how their captors project images into their minds of huge, atomic mushroom clouds looming ominously over our cities in the near future. (6)

In one prime example, after an alleged alien abduction in Texas in 1973, "Tammy" began to have vivid dreams of a nightmarish, futuristic Earth that had been reduced to ruins as a result of localized nuclear skirmishes and a lethal virus of unknown origins. And, all the while, foreboding flying saucer style vehicles would soar ominously above, patiently counting down the weeks and days to our complete destruction. (7)

While such claims proliferate in the UFO literature, it is illuminating indeed to note that Dennis Wheatley picked up on two specific UFO issues–namely the insect-like nature of the aliens and their weird obsession with projecting imagery of Armageddon–at a time when both issues were barely discussed. Perhaps it was all a coincidence. Or perhaps Wheatley's long lasting, deep governmental and military connection allowed him access to a dark, secret truth pertaining to a real alien presence.

If the latter, then this sounds very much like the experience of the late UFO contactee Howard Menger, the author of the science fiction style book *From Outer Space to You,* which dealt with Menger's own alleged encounters with aliens. Notably, Menger had informed UFO writers Gray Barker and Jim Moseley that his book was, in reality, a form of "fiction-fact" that had been carefully encouraged and nurtured by Pentagon staff who had asked Menger to participate in a clandestine experiment to test the public's reaction to tales of extraterrestrial contact. (8)

The examples continue. According to the biographical note on the dust jacket of Ralph Noyes' 1985 novel, *A Secret Property*:

Ralph Noyes was born in the tropics and spent most of his childhood in the West Indies. He served in the RAF from 1940 to 1946 and was commissioned as aircrew, engaging in active service in North Africa and the Far East. He entered the civil service in 1949 and served in the Air Ministry and subsequently the unified Ministry of Defense. In 1977 he retired early from the civil service to take up a writing career, leaving in the grade of under Secretary of State. He has since published several pieces of shorter fiction, most of them on speculative themes.

For nearly four years, until late 1972, Ralph Noyes headed a division in the central staffs of the Ministry of Defense which brought him in touch with the UFO problem. Since his retirement he has become increasingly interested in this subject, among others which lie on the fringes of present understanding. He sees speculative fiction as the ideal mode for grappling with these unusual areas of experience. But *A Secret Property* is not only fiction but also "faction"–at least to the extent of drawing on Ralph Noyes's lengthy background in the Royal Air Force and the Ministry of Defense. (9)

The description of Noyes that his publisher presented is made all the more provocative by virtue of the fact that, in its science fiction format, *A Secret Property* specifically dealt with what is perhaps the most well-known UFO incident in the British Isles: the alleged landing, on December 26, 1980, of an alien spacecraft at Rendlesham Forest, Suffolk. The event involved numerous United States Air Force personnel from the nearby Royal Air Force Bentwaters military base–including Colonel Charles Halt, who prepared an official memorandum on the affair–who were witness to a small, triangular-shaped UFO that touched down in the forest, and, according to some witnesses, disgorged a number of small alien beings. The incident was reportedly the subject of a high-level, U.S. Government-orchestrated cover-up and conspiracy. (10)

As with the real story, Noyes' novel focuses its attention upon classified government experiments, official secrecy, obfuscation, and denial at the highest level, and a very real–but ultimately unexplained–UFO presence in our midst. When *A Secret Property* was published, rumors churned wildly that Noyes was writing the literal truth about Rendlesham, albeit under the guise of sci-fi. Certainly, Noyes's career with the Ministry of Defense brought him into direct contact with the complexities of the UFO subject, as he admitted to investigative writers Andy Roberts and David Clarke: "In the several capacities which brought me into touch with UFO reports during my 28 years in the MoD, I encountered several reports, particularly those from military establishments, which indicated 'high strangeness.' I, and military colleagues, had little doubt something had taken place for which we had no explanation." (11)

More intriguingly, Noyes advised Roberts and Clarke that:

There is no doubt at all that the MoD played a thoroughly dishonest game over the Rendlesham affair...The case itself is complex. I have given my own views about it–essentially that Halt and several others came face to face with a striking manifestation of the "UFO phenomenon," whatever that may be, in the December of 1980. Other commentators may disagree; alternative theories abound. My only immediate point is that the MoD have resisted all attempts to obtain a sensible statement, even under sustained pressure to the Defense Secretary from Lord Hill-Norton. Why? Simply, I think, because it embarrasses them. Either they must admit that a senior USAF officer at a highly sensitive base in the UK went out of his mind in December 1980, with unthinkable potential consequences in defense terms, or they must acknowledge publicly that weird things occur for which no explanation is at present possible. Can we be surprised that they stalled and cheated? I would have done the same had I had the ill luck to be in post at the relevant time. (12)

Whether based upon secret, insider knowledge or simply a work of sci-fi, *A Secret Property* was written by someone with undeniable and deep connections to the strange world of the British Government's UFO investigations.

Speaking of which, there is a "Man from the Ministry" named Nick Pope who deserves a chapter all to himself.

■■ I II 21 II I ■■

THUNDER CHILD

"It's extremely strange that on the one hand the MoD is publicly so dismissive about UFOs; and yet on the other it bent over backwards to provide assistance to a TV company producing a science-fiction drama which starts with the RAF shooting down a UFO."

In 1958 author Gavin Gibbons penned a science fiction novel titled *By Space Ship to the Moon*, which involved the landing of an alien spacecraft on the Berwyn Mountain Range in North Wales. (1) Some might say that Gibbons was somewhat of a prophet as on the night of January 23, 1974, an event occurred on the Berwyns that has come to be known within the UFO research community as the British Roswell.

The English researcher Andy Roberts says:

Prehistoric man lived and worshipped on the mountains leaving behind him a dramatic, ritual landscape dotted with stone circles...Folklore tells us that these mountains are haunted by many types of aerial phenomena, including the spectral Hounds of Hell: those who saw them recalled how they flew through the night sky baying as though pursued by Satan himself. To the south of the Berwyn's, at Llanrhaedr-ym-Mochnant, the locals were plagued by a "flying dragon"–intriguingly, a common name for UFOs in times gone by.

It is against this backdrop of history and myth that on the evening of January 23, 1974 an event took place on the Berwyn Mountains that was to perplex locals and spawned a veritable cascade of rumours, culminating in an incredible claim that, if true, would irrevocably change our view of history and make us revise our plans for the future of both our planet and our species. The claim was that a UFO piloted by extraterrestrials crashed, or was shot down, on the mountain known as Cader Berwyn and that the alien crew, some still alive, were whisked off to a secret military installation in the south of England for study. (2)

Since then, the issue of what did or did not occur on the Berwyn Mountains on the night in question has been the subject of several books, intense controversy, heated debate, and, at times, unbridled fury. That something happened at around 8.30 p.m. on the night in question is not in any doubt, however.

Tales of strange lights in the sky, explosions on the Berwyns, cordoned-off mountain roads, and Government conspiracies to hide the dark, alien truth abound and have done now for decades. Andy Roberts, however, takes a distinctly down-to-earth approach to the story. He believes that the UFO crash was nothing more than the misperception of a meteorite shower and an earth-tremor, as well as poachers on the mountainside who were armed with powerful lamps, all topped off with unbridled paranoia and rumor run riot. Others believe that perhaps a military aircraft carrying Top Secret equipment crashed on the Berwyn range.

But as to the UFO angle, certainly the most sensational story surfaced in 1996 via English police sergeant Tony Dodd, who served on the force for 25 years. When the story was first revealed in the pages of the now-defunct but popular British newsstand publication, *UFO Magazine*, Dodd steadfastly refused to reveal the real name of his source for the story, as he continued to do throughout his time as a UFO investigator, and instead gave him the pseudonym of "James Prescott." Dodd also claimed to have seen Prescott's military records.

Prescott told Dodd that in January 1974 he was stationed at an Army barracks in the south of England. "I cannot name my unit or barracks as they are still operational," said Prescott, who detailed how on January 18, 1974, he and his colleagues were put on "stand-by at short notice." Twenty-four hours later, the unit was directed to make its way towards the city of Birmingham.

"We then received orders to proceed with speed towards North Wales," Prescott elaborated. "We were halted in Chester in readiness for a military exercise we believed was about to take place. On 20 January, the communication to us was 'hot.' At approximately 20:13 hours we received orders to proceed to Llangollen in North Wales and to wait at that point."

On arrival at Llangollen, recalled Prescott, the unit noticed a great deal of "ground and aircraft activity" in the area. Extraordinary events were allegedly unfolding. But it was shortly after 11:30 p.m. when things really began to take shape.

"We, that is myself and four others, were ordered to go to Llanderfel and were under strict orders not to stop for any civilians," said Prescott. The team soon reached Llanderfel, whereupon they were ordered to load two large oblong boxes into their vehicle. "We were at this time warned not to open the boxes, but to proceed to [the Chemical and Biological Defense Establishment at] Porton Down, [Wiltshire], and deliver the boxes."

A number of hours later, they reached Porton Down and the mysterious cargo was quickly taken inside the facility. "Once inside," explained Prescott, "the boxes were opened by staff at the facility in our presence. We were shocked to see two creatures which had been placed inside decontamination suits."

The staff at Porton began the careful task of opening the suits. "When the suits were fully opened it was obvious the creatures were clearly not of this world and, when examined, were found to be dead. What I saw in the boxes that day," Prescott told Dodd, "made me change my whole concept of life.

"The bodies were about five to six feet tall, humanoid in shape, but so thin they looked almost skeletal with a covering skin. Although I did not see a craft at the scene of the recovery, I was informed that a large craft had crashed and was recovered by other military units."

Most remarkable was what Prescott had to say next: "Sometime later we joined up with the other elements of our unit, who informed us that they had also transported bodies of 'alien beings' to Porton Down, but said that their cargo was still alive." In conclusion, Prescott added that this was "the only time I was ever involved in anything of this nature. This event took place many years ago and I am now retired from the Armed Forces." (3)

Although work at Porton Down had originally begun in March 1916, it was not until 1940 that the installation became the central hub of British interest in biological warfare. Following the outbreak of the Second World War, a highly secret and independent group—the Biology Department, Porton—was established by the War Cabinet, with a specific mandate to investigate the reality of biological warfare and to develop a means of retaliation in the event that biological warfare was utilized against the United Kingdom and its people. By 1946, the name of the wartime group had become the Microbiological Research Department. A decade later, the biological warfare research of Porton Down's staff had become solely defensive in nature, and in 1957 it was re-named the Microbiological Research Establishment.

By the 1970s MRE was placed under the aegis of a civil authority, and on April 1, 1979, it became known as the Center for Applied Microbiology and Research. In 1995, the MRE became part of the Defense Evaluation and Research Agency (DERA), and six years later DERA split into two organizations: QinetiQ, a private company, and the Defense Science and Technology Laboratory, which remains an agency of the Min-

Nick Pope, a real Fox Mulder?

istry of Defense. Today, Porton Down is known as DSTL, Porton Down. (4)

In 1996, the same year that James Prescott's story surfaced, Simon & Schuster's London office published a book titled *Open Skies, Closed Minds*. (5) Written by a man named Nick Pope, it told the true story of his 1991-to-1994 study of UFO reports for the British Ministry of Defense. *Open Skies, Closed Minds* instantly became a best-seller for Pope, who instantly–much to the delight of his publicist, one strongly suspects–became known as "Britain's Fox Mulder" in the eyes of the nation's media, primarily because he was publicly stating his belief that some of the UFO reports that crossed his desk strongly suggested that aliens were visiting the Earth. The book was followed, twelve months later, by *The Uninvited*, a study by Pope of the so-called "alien abduction" phenomenon. (6)

Then in 1999, Pope wrote a science fiction novel titled *Operation Thunder Child,* which dealt with the emotive topic of hostile extraterrestrials attacking the Earth. When the book was published, however, rumors quickly spread within the British UFO research community that Pope was telling, in a strictly science fiction format, a very real and highly secret truth that he was legally unable to reveal in a non-fiction book.

Regardless of whether or not this was indeed the case, in *Operation Thunder Child*, alien bodies recovered from a UFO crash are taken to the Chemical and Biological Defense Establishment at Porton Down–precisely the same location where, it was alleged, James Prescott had said alien bodies found on the Berwyn Mountains, North Wales were taken in January 1974. And, interestingly enough, Pope has admitted that: "I discussed with various official sources before writing the book, so that the plot was as realistic as possible in dealing with how the government and military would respond to an alien invasion."

Notably, he added: "The final manuscript had to be submitted for official clearance and various details were changed to avoid compromising national security." (7) On the eve of publication of the book, I questioned Pope vigorously regarding the claims and rumors that *Operation Thunder Child* was basde more upon secret science-fact than science-fiction. His comments were illuminating:

Even to you, Nick, I can't comment on that. But let's put it this way: *Operation Thunder Child* is going to be more controversial than *Open Skies, Closed Minds* or *The Uninvited*. And, indeed, the Ministry of Defense may have more of a problem with it. Mainly because it's going to feature real locations, real weapon systems, real tactics, real doctrine and real crisis management techniques. It's going to blend my knowledge and experience of UFOs with my knowledge of crisis management–such as my involvement in the Gulf War where I worked in the Joint Operations Center. (8)

Moreover, by Pope's own admission, he had a great deal of inside help when it came to researching the subject matter, as he made clear in the book's Acknowledgements:

Finally, but perhaps most crucially, there are those who, for a number of reasons, I am not able to name. I was helped with this book by a wide range of experts from various different agencies, who supplemented my own knowledge with their insights into the world of politics, science, military doctrine and much else besides. (9)

It is interesting to note that Pope's novel included a section on alien bodies being taken for analysis to none other than Porton Down. Of course, Pope, at the time a regular contributor to *UFO Magazine*, would have been keenly aware of the James Prescott controversy and may simply have included the Porton Down angle in his book to help perpetuate the air of mystery and intrigue about himself that he has been very careful to cultivate since publicly announcing his belief in the existence of aliens.

Even stranger, in 1998, the year before Nick Pope's *Operation Thunder Child* was published, the British Ministry of Defense, in a wholly unprecedented move, gave a huge amount of technical assistance, and extensive support, to a BBC television production titled *Invasion Earth*. Based on a novel written by science fiction writer Harry Harrison and set in Scotland, the six-part series featured a race of aliens known as the Echoes who come to Earth to escape from hostile, inter-dimensional aliens called the NDs. Inevitably, this action on the part of the MoD led to rumors within the UFO research community that this was all part of a less-than-subtle attempt by the British Government to get the general public thinking about the possibility that real-life aliens–potentially hostiles ones–were secretly among us. (10)

A Ministry of Defense source specifically referred to me by Nick Pope made a number of perceptive comments on the matter of *Invasion Earth*:

It's extremely strange that on the one hand the MoD is publicly so dismissive about UFOs; and yet on the other it bent over backwards to provide assistance to a TV company producing a science-fiction drama which starts with the RAF shooting down a UFO. Normally, the Ministry of Defense only helps film and TV companies where it believes that significant benefits will fall to the MoD in terms of recruiting, training or public relations. This was the case, for example, with our participation in the James Bond film, *Tomorrow Never Dies*. What, one wonders, did the MoD think it had to gain from helping to perpetuate a view that the Royal Air Force were virtually at war with extraterrestrials? Questions about our participation in this project were raised at the highest level within the Ministry of Defense. (11)

But most notable of all, in *Invasion: Earth*, aliens from a captured, crashed UFO were taken to...Porton Down. The question of whether or not the account of James Prescott, Nick Pope's science fiction novel *Operation Thunder Child*, and the Ministry of Defense's unprecedented assistance given to the production of the BBC's *Invasion: Earth* science fiction drama series were all integral parts of a carefully crafted and subtle attempt on the part of the British Government to acclimatize the British public to the idea that aliens existed, that UFOs had crashed on British soil, and that their dead crews had been taken to Porton Down, still resounds and resonates more than a decade later.

■ ■ ■ ▎ ▎ 22 ▎▎ ■ ■ ■

9-11

"I woke up on September 11 and saw it on TV and the first thing I thought of was The Lone Gunmen.*"*

The Lone Gunmen were a trio of endearing, but geek-like, characters who made guest appearances on television's most paranoid and paranormal science fiction show of the 1990s, *The X-Files*. Full-on conspiracy theorists, they often gave assistance to FBI Agents Mulder and Scully in various alien-dominated adventures, as well as being the authors of an underground newspaper titled *The Magic Bullet Newsletter*. And they were hardly conventional. Lacking conventional employment, they lived in a loft-apartment together, rarely surfaced during daylight hours, and drove around in an old 1970s Volkswagen van.

They were: Melvin Frohike, a 1960s radical who was unashamedly hot for Scully; John Fitzgerald Byers, formerly an employee of the FCC, and perhaps best remembered for his line to Mulder: "That's what we like about you, Mulder. Your ideas are even weirder than ours;" and Richard Langly, a highly-skilled computer hacker and a big fan of the punk rock band the *Ramones*. (1)

So popular were the Lone Gunmen with the fans of *The X-Files* that, in 2001, they received the ultimate accolade after years of playing second fiddle to Mulder and Scully: namely, a short-lived, spin-off series of their very own on the Fox network starting on March 4, 2001. (2) It began in a style that still creates controversy to this very day, but certainly not for rea-

Author Nick Redfern (right) with actor Dean Haglund who played "Langly" in The Lone Gunman.

sons that could be foreseen at the time: the controversy centers around the fact that this episode of *The Lone Gunmen* dealt with the hijacking of a Boeing 727 passenger aircraft by a hostile computer hacker, who then takes control of the plane's computer flight system and directs it to fly from its departure point in Boston straight into one of the towers of the New York World Trade Center.

Indeed, the climactic sequence shows the 727 heading straight for one of the twin towers. Thanks to the efforts of the Lone Gunmen, who, at the last minute, succeed in hacking into the computer-controlled system, the pilots are finally able to regain control of the plane at the last second and manage to avoid the tower–by inches. A special aerial crew that used a helicopter to fly low over Manhattan at night and directly toward the World Trade Center filmed the background footage for the plane's approach to the twin towers during the spring of 2000.

In the show, the purpose of this atrocity is to increase the United States' military defense budget by blaming the attack on foreign dictators who are "begging to be smart-bombed." In Australia, the episode aired on August 30, 2001, less than two weeks before the 9-11 attacks. (3)

Writer Christopher Bollyn has observed that: "...rather than being discussed in the media as a prescient warning of the possibility of such an attack, the pilot episode of *The Lone Gunmen* series seemed to have been quietly forgotten. While an estimated 13.2 million Fox TV viewers are reported to have watched the pilot episode...when life imitated art just six months later on 9-11, no one in the media seemed to recall the program." (4)

But others certainly did remember.

"I woke up on September 11 and saw it on TV and the first thing I thought of was *The Lone Gunmen*," recalled Frank Spotnitz, one of the show's four executive producers. "But then in the weeks and months that followed, almost no one noticed the connection. What's disturbing about it to me is, you think as a fiction writer that if you can imagine this scenario, then the people in power in the government who are there to imagine disaster scenarios can imagine it, too." (5)

Robert McLachlan, the director of photography on the series concurred: "It was odd that nobody referenced it. In the ensuing press nobody mentioned that [9-11] echoed something that had been seen before." (6)

Jeffrey King, a researcher who had delved deep into the controversy surrounding the 9-11 attacks, asked the questions: "Is this just a case of life imitating art, or did Carter and his associates know something about the upcoming attacks? Was this an attempt to use the highly visible platform of the first episode of a new series (and a spin-off from the very popular

X-Files) to make enough people aware of the scenario that it would become too risky to implement? Or was it just one of those ideas that was 'in the air' at the time, an expression of the zeitgeist?" (7)

What really happened on that fateful day in 2001 continues to provoke deep controversy, both in the real world and–thanks to *The Lone Gunmen*–in the world of sci-fi, too.

■ ■ I I I I 23 I I I ■ ■ ■

PROJECT TELEPORT

"Beginning in the 1980s developments in quantum theory and general relativity physics have succeeded in pushing the envelope in exploring the reality of teleportation."

For fans of sci-fi, "Beam me up, Scotty" is perhaps the most widely, and instantly, recognized quote of all. Although attributed to *Star Trek's* Captain James T. Kirk, it is ironic that those four specific words were never actually uttered in that particular order in even a single episode of what is probably the world's most-watched science fiction television series of all time. Nevertheless, they are words that are now firmly ingrained within the minds of whole generations of devotees of the often-repeated series that was created by Gene Rodenberry and that ran from 1966 to 1968. As anyone who has ever watched *Star Trek* will know, derivations of the famous phrase were routinely used whenever Kirk, Spock, McCoy, and the rest of the crew of the *Enterprise* needed to travel from one location to another via what today we routinely refer to as teleportation. (1)

The word teleportation was coined in the early 1900s by the American writer and renowned chronicler of all-things weird, Charles Fort, to describe something that fascinated him, namely, the unexplained disappearances and appearances of people, animals, and objects. Having combined the Greek prefix "tele-" (meaning "distant") with the latter part of the word "transportation," teleportation was born, and was first used by Fort in his 1931 book *Lo!* Fort noted: "Mostly in this book I shall special-

REPORT DOCUMENTATION PAGE			Form Approved OMB No. 0704-0188
Public reporting burden for this collection of information is estimated to average 1 hour per response, including the time for reviewing instructions, searching existing data sources, gathering and maintaining the data needed, and completing and reviewing this collection of information. Send comments regarding this burden estimate or any other aspect of this collection of information, including suggestions for reducing this burden to Department of Defense, Washington Headquarters Services, Directorate for Information Operations and Reports (0704-0188), 1215 Jefferson Davis Highway, Suite 1204, Arlington, VA 22202-4302. Respondents should be aware that notwithstanding any other provision of law, no person shall be subject to any penalty for failing to comply with a collection of information if it does not display a currently valid OMB control number. **PLEASE DO NOT RETURN YOUR FORM TO THE ABOVE ADDRESS.**			
1. REPORT DATE (DD-MM-YYYY) 25-11-2003	2. REPORT TYPE Special	3. DATES COVERED (From - To) 30 Jan 2001 – 28 Jul 2003	
4. TITLE AND SUBTITLE Teleportation Physics Study		5a. CONTRACT NUMBER F04611-99-C-0025	
		5b. GRANT NUMBER	
		5c. PROGRAM ELEMENT NUMBER 62500F	
6. AUTHOR(S) Eric W. Davis		5d. PROJECT NUMBER 4847	
		5e. TASK NUMBER 0159	
		5f. WORK UNIT NUMBER 549907	
7. PERFORMING ORGANIZATION NAME(S) AND ADDRESS(ES) Warp Drive Metrics 4849 San Rafael Ave. Las Vegas, NV 89120		8. PERFORMING ORGANIZATION REPORT NO.	
9. SPONSORING / MONITORING AGENCY NAME(S) AND ADDRESS(ES) Air Force Research Laboratory (AFMC) AFRL/PRSP 10 E. Saturn Blvd. Edwards AFB CA 93524-7680		10. SPONSOR/MONITOR'S ACRONYM(S)	
		11. SPONSOR/MONITOR'S REPORT NUMBER(S) AFRL-PR-ED-TR-2003-0034	
12. DISTRIBUTION / AVAILABILITY STATEMENT Approved for public release; distribution unlimited.			
13. SUPPLEMENTARY NOTES			

14. ABSTRACT
This study was tasked with the purpose of collecting information describing the teleportation of material objects, providing a description of teleportation as it occurs in physics, its theoretical and experimental status, and a projection of potential applications. The study also consisted of a search for teleportation phenomena occurring naturally or under laboratory conditions that can be assembled into a model describing the conditions required to accomplish the transfer of objects. This included a review and documentation of quantum teleportation, its theoretical basis, technological development, and its potential applications. The characteristics of teleportation were defined and physical theories were evaluated in terms of their ability to completely describe the phenomena. Contemporary physics, as well as theories that presently challenge the current physics paradigm were investigated. The author identified and proposed two unique physics models for teleportation that are based on the manipulation of either the general relativistic spacetime metric or the spacetime vacuum electromagnetic (zero-point fluctuations) parameters. Naturally occurring anomalous teleportation phenomena that were previously studied by the United States and foreign governments were also documented in the study and are reviewed in the report. The author proposes an additional model for teleportation that is based on a combination of the experimental results from the previous government studies and advanced physics concepts. Numerous recommendations outlining proposals for further theoretical and experimental studies are given in the report. The report also includes an extensive teleportation bibliography.

15. SUBJECT TERMS
teleportation; physics; quantum teleportation; teleportation phenomena; anomalous teleportation; teleportation theories; teleportation experiments; teleportation bibliography

16. SECURITY CLASSIFICATION OF:			17. LIMITATION OF ABSTRACT	18. NUMBER OF PAGES	19a. NAME OF RESPONSIBLE PERSON Franklin B. Mead, Jr.
a. REPORT Unclassified	b. ABSTRACT Unclassified	c. THIS PAGE Unclassified	A	88	19b. TELEPHONE NO (include area code) (661) 275-5929

Standard Form 298
(Rev. 8-98)
Prescribed by ANSI Std. 239.18

A research study on teleportation prepared for the U.S. Air Force.

ize upon indications that there exists a transportory force that I shall call Teleportation." (2)

According to an IBM Research Report:

Teleportation is the name given by science fiction writers to the feat of making an object or person disintegrate in one place while a perfect replica appears somewhere else. How this is accomplished is usually not explained in detail, but the general idea seems to be that the original object is scanned in such a way as to extract all the information from it, then this information is transmitted to the receiving location and used to construct the replica, not necessarily from the actual material of the original, but perhaps from atoms of the same kinds, arranged in exactly the same pattern as the original...A few science fiction writers consider teleporters that preserve the original, and the plot gets complicated when the original and teleported versions of the same person meet; but the more common kind of teleporter destroys the original, functioning as a super transportation device, not as a perfect replicator of souls and bodies. (3)

Despite the fact that any mention of teleportation will forever conjure up images of Captain Kirk and Co. doing battle with hostile aliens on far-away planets, the subject has a long history within the annals of sci-fi. Quite possibly the earliest use of teleportation as an integral part of the plot was within the pages of David Page Mitchell's 1877 story "The Man without a Body," in which a scientist scrambles a cat's atoms and transmits them via telegraph-wire. When the scientist becomes the guinea-pig for his very own experiments, however, disaster results when the telegraph's battery dies and only his disembodied head is teleported. (4) Similarly, Sir Arthur Conan Doyle's 1927 story "The Disintegration Machine" told a similar tale (5), as did A.E. van Vogt's *World of Null-A*, which was published in the August 1945 issue of *Astounding Science fiction* (6), and Algis Budrys' *Rogue Moon* of 1960. (7)

But perhaps most memorable, and grisly, was George Langelaan's "The Fly" that appeared in *Playboy* magazine in June 1957. The story tells the tale of a brilliant scientist who unlocks the secrets of teleportation and decides to experiment upon himself; only things to go catastrophically wrong when, on one occasion, he neglects to notice that a fly has entered the teleporting device with him. As a result, the genes and DNA of the two are combined at the moment of teleportation, and a literal monster is created. Made into a hit movie in 1958 that starred David "Al" Hedison (later of *Voyage to the Bottom of the Sea* fame), and a graphic, special-effects-driven remake with Jeff Goldblum in 1986, *The Fly* is a creepy, dark tale of what can go wrong when science begins to wildly delve into – and fuse with – the realm of the unknown. (8)

While the overwhelming majority of people surely consider teleportation to be pure science fiction and nothing else, for years, the U.S. Air Force has secretly taken an interest in this strange–but potentially world-changing–subject. And for firm evidence of this, we have to turn our attention to something known as the "Teleportation Physics Study."

The Air Force Research Laboratory of Air Force Materiel Command quietly contracted the study to Eric W. Davis of a Las Vegas-based outfit called Warp Drive Metrics. And in August 2004 the military made Davis' report available to the general public and the media.

Davis explains:

This study was tasked with the purpose of collecting information describing the teleportation of material objects, providing a description of teleportation as it occurs in physics, its theoretical and experimental status, and a projection of potential applications. The study also consisted of a search for teleportation phenomena occurring naturally or under laboratory conditions that can be assembled into a model describing the conditions required to accomplish the transfer of objects.

Interestingly, the Davis report noted that there appeared to be keen interest in official circles with respect to teleportation and its potential applications by the Department of Defense:

The late Dr. Robert L. Forward stated that modern hard-core SciFi literature, with the exception of the ongoing Star Trek franchise, has abandoned using the teleportation concept because writers believe that it has more to do with the realms of parapsychology/paranormal (a.k.a. psychic) and imaginative fantasy than with any realm of science. Beginning in the 1980s developments in quantum theory and general relativity physics have succeeded in pushing the envelope in exploring the reality of teleportation. As for the psychic aspect of teleportation, it became known to Dr. Forward and myself, along with several colleagues both inside and outside of government, that anomalous teleportation has been scientifically investigated and separately documented by the Department of Defense.

Davis's report carefully noted that there were a number of definitions for what might constitute teleportation:

1. Teleportation – SciFi: the disembodied transport of persons or inanimate objects across space by advanced (futuristic) technological means. We will call this sf- Teleportation, which will not be considered further in this study.
2. Teleportation – psychic: the conveyance of persons or inanimate objects by psychic means. We will call this p-Teleportation.
3. Teleportation – engineering the vacuum or spacetime metric: the conveyance of persons or inanimate objects across space by altering the properties of the spacetime vacuum, or by altering the spacetime metric (geometry). We will call this vm-Teleportation.
4. Teleportation – quantum entanglement: the disembodied transport of the quantum state of a system and its correlations across space to another system, where system refers to any single or collective particles of matter or energy such as baryons (protons, neutrons, etc.), leptons (electrons, etc.), photons, atoms, ions, etc. We will call this q-Teleportation.
5. Teleportation – exotic: the conveyance of persons or inanimate

objects by transport through extra space dimensions or parallel universes. We will call this e-Teleportation.

The "Teleportation Physics Study" is highly technical in nature, but it is worth noting Davis's conclusions with respect to the five areas of teleportation described above. He concludes that, based on present day capabilities, "P-Teleportation" would seem to offer the greatest potential:

P-Teleportation, if verified, would represent a phenomenon that could offer potential high-payoff military, intelligence and commercial applications. This phenomenon could generate a dramatic revolution in technology, which would result from a dramatic paradigm shift in science. Anomalies are the key to all paradigm shifts!

In a section of the Study titled Recommendations, Davis added:

A research program...should be conducted in order to generate p-Teleportation phenomenon in the lab. An experimental program...should be funded at $900,000–1,000,000 per year in parallel with a theoretical program funded at $500,000 per year for an initial five-year duration. (9)

There is an interesting science fiction tie-in to Eric Davis's "Teleportation Physics Study," too. Among those listed for "Primary Distribution" of the document, one was Dr. Greg Benford, of the University of California's Physics Department. Born in Mobile, Alabama in 1941, Benford is also a renowned science fiction author. His story "Stand-In" appeared in the June 1965 issue of the *Magazine of Fantasy and Science fiction*, and in 1969, he began writing a regular science column for *Amazing Stories*. His Galactic Center Saga began with the 1977 title *In the Ocean of Night*, which described a galaxy in which sentient, organic life is engaged in constant warfare with sentient, mechanical life. His 1980 novel, *Timescape*, won the prestigious Nebula Award.

Notably, in the 1990s, Benford wrote *Foundation's Fear*, which was one of an authorized sequel trilogy to Isaac Asimov's Foundation series. Other novels written by Benford and published in the 1990s include several near-future science thrillers: *Cosm*, *The Martian Race*, and *Eater*. In addition, Benford has proposed a corollary to renowned science fiction author Arthur C. Clarke's third law: "Any technology distinguishable from magic is insufficiently advanced." (10)

Perhaps taking a hint from the distribution of Eric Davis' Study to a science fiction author, the Air Force apparently concluded that the whole matter of teleportation was one that should remain in the world of sci-fi. When the Air Force declassified the Study, Lawrence Krauss of Case Western Reserve University and the author of *The Physics of Star Trek*, stated: "It is in large part crackpot physics," and added that it contained "some things adapted from reasonable theoretical studies, and other things from nonsensical ones." (11)

Perhaps the Air Force, after reading Davis's document, agreed: "The views expressed in the report are those of the author and do not necessarily reflect the official policy of the Air Force, the Department of Defense or the U.S. Government," was the statement made by the Air Force's Research Laboratory when questioned by *USA Today*. (12)

Asked why the Laboratory had secretly sponsored the study, AFRL spokesman Ranney Adams said: "If we don't turn over stones, we don't know if we have missed something."

Significantly, the AFRL added that: "There are no plans by the AFRL Propulsion Directorate for additional funding on this contract." (13)

Unless circumstances change drastically–or the whole subject has gone undercover–it would seem that teleportation is destined to remain purely within the realm of science fiction for a very long time indeed.

■ ■ ■ I I II 24 II I ■ ■ ■

SCIENCE FICTION SPECIAL-EFFECT
OR SECRET EVIDENCE?

*"There was something lying on the autopsy table,
and it wasn't human..."*

On January 13, 1995, Reg Presley, lead singer with the 1960s rock band, *The Troggs*, was interviewed on the British BBC television talk-show, *Good Morning with Anne and Nick* and disclosed he had then recently viewed a sensational piece of film footage that purportedly displayed the autopsy of an unusual body recovered from the wreckage of an equally unusual air-craft found near the White Sands Missile Range, New Mexico, in the early summer of 1947. The footage had allegedly been filmed by a now-elderly cameraman who had served with the Army Air Forces at the time. (1) It transpired that the footage was in the possession of one Ray Santilli, who was described as "an entrepreneur whose business is making videos." (2)

At the time, Santilli described the background to the story: "As a result of research into film material for a music docu-mentary I was in Cleveland, Ohio, USA in the summer of 1993. [While] there I had identified some old film material taken by Universal News in the summer of 1955. As Universal News no longer existed I needed the film to investigate the source of the film and was able to determine that the film was shot by a then local freelance cameraman. He had been employed by Universal News because of a Film Union strike in the summer of 1955.

"The cameraman was located, following which a very straightforward negotiation took place for his small piece of film, i.e. cash for three minutes of film. Upon completion of this the cameraman asked if I would be interested in purchasing outright very valuable footage taken during his time in the forces. He explained that the footage in question came from the Roswell crash; that it included debris and recovery footage and, of most importance, autopsy footage." (3)

Since later pronouncements from Ray Santilli somewhat contradicted his original account of how he came to acquire the controversial film, he conceded: "I still maintain that the story of the film's acquisition is true. Certain non-relevant details were only changed to stop people getting to the cameraman." (4)

On May 5, 1995, the film was finally shown to a select audience at the Museum of London. And thus was born the controversy surrounding the now-notorious Alien Autopsy film—a controversy that has now raged for nearly a decade-and-a-half with no end in sight. One of those present at the Museum of London presentation of the footage was former British Ministry of Defense UFO investigator-turned-science fiction novelist, Nick Pope. He recalls the day in question: "I won't say that I was keeping a low profile at the Museum of London, but I was certainly not advertising my presence. I wasn't, like a number of people, wearing a name badge or going out of my way to speak to the media.

"Well, I turned up; and there was a lectern at the front of the auditorium and there was a kind of expectant atmosphere. I was expecting Ray Santilli, whom I'd heard about but not met, to introduce the film in some way. But to my surprise, and I think to the surprise and disgust of just about everyone there, there was no introduction: the film simply started and then stopped.

"I don't have a particularly strong constitution, and I would say there was a kind of awkward atmosphere. I could smell the sweat and the distaste at one point. Everyone had gone in a light-hearted mood, particularly the journalists. They were thinking: this is a Friday; there's a little bit of a party atmosphere.

"But that mood didn't last long; a rather shocked hush fell over the auditorium. Afterwards, the lights went out and people were expecting an announcement. That announcement didn't come. Now, one or two of the journalists recognized Ray Santilli at the back, and in a fairly aggressive and angry way, they surrounded him and started firing questions. I recall he was almost physically picked up and escorted from the room by his minders or his commercial backers, whoever they were. There were certainly some people there who didn't want him placed in a position where he had to answer the questions that were being fired at him: 'Where did you get this? Who took it? Can we speak to the cameraman?'" (5)

And what was Pope's assessment of the film?

"There was something lying on the autopsy table, and it wasn't human…probably around five feet, perhaps a little less. It was essentially humanoid, with a bulbous, hairless head. The eyes seemed slightly larger than ours…the nose and mouth were basically humanoid…and the mouth was frozen in an expression of terror. The torso looked muscular, especially the upper arms and thighs. It had six fingers on its hands and six toes on its feet. The upper [right] leg appeared to be seriously injured, and the [right] hand almost severed at the wrist. These, presumably, were injuries sustained in the crash." (6)

There can be no doubt that the film, and its attendant years of controversy, firmly split the UFO research community into several camps: some believed it was the genuine article; others considered it to be nothing more than an ingenious hoax generated by special-effects experts who worked in the field of cinematic sci-fi; and a number of commentators took the view that the film was a prime example of U.S. Government-orchestrated disinformation to obfuscate the real nature of the Roswell event.

More than a decade would pass before the next major development in the story surfaced. On April 4, 2006, Britain's SKY Television show *Eamonn Investigates* revealed that the infamous Alien Autopsy film that had tantalized and intrigued so many for years was nothing more than an elaborate hoax. Ray Santilli told host Eamonn Holmes that he was responsible for the creation of the footage with the help of colleague Gary Shoefield and special-effects expert John Humphreys, who worked on the British science fiction show *Dr. Who* and on the fantasy movie *Charlie and the Chocolate Factory*. Santilli continued to assert that he did secure original footage from a still-unidentified cameraman, however. (7)

Days after Santilli made his confession on *Eamonn Investigates*, the BBC reported: "Ray Santilli and Gary Shoefield now claim in 1992 that they originally saw twenty-two cans of film, averaging four minutes in length, shot in 1947 by a US Army cameraman in Roswell covering an alien autopsy. However, by the time he returned to purchase the footage two years later, the footage had degraded from humidity and heat with only a few frames staying intact. They now claim that they 'restored the footage' by filming a fake autopsy on a fake alien 'based upon what they saw.'" (8)

According to Santilli's story, a set was carefully constructed in the living room of an empty apartment at Rochester Square, Camden Town, London. Humphreys was employed to construct two alien bodies over a period of three weeks, using casts containing a sheep brain that was set in Jello, chicken entrails, and knuckle joints obtained from S.C. Crosby Wholesale Butchers in Smithfield Meat Market, London. (9)

When questioned by the BBC, Humphreys stated: "Well,

it started when Ray and Gary went to the States to get hold of some unseen film of rock stars. They managed to buy some but then they were approached by a guy who said he had footage of an alien autopsy. At the time they were very spooked–they honestly didn't know what they were looking at. But the problem was the film was in very poor condition, it was disintegrating. So they asked me if I could interpret what I could see and help them to restore it. In effect, it was a documentary. But what you see in the original 1995 film, the alien, is what I made." (10)

"So was it a hoax?" demanded the BBC. Notably, Humphreys was distinctly diplomatic when it came to providing a definitive answer to that question: "It was a long time ago, and you'd have to ask Ray and Gary what they were doing. Basically, they explained that they had some damaged film and they needed my help to re-create it. It wasn't presentable in the form that they had. If you imagine, it was like having pieces of a broken statue and trying to put it together. Whether there was a hoax or not…well that's not for me to say. But it was an exciting time, and an exciting thing to be involved in." (11)

It must be noted too that in the Alien Autopsy film, the "doctors" carefully remove from the eyes of the creature two, large, black lenses that reveal perfectly human-looking eyes underneath. Interestingly, precisely this same scenario was utilized in an episode of a British science fiction television series of 1970 titled *UFO*, in which similar lenses are removed from the body of a dead alien during the course of an autopsy. (12)

And while the world's media has firmly embraced Santilli's confession that the "alien body" that is shown in the film was merely the skilled handiwork of science fiction special effects artists, the controversy continues for one specific reason: namely, the testimony of numerous, highly credible, people who claim to have seen the Alien Autopsy film long before Ray Santilli made it available to the world at large.

The respected British UFO investigator, Jenny Randles, has made an intriguing comment with regard to an offer of alleged Top Secret documents on crashed UFOs that had been made to her in late 1986 by a British Army source that she calls "Robert." According to Randles, Robert had then recently left the military and had personal access to certain UFO files that had been surreptitiously removed from Wright-Patterson Air Force Base, Dayton, Ohio, and provided to the British Army by a source at Wright-Patterson.

From there, sources in the Army were determined to forward this documentation on to Randles for circulation and dissemination to the public. However, the transfer of the classified material to Randles never occurred, and to this day Randles remains unsure of what motivated this bizarre episode. Her comments on this strange, cloak-and-dagger episode are notable, however, and highly relevant to the Alien Autopsy film.

Randles says that within the files that Robert described to her in 1986 were photographs that sound very much like photographic images that had been lifted directly from the Alien Autopsy film: "Bear in mind," Randles said, "1986 was years before the Autopsy film surfaced. In fact, the connections with the Autopsy film and with what Robert told me are chillingly similar. One of the impressions that you get from viewing the Alien Autopsy footage is that the body is very human-like; and is around five foot in height. I have to say, it struck me as soon as I saw the footage that this was *very* similar to what Robert had described." (13)

Two reports that may have a direct bearing on the Alien Autopsy film came from the premier collector of UFO crash-retrieval accounts, the late Leonard Stringfield. In 1980, in *The UFO Crash Retrieval Syndrome*, Stringfield related the testimony of a former "Air Force radar specialist, who in the spring of 1953 was "summoned to view a film at the base theater" while stationed at Ft. Monmouth, New Jersey.

The film, Stringfield was told, showed "a desert scene dominated by a silver disc-shaped object imbedded in the sand with a domed section at the top." The source of the story advised Stringfield that the UFO had been recovered in New Mexico in 1952. It was fifteen to twenty feet in diameter and was surrounded by "ten to fifteen military personnel dressed in fatigues."

Stringfield's informant told him that the movie then jumped to another scene. According to the man's recollection: "Now in view were two tables, probably taken inside a tent, on which were dead bodies. Two were on one table; one on the other. The bodies appeared little by human standards and most notable were the heads, all looking alike, and all being large compared to their body sizes. They looked Mongoloid, with small noses, mouths, and eyes that were shut." Interestingly, Stringfield was told that the man and his colleagues were ordered by a superior officer not to discuss what they had seen with anyone and merely to "think about the movie." Two weeks later, T.E. was told: "Forget the movie you saw; it was a hoax."

Stringfield's source added that: "The 5-minute long movie was not a Walt Disney production. It was probably shot by an inexperienced cameraman because it was full of scratches, and had poor coloring and texture." Even though the footage viewed by T.E. was reportedly taken five years after the Alien Autopsy film was allegedly made, there can be no doubt that the description of the film being of poor texture, and the fact that it seemed to have been filmed by an inexperienced cameraman, seems to tally very closely with the out-of-focus, poor-quality segments of footage that Ray Santilli thrust upon the world in 1995. (14)

Similarly, in his report *UFO Crash/Retrievals: Is the Cover-Up Lid Lifting?* Leonard Stringfield wrote: "In 1985, Chris Coffey, of Cincinnati, who was a close friend of astronaut Ellison Onizuka, revealed to me that she had asked him when they met after one of his visits to Wright-Patterson AFB, about his interest in UFOs. He admitted he kept an open mind on the subject and added that his curiosity was aroused when he and a select group of air force pilots, at McClelland AFB in 1973, were shown a black-and-white movie film featuring 'alien bodies on a slab.' In his state of shock, he said he remembered saying aloud, 'Oh, my God!' Chris, knowing my work in C/R [Crash/Retrievals], had arranged for me to meet Onizuka to discuss UFOs after his scheduled flight on the space shuttle *Challenger*. As it turned out, fate intervened when the shuttle exploded." (15)

A former employee of the British Government's Home Office, who is known to me, also claims to have seen footage practically identical to the famous Alien Autopsy footage. In this case, the year was 1989 and the location was a London office that belonged to the British Ministry of Defense. During a briefing given by representatives of British and American intelligence, those present were shown a film that eerily paralleled the Santilli footage and displayed a very similar body.

The Home Office personnel who received the briefing were initially told that the body in the footage was that of an extraterrestrial recovered from a UFO crash in New Mexico nearly sixty years ago. However, the possibility was later discussed that it may have been related to dark and disturbing experimentation undertaken on handicapped human subjects in 1947, somewhat akin to the so-called "Human Radiation Experiment" scandal that spanned the 1940s to the 1970s, the details of which surfaced under the Clinton Administration during the 1990s. (16)

Philip Mantle has secured the testimony of a number of individuals who claimed to have seen the Santilli film decades ago, too. One source, Jack Bryan, told Mantle that his father was a military cameraman who had been "assigned" to the

UFO crash site at Roswell, New Mexico in 1947. According to Bryan, in the 1950s his father had shown him "a few stills" that appeared to have been taken from the Alien Autopsy footage.

Mike Maloney, Group Chief Photographer with the British *Daily Mirror* newspaper, informed Mantle that during the 1970s he had the opportunity to visit the offices of the Disney Corporation in California. While there, Maloney elaborated, he viewed a piece of footage that was almost certainly linked with the film that Ray Santilli made available years later. As Maloney said: "The film I saw all those years ago was shot, I would suggest, by somebody who could control a camera but it wasn't a brilliant piece of footage, but it was fascinating… There was an alien lying on a table like it was before it had be operated on, but it had some incisions in it. I was told that the alien had originally been alive but was now dead and that this was some sort of post mortem to try and discover the cause of death." (17)

Highly intriguing is the fact that, as the late UFO author Georgina Bruni noted, Mike Maloney was friends with Disney's Ward Kimball, who was deeply interested in UFOs, and whose involvement with Wernher von Braun, and with the U.S. Air Force on a proposed UFO-themed television documentary in the 1950s is detailed in Chapter Two of this book: *Kirby Conspiracies*. (18)

Diana Lyons, a retired physiotherapist, advised Philip Mantle that, at some point between 1970 and 1973, her father, a radiologist named Dr. Geoffrey Hordle, showed her a number of photographs that she believes may have come from the Alien Autopsy film. Lyons' reasoning is that both the Santilli film and the photographs that she saw displayed a creature with six fingers and toes. (19)

The fact that so many people apparently viewed the Alien Autopsy film or aspects of it at least, long before Santilli's copy surfaced into the public domain will doubtless ensure that those who believe the film to be real will say that it is Santilli's science fiction special-effects-laden confession that is the hoax and not the film itself.

While Santilli's confession should have laid matters to rest, it has, ironically, only succeeded in stirring up even more controversy. But the fact that this confession surfaced at precisely the same time that a major new movie on the saga, titled *Alien Autopsy*, opened in British cinemas may mean that more controversy is precisely what Ray Santilli was looking for.

■ ■ ■ ■ ‖ 25 ‖ ■ ■ ■

Serpo and the Science fiction Spy

"The 'Project SERPO' report was part of an attempt to trump the Soviets. Its aim was to make them believe that we had acquired lethal extraterrestrial energy devices."

There is a truly dizzying amount of information, disinformation, and misinformation available on UFOs, but the subject is sadly lacking in verifiable facts. But even the wildest unverifiable stories about UFOs pale into absolute insignificance when placed up against a startling, and highly controversial, saga that began in early November 2005.

That month a person, who dubbed himself, or herself, Anonymous and who claimed to be a former employee of the super-secret Defense Intelligence Agency (DIA), surfaced with a controversial tale about having read something that would become known as "The Serpo Documents," purportedly classified files that detailed a close encounter of a truly extraordinary kind between representatives of the Earth and those of an alien race.

According to the documentation supplied by Anonymous:

I am a retired employee of the U.S. Government. I won't go into any great details about my past, but I was involved in a special program. As for Roswell, it occurred, but not like the story books tell. There were two crash sites: one southwest of Corona, New Mexico and the second site at Pelona Peak, south of Datil, New Mexico.

The crash involved two extraterrestrial aircraft. The Corona site was found a day later by an archaeological team. This team reported the crash site to the Lincoln County Sheriff's department. A deputy arrived the next day and summoned a state police officer. One live entity was found hiding behind a rock. The entity was given water but declined food. The entity was later transferred to Los Alamos.

The information eventually went to Roswell Army Air Field. The site was examined and all evidence was removed. The bodies were taken to Los Alamos National Laboratory because they had a freezing system that allowed the bodies to remain frozen for research. The craft was taken to Roswell and then onto Wright Field, Ohio.

The second site was not discovered until August 1949 by two ranchers. They reported their findings several days later to the sheriff of Catron County, New Mexico. Because of the remote location, it took the sheriff several days to make his way to the crash site. Once at the site, the sheriff took photographs and then drove back to Datil.

Sandia Army Base, Albuquerque, New Mexico was then notified. A recovery team from Sandia took custody of all evidence, including six bodies. The bodies were taken to Sandia Base, but later transferred to Los Alamos.

The live entity established communications with us and provided us with a location of his home planet. The entity remained alive until 1952, when he died. But before his death, he provided us with a full explanation of the items found inside the two crafts. One item was a communication device. The entity was allowed to make contact with his planet.

Somehow, I never knew this information, but a meeting date was set for April 1964 near Alamogordo, New Mexico. The Aliens landed and retrieved the bodies of their dead comrades. Information was exchanged. Communication was in English. The aliens had a translation device.

In 1965, we had an exchange program with the aliens. We carefully selected 12 military personnel; ten men and two women. They were trained, vetted and carefully removed from the military system. The 12 were skilled in various specialties.

Near the northern part of the Nevada Test Site, the aliens landed and the 12 Americans left. One entity was left on Earth. The original plan was for our 12 people to stay 10 years and then return to Earth.

But something went wrong. The 12 remained until 1978, when they were returned to the same location in Nevada. Seven men and one woman returned. Two died on the alien's home planet. Four others decided to remain, according to the returnees. Of the eight that returned, all have died. The last survivor died in 2002.

The returnees were isolated from 1978 until 1984 at various military installations. The Air Force Office of Special Investigations (AFOSI) was responsible for their security and safety. AFOSI also conducted debriefing sessions with the returnees. (1)

That, in brief, is the extraordinary story of Anonymous. But is it true? Is it a bizarre and outrageous hoax? Or is it something even stranger? The debate raged endlessly when the story first surfaced. Indeed, one aspect of the story that divided the UFO research community was the fact that the description of the so-called "exchange program" as revealed by Anonymous sounded suspiciously like the closing scenes of Steven Spielberg's epic science fiction production *Close Encounters of the Third Kind* that sees a team of specially trained personnel embarking on just such an excursion to a far-off alien world.

Significantly, and on this particular point, William J. Birnes—the publisher of *UFO* magazine and one of the team-members on the History Channel's *UFO Hunters* series—notes that one of the Serpo-related claims was that: "The basis of this story made its way to Steven Spielberg and was part of the background for his 1977 movie *Close Encounters of the Third Kind*." (2)

Despite the controversial nature of this assertion, it should not be forgotten that, according to UFO researcher Grant Cameron, the Government had indeed provided "some input" to both of Spielberg's UFO-dominated movies: *Close Encounters of the Third Kind* and *E.T.* And respected investigative writer Greg Bishop has reported that: "One former AFOSI [Air Force Office of Special Investigations] Special Agent… maintains that there was someone in the production office at Spielberg's company who received checks from an unnamed government agency in order to help finance the film and push a particular message of wonder and friendly aliens." (3)

Interestingly, the best-selling author Whitley Strieber, who wrote a science fiction novel titled *Majestic* that had the infamous Roswell crash as its central theme, was told a similar story more than a decade ago that closely matched that of Anonymous. At a UFO conference held in Gulf Breeze, Florida in the early 1990s, an old man told Strieber that he could prove he was from another planet, adding only one word after that, which Strieber thought was "Serpico." Strieber now wonders if he misheard the word "Serpo." (4)

The most intriguing development in the Serpo saga, however, began on January 25, 2006, when an alleged former employee of the British Ministry of Defense at Whitehall, London, identifying himself or herself only as Chapman, posted the following to the online "Above Top Secret" discussion forum on the internet with regard to the Serpo documents:

Interesting reading. However, these are NOT real events that are being described here, although the document they come from IS REAL. I saw this information in 1969 or '70 in Whitehall. Originally it was a CIA document authored by a lady named Alice Bradley Sheldon. Its main purpose, if you will pardon the phrase, was to "scare the crap out of the Soviets" in response to them scaring the crap out of us.

In the '60s, during the warmer part of the Cold War, the KGB successfully led the U.S. Government to believe that a number of nuclear devices had been concealed in disused mines and caves close to four (4) large American cities. These bombs could be detonated by sleeper agents at any time Moscow wished. It was not completely disproved that this was fake until 1980.

The "Project SERPO" report was part of the CIA's riposte

to this and an attempt to trump the Soviets. Its aim was to make them believe that we had acquired lethal extraterrestrial energy devices and that we had a cozy friendship with these all-powerful EBENs [Note: EBEN is allegedly a classified term used by American Intelligence to describe aliens. It is said to derive from the term Extraterrestrial Biological Entity] who would be very unhappy if Moscow attempted to harm the United States in any way. To a degree I believe this effort was effective to begin with.

However, it came unstuck when the CIA tried to overreach the information by ADDING PHOTOGRAPHS and also trying to spook allies such as ourselves who were better equipped to analyze the information and bugged to the hilt by the KGB.

Why this information is being released again now I do not know. Possibly in the past the DIA could have BEEN FOOLED BY THE CIA into believing that "Project SERPO" was a real event and the ANONYMOUS source may genuinely want to release this information. Alternatively the DIA may have got it direct from the KGB most likely with a few choice modifications added by them. (5)

Despite the fact that many UFO researchers who believe the Serpo documents to be genuine dismissed Chapman's account when it surfaced, his or her claim that the papers were allegedly written by one Alice Bradley Sheldon is a notable one, chiefly because of the intriguing fact that Sheldon had a background in both clandestine, international espionage and the world of sci-fi. In other words, if the CIA had wanted to employ someone who was sufficiently skilled and imaginative to concoct a bogus science fiction oriented story to both deceive and alarm the Soviets, then Sheldon would arguably have been the perfect candidate.

Sheldon was born in 1915 to Mary Hastings Bradley – noted author of travel books – and an attorney and African explorer, Herbert Bradley. Even as a child, Sheldon's life was an extraordinary one: in 1921, she journeyed with her parents on an Africa safari that was to last for more than a year. Having

a keen interest in art, Sheldon began a career as a graphic artist and a professional painter, and in 1934 began a marriage to
William Davey. It was a marriage that would not last, however. In 1941, she accepted a position as art critic for the *Chicago
Sun*. After the United States joined the Second World War following the Japanese attack on Pearl Harbor in December 1941,
however, Sheldon joined the military, and was assigned to Air
Intelligence.

At the close of hostilities in 1945, she married one Hun-
tington Sheldon, and in the following year received her military discharge, having achieved the rank of Major. In 1952,
the Sheldon's moved to Washington, D.C., after they had been
"invited" to join the CIA. The full and precise details of Sheldon's work for the CIA are unknown; however, it has been
confirmed that, until she resigned from the CIA in 1955 to further her education, Sheldon acted as a fully-fledged spy in the
Near East and as a photo-analyst.

In 1967, she made a decision to try and pursue a career
in writing full-time, and specifically within the field of sci-fi,
a subject for which she had a deep fascination. Rather than
do so under her real name, however, Sheldon took on a male
persona and the pseudonym of James Tiptree, Jr. And so it was
that, in 1968, the career of the former Army Major and CIA
spy began to follow a new and intriguing path.

In 1973, a collection of Sheldon's short stories, that she began to write in the late 1960s, was published under the title of
Ten Thousand Light Years from Home. In 1975, a second volume, *Warm Worlds and Otherwise*, followed. It was also in 1975
that her first full-length novel, *Up the Walls of the World*, was
published.

It is highly ironic that Tiptree's work was widely admired
in the 1970s for the fact that "he" was unafraid to delve into
women's issues. But as Sheldon's work progressed, so did rumors within the world of science fiction writing that suggested

James Tiptree, Jr., was really an alias for an unknown woman. Sheldon continued to write science fiction with *Out of the Everywhere and Other Extraordinary Visions* and *Brightness Falls from the Air* published in 1981 and 1985 respectively. Tragedy struck on May 19, 1987, however, when she mercy killed her 84-year-old blind, bedridden, and ailing husband, and then took her own life via a bullet to the head. (6)

We may never know for sure if this extraordinary woman, who seemingly moved effortlessly within the realms of secret international espionage, the military, and sci-fi, really did pen the Serpo documents for her former employers at the CIA as part of a clandestine operation designed to alarm the Soviets, but the story does not end there.

One of those who asserted that the Serpo documents told a very real story is a man named Richard Doty, a retired Special Agent with the Air Force Office of Special Investigations (AFOSI). Doty has said that: "During a briefing in 1984 I read a document which mentioned an exchange program between an alien race and twelve U.S. military personnel." Although Doty states that the document "did not mention any specific details," he claims that in 1991 he was told the truth of the program by a "Colonel Jack Casey, retired Air Force Intelligence." (7)

According to Doty, Casey told him that: "In 1965, twelve U.S. military men were placed on an extraterrestrial spacecraft and flew to an alien planet some 40 light years away. The exchange program lasted until 1978 when the team returned. Some of the twelve died on the alien planet and by 1991, when I was given this information, some had died since. The final briefing of the returnees is still classified. Note: all the team are now dead, the last surviving until 2002." (8)

There is a very strange footnote to the story of Richard Doty, too, as UFO authority and writer Greg Bishop has learned: "Years after his AFOSI involvement, Doty's career reached an apotheosis of sorts when he was actually invited to become a consultant for *The X-Files*, a position he says he held from 1994 to 1996. In time, he also wrote the screenplay for an episode, "The Blessing Way," which aired on September 22, 1995, although producer Chris Carter received writing credit. Doty also appeared as an extra in two episodes: "Anasazi," which aired on May 19, 1995, and "Paper Clip," shown on September 29 of the same year. He tried to write another, but says that it was 'killed' by a government agency that he was required to run everything past before turning any of it in for production." (9)

Very ironically, the aforementioned "Paper Clip" episode of *The X-Files*, in which Doty appeared as an extra, specifically dealt with the way in which the UFO subject had been used as camouflage for secret government projects and experiments. (10)

Greg Bishop is convinced that the Serpo documents are a part of an ongoing plan designed to flood the UFO research community with science fiction style disinformation in an effort to smoke out foreign espionage agents, secretly positioned within the continental United States, who subsequently follow their scent. (11)

Bishop just might be correct.

CONCLUSIONS

Having now digested a veritable wealth of information relative to high-level government secrecy and sci-fi, there can be absolutely no doubt whatsoever that the two worlds have crossed paths on many occasions–and for an absolute multiplicity of reasons, too.

As we have seen, government, military and intelligence agencies from the United States, Russia, and Britain have very carefully and secretly utilized and exploited science fiction for espionage and disinformation purposes; the story of the CIA and the *Lord of Light*, and the KGB's unfortunate use of fantasy literature as a direct springboard for creating spurious tales about the nature and origin of HIV and AIDS are both prime examples of just such a scenario.

Science fiction has also acted as a useful tool when it comes to encouraging revolutionary ideas for research into new–and secret–groundbreaking technologies such as invisibility, teleportation, and the creation of half-human super-soldiers. The fact that these technologies still elude us (as far as the general public and the media are concerned, at least) is perhaps secondary to the fact that without the enterprising vision of the science fiction authors who created them and made them famous in a fictional setting, it is highly unlikely that similar scenarios would ever have been considered possible in the real world.

When it comes to government agents secretly using science fiction as a convenient mouthpiece to subtly acclimatize the public to the idea that alien beings really are amongst us, the jury still seems to be very much out on this particularly controversial and thought-provoking issue. Granted, the stories relating to Steven Spielberg, *E.T.*, and *Close Encounters of the Third Kind*; Nick Pope and *Operation Thunder Child*; Ralph Noyes and *A Secret Property*; and the British military's unprecedented assistance given to the BBC science fiction drama series *Invasion Earth* are all deeply provocative but thus far ultimately—and admittedly—unproven. In time, perhaps, the full and unexpurgated stories relating to these intriguing topics will surface, and definitive answers will finally be in-hand. Official concern over science fiction is something that seems to have been borne out on both sides of the Atlantic on several occasions; that Mikel Conrad's 1950 movie *The Flying Saucer* was rumored to include footage of real UFOs in flight worried the U.S. Air Force just about as much as the 1965 British TV production *The War Game* bothered the British Government. And, as the FBI's previously secret files on science fiction authors L. Ron Hubbard and Philip K. Dick have graphically revealed, their private lives were nearly as strange as the subjects they wrote about.

The old adage aside, fiction (and particularly science fiction) is still stranger than truth. But when it comes to the potent cocktail of government, science fiction, and the paranormal—not by much!

REFERENCES

Chapter 1: *Martian Mysteries*
1. *Gulliver's Travels*, Jonathan Swift, Penguin Classics, 2003
2. Ibid. *Jonathan Swift, The Literature Network*, http://www.online-litera-ture.com/swift/; *Jonathan Swift: A Brief Biography*, http://www.victorian-web.org/previctorian/swift/bio.html; *Jonathan Swift*, http://en.wikipedia.org/wiki/Jonathan_Swift
3. *Gulliver's Travels*, Jonathan Swift, Penguin Classics, 2003
4. *Mars: Extreme Planet*, National Aeronautics and Space Administration (NASA), http://mpfwww.jpl.nasa.gov/facts/moons.html
5. *Voltaire: Author & Philosopher, 1694-1778*, http://www.lucidcafe.com/library/95nov/voltaire.html;
Voltaire's Page, http://www.geocities.com/Athens/7308/;
Micromegas, http://www.wondersmith.com/scifi/micro.htm;
Micromegas, Voltaire, http://www.timelineindex.com/content/view/702
6. *Johannes Kelper: His Life, His Laws and Times*, National Aeronautics and Space Administration, http://kepler.nasa.gov/johannes/
7. *Kepler's Somnium: Science fiction and the Renaissance Scientist*, Gale E. Christianson, http://www.depauw.edu/sfs/backissues/8/christianson8art.htm
8. *Jonathan Swift's Martian Moons Right On*, Ed Hatton, *Irish American Post*, Vol. 5, Issue 3, October 2004, http://www.gaelicweb.com/irishampost/year2004/10oct/featured/featured08.html;
Kepler, Johannes, New World Encyclopedia, http://www.newworldencyclopedia.org/entry/Johannes_Kepler;
Johannes Kepler: From "Mysteries" to "Harmony," http://www.goldenmu-seum.com/0404Kepler_engl.html
The Galileo Project, http://galileo.rice.edu/sci/observations/saturn.html

Chapter 2: *Kirby Conspiracies*
1. *After the Martian Apocalypse*, Mac Tonnies, Paraview-Pocket Books, 2004
2. Ibid.
3. *A New View of the Famous Face on Mars*, Alan Boyle, http://www.msnbc.msn.com/id/3077691/
4. *Tom Corbett, Space Cadet*, http://www.solarguard.com/tchome.htm;
Tom Corbett, Space Cadet,
http://en.wikipedia.org/wiki/Tom_Corbett,_Space_Cadet;

5. *The Moon Pyramid*, http://www.solarguard.com/tcreel1.htm; *The "Tom Corbett Lunar Pyramid" - Tying It All Together*, Steve Troy, 2000, http://www.solarguard.com/tcreel1.htm; *Tetrahedrons, Faces on Mars, Exploding Planets, Hyperdimensional Physics, -- and Tom Corbett, Space Cadet?! What Did They Know, and When Did They Know it?*, http://www.enterprisemission.com/corbett.htm *Kenn, Kirby & Conspiracies*, Nick Redfern, *UFO Mystic*, http://www.ufomystic.com/the-redfern-files/kenn-kirby-conspiracies/
6. Ibid.
Jack Kirby Museum, http://kirbymuseum.org/catalogue/view.php?pp=4078; *Forbidden Planet...Mars*, Richard Hoagland, http://www.enterprisemission.com/forbidden-planet.htm, 2006; *The Face of Mars in 1958 Comic Book!*, http://www.abovetopsecret.com/forum/thread296386/pg1; *Cydonia Quest, The Occasional Journal*, No. 10, March 1, 2006, http://bobwonderland.supanet.com/journal_11.htm
7. *Cydonia Quest, The Occasional Journal*, No. 10, March 1, 2006, http://bobwonderland.supanet.com/journal_11.htm
8. *Forbidden Planet...Mars*, Richard Hoagland, http://www.enterprisemission.com/forbidden-planet.htm, 2006;
9. *Robert A. Heinlein, A Biography* by William H. Patterson, Jr., http://www.heinleinsociety.org/rah/biographies.html; *Robert. A. Heinlein*, http://en.wikipedia.org/wiki/Robert_A._Heinlein
10. *Dr. Wernher von Braun*, NASA, http://history.msfc.nasa.gov/vonbraun/bio.html
11. *Ley*, http://www.astronautix.com/astros/ley.htm; *Willy Ley*, http://en.wikipedia.org/wiki/Willy_Ley
12. *Disney, UFOs and Disclosure*, Grant Cameron, July 11, 2002, http://www.rense.com/general27/dis.htm
13. *Disclosure Pattern: A Disney Connection?*, Grant Cameron, Grant Cameron, http://www.presidentialufo.com/disclosure&disney.htm
14. *Ward Kimball*, http://en.wikipedia.org/wiki/Ward_Kimball; *Ward Kimball*, http://www.imdb.com/name/nm0453832/bio
15. *Report of Scientific Advisory Panel on Unidentified Flying Objects Convened by Office of Scientific Intelligence*, Central Intelligence Agency, January 14-18. 1953
16. Ibid.
17. *The Disney-von Braun Collaboration and Its Influence on Space Exploration*, Mike Wright, Marshall Space Flight Center Historian, http://www.

artgomperz.com/a2000/mar/v.htm
18. *Lord of Light*, http://en.wikipedia.org/wiki/Lord_of_Light;
Lord of Light, Roger Zelanzy, Methuen, 1986
19 *The CIA, the Lord of Light Project, and ScienceFictionLand*, http://www.lordoflight.com/cia.html
20. Ibid.
A Classic Case of Deception: CIA Goes Hollywood, Antonio J. Mendez, *Studies in Intelligence*, Central Intelligence Agency, Winter 1999-2000, https://www.cia.gov/library/center-for-the-study-of-intelligence/csi-publications/csi-studies/studies/winter99-00/art1.html;
How the CIA Used a Fake Science fiction Flick to Rescue Americans from Tehran, Joshuah Bearman, *Wired Magazine*, Issue 15, 2005;
"Lord of Light" in Tehran, Scott Rosenberg's Wordyard, http://www.wordyard.com/2007/04/27/lord-of-light/;

Chapter 3: The Tunguska Explosion

1. *The Fire Came By*, John Baxter & Thomas Atkins, Macdonald & Janes, 1975; *The Tunguska Event*, Rupert Furneaux, Nordon Publishers, 1977
2. *Sibir*, July 2, 1908
3. *Krasnoyaretz*, July 13, 1908
4. *Eyewitness Accounts of Tunguska Crash*, N.V. Vasilev, A.F. Kovalevsky, S.A. Razin, L.E. Epiktetova, http://tunguska.tsc.ru/ru/science/1/0
5. Ibid.
6. *Tunguska Phenomenon*, David Darling, http://www.daviddarling.info/encyclopedia/T/Tunguska.html
7. *The Fire Came By*, John Baxter & Thomas Atkins, Macdonald & Janes, 1975
8. *The Tunguska Event*, Matthew Wittnebel & Andrew Mann, *The Lone Conspirators*, http://home.flash.net/~manniac/tunguska.htm
9. *The Unknown Tunguska*, Vladimir V. Rubtsov, *Fate*, May 2001
10. *Russian Alien Spaceship Claims Raise Eyebrows, Skepticism*, Robert Roy Britt, http://www.space.com/scienceastronomy/tunguska_event_040812.html, August 12, 2004
11. *Tunguska Phenomenon*, David Darling,
http://www.daviddarling.info/encyclopedia/T/Tunguska.html
12. *Astronauts*, http://english.lem.pl/index.php/works/novels/astronauts;
http://en.wikipedia.org/wiki/Tunguska_event_in_fiction
13. *And Having Writ*, Donald R. Bensen, Ace Books 1979
14. *Chekhov's Journey*, Ian Watson, Littlehampton Book Services Ltd., 1983
15. *Storming the Cosmos*, Bruce Sterling & Rudy Ricker, published in *Trans-*

real! by Rudy Rucker, Cambrian Publishers, 1991

16. *Tunguska event in fiction*, http://en.wikipedia.org/wiki/Tunguska_event_in_fiction

17. *Tunguska*, The X-Files, Episode 8, Season 4, Episode 8, November 24, 1996 & *Terma*, The X-Files, Episode 9, Season 4, December 1, 1996

18. Interview, September 14. 2005

Chapter 4: *Planet of the Ape-Men*

1. *H.G. Wells, The Literature Network*, http://www.online-literature.com/wellshg/;

Herbert George Wells, 1866-1946, http://www.kirjasto.sci.fi/hgwells.htm;

Spartacus Educational, http://www.spartacus.schoolnet.co.uk/Jwells.htm;

H.G. Wells, Biography, http://www.geocities.com/Athens/Marble/5652/

2. *The Island of Dr. Moreau*, Bantam Classics, 1994;

The Island of Dr. Moreau Study Guide, http://www.gradesaver.com/the-island-of-dr-moreau/study-guide/short-summary/;

The Island of Dr. Moreau, http://en.wikipedia.org/wiki/The_Island_of_Doctor_Moreau

3. *Pierre Boulle, 1912-1994*, http://www.kirjasto.sci.fi/boulle.htm

4. *Planet of the Apes: The Forbidden Zone*, http://www.theforbidden-zone.com/index.shtml

5. *Scientist Sent to Africa in Stalin's Plan for Species That Felt no Pain*, The Scotsman, April, 29, 2008, http://heritage.scotsman.com/science/Scientist-sent-to-Africa-in.4029006.jp

6. *Ilya Ivanovich Ivanov (Biologist)*, http://en.wikipedia.org/wiki/Ilya_Ivanovich_Ivanov_(biologist)

7. *Stalin's Mutant Ape Army*, Jerome Starkey, freerepublic.com, December 20, 2005, http://www.freerepublic.com/focus/f-news/1543814/posts;

Stalin's Army of Mutant Ape-Men, Sky News, December 20, 2005, http://news.sky.com/skynews/Home/Sky-News-Archive/Article/200806413482528;

Stalin's Half-Man, Half-Ape Super Warriors, Chris Stephen & Allan Hall, The Scotsman, December 20, 2005, http://news.scotsman.com/latestnews/Stalins-halfman-halfape-superwarriors.2688011.jp

8. *Stalin-Wells Talk*, http://www.lib.monash.edu.au/exhibitions/communism/com107.html

Chapter 5: *Project Invisibility*

1. *The Invisible Man*, H.G. Wells, Tor Classics, 1992

2. *The Invisible Man (film)*, http://en.wikipedia.org/wiki/The_Invisible_Man_(film)

3. *Predator*, http://www.imdb.com/title/tt0093773/
4. *Hollow Man*, http://www.imdb.com/title/tt0164052/
5. *B-2 Spirit*, http://www.af.mil/factsheets/factsheet.asp?fsID=82
6. *UFO Secrets*, Charles R. Smith, *Newsmax*, January 15, 2004, http://archive.newsmax.com/archives/articles/2004/1/14/222343.shtml
7. Ibid.
8. *Weapons of the Future are Here*, Charles R. Smith, *Newsmax*, February 11, 2005, http://archive.newsmax.com/archives/articles/2005/2/10/202311.shtml
9. *Thin Air*, George Eaton Simpson & Neal R. Burger, Dell, 1977
10. *The Philadelphia Experiment*, http://www.imdb.com/title/tt0087910/
11. *The Philadelphia Experiment*, Charles Berlitz & William L. Moore, Fawcett, 1995; *Secrets of the Unified Field*, Joseph P. Farrell, Adventures Unlimited Press, 2008;
The Philadelphia Experiment and Other UFO Conspiracies, Brad Steiger, Sherry Steiger & Alfred Bielek
12. *Information Sheet: Philadelphia Experiment*, U.S. Navy, http://www.history.navy.mil/faqs/faq21-2.htm
13. *The Case for the UFO*, Morris Jessup, Bantam, 1955; Morris K. Jessup, http://en.wikipedia.org/wiki/Morris_K._Jessup;
14. Ibid.
15. *What is Unified Field Theory?* Andrew Zimmerman, http://physics.about.com/od/quantumphysics/f/uft.htm
16. *Information Sheet: Philadelphia Experiment*, U.S. Navy, http://www.history.navy.mil/faqs/faq21-2.htm
17. *The Case for the UFO*, Morris Jessup, Bantam, 1955; Morris K. Jessup, http://en.wikipedia.org/wiki/Morris_K._Jessup; *The Philadelphia Experiment*, Charles Berlitz & William L. Moore, Fawcett, 1995
18. Ibid.
19. Ibid.
20. Ibid.
21. *Information Sheet: Philadelphia Experiment*, U.S. Navy, http://www.history.navy.mil/faqs/faq21-2.htm
22. *The Jessup Dimension*, Anna Lykins Genzlinger, Saucerian Press, 1981
23. *Information Sheet: Philadelphia Experiment*, U.S. Navy, http://www.history.navy.mil/faqs/faq21-2.htm
24. Ibid.
25. Ibid.
26. Ibid.
27. Ibid.

28. Ibid.

29. Ibid.

30. *Photographs Show a Man Becoming Invisible, Popular Mechanics*, May 1934

31. *Brains Trust*, BBC, December 21, 1943

32. Newspaper clipping reproduced in *The Philadelphia Experiment*, Charles Berlitz & William L. Moore, Fawcett, 1995

33. Ibid.

34. Ibid.

35. Interview, February 18, 1999

36. *The Philadelphia Experiment: Update*, William L. Moore, William L. Moore Publications, 1984

Chapter 6: The Strange World of Kirk Allen

1. *The Fifty Minute Hour: A Collection of True Psychoanalytic Tales*, Robert Lindner, Bantam, 1956

2. Ibid.
Revelations: Alien Contact and Human Deception, Jacques Vallee, Anomalist Books, 2008;
The Case of Kirk Allen, Jacques Vallee, http://www.brainsturbator.com/articles/the_case_of_kirk_allen_by_jacques_vallee/

3. Ibid.

4. *The Manhattan Project: An Interactive History*, U.S. Department of Energy, http://www.cfo.doe.gov/me70/manhattan/;
Manhattan Project, http://en.wikipedia.org/wiki/Manhattan_Project

5. *The Fifty Minute Hour: A Collection of True Psychoanalytic Tales*, Robert Lindner, Bantam, 1956;
Revelations: Alien Contact and Human Deception, Jacques Vallee, Anomalist Books, 2008;
The Case of Kirk Allen, Jacques Vallee, http://www.brainsturbator.com/articles/the_case_of_kirk_allen_by_jacques_vallee/

6. *The Demon-Haunted World; Science as a Candle in the Dark*, Carl Sagan, Ballantine Books, 1997

7. *The Remarkable Science fiction of Cordwainer Smith*, http://www.cordwainer-smith.com/;
About Cordwainer Smith, http://www.fantasticfiction.co.uk/s/cordwainer-smith/;
Cordwainer Smith, http://en.wikipedia.org/wiki/Cordwainer_Smith;

8. *A Psychologist Investigates Cordwainer Smith*, Alan C. Elms, *Alan C. Elms Virtual Library*, http://www.ulmus.net/ace/csmith/investigatingsmith.html;

Behind the Jet-Propelled Couch: Cordwainer Smith & Kirk Allen, Alan C. Elms, *New York Review of Science fiction* , May 2002, http://www.ulmus. net/ace/csmith/behindjetcouch.html
9. Ibid.

Chapter 7: *The Dwarf, the Deros, and the Discs*
1. *The Coming of the Saucers*, Kenneth Arnold & Ray Palmer, Legend Press, 1996
2. *Raymond A. Palmer - Summary Bibliography*, http://www.isfdb.org/cgi-bin/ea.cgi?Raymond_A._Palmer; *Raymond A. Palmer*, http://en.wikipedia.org/wiki/Raymond_A._Palmer
3. Ibid.
4. *Raymond A. Palmer*, http://www.absoluteastronomy.com/topics/Raymond_A._Palmer;
5. *Raymond A. Palmer*, http://en.wikipedia.org/wiki/Raymond_A._Palmer
6. *The Shaver Mystery and the Inner Earth*, Timothy Green Beckley, Mokelumne Hill Press, 1985; *The Shaver Mystery and the Truth about Earth's Past*, http://www.bbc.co.uk/dna/h2g2/A676244; *Amazing Stories*, March 1945
7. *Maury Island UFO*, Kenn Thomas, Illuminet Press, 1999
8. Ibid.
9. Ibid.
10. *The Coming of the Saucers*, Kenneth Arnold & Ray Palmer, Legend Press, 1996
11. *Amazing Stories*, September 1946
12. *The Man Who Invented Flying Saucers*, John A. Keel, *Grey Lodge Occult Review*, http://www.greylodge.org/occultreview/glor_005/saucermythos.htm
13. *The Coming of the Saucers*, Kenneth Arnold & Ray Palmer, Legend Press, 1996; *Maury Island UFO*, Kenn Thomas, Illuminet Press, 1999; *1947 - Maury Island UFO Crash*, http://ufos.about.com/od/ufofolkloremythlegend/p/mauryisland.htm
14. *Tacoma News*, May 10, 1946
15. *Nasa, Nazis & JFK*, William Torbitt, Adventures Unlimited Press, 1996; *Notorious Fred Crisman, Part II*, Kalani & Katiuska Hanohano, *UFO Magazine*, Vol. 9, No. 1, 1994
16. "The Maury Island Caper," John Keel, *UFOs: 1947-1987*, edited by Hilary Evans & John Spencer, Fortean Tomes, 1987

17. *Maury Island UFO*, Kenn Thomas, Illuminet Press, 1999;
The Octopus, Kenn Thomas & Jim Keith, Feral House, 2003
18. *Amazing! Astounding! Incredible! Pulp Science fiction , Forrest J Acker-man's World of Science fiction* , Forrest J Ackerman, RR Donnelley & Sons Company, 1997
19. Ibid. *Raymond A. Palmer*, http://en.wikipedia.org/wiki/Raymond_A._ Palmer
20. *Raymond A. Palmer*, http://en.wikipedia.org/wiki/Raymond_A._Palm-er
21. *Maury Island UFO*, Kenn Thomas, Illuminet Press, 1999
22. *Kenneth Arnold*, http://en.wikipedia.org/wiki/Kenneth_Arnold
23. *Maury Island UFO: Fred Crisman and Covert Infiltration of Ufology*, Kenn Thomas, 2001, http://www.disinfo.com/archive/pages/article/id904/pg1/in-dex.html
24. *Liquidation Of The UFO Investigators!*, Otto O. Binder, *Saga's Special UFO Report*, Vol. II, 1971

Chapter 8: *Roswell*

1. *Body Snatchers in the Desert: The Horrible Truth at the Heart of the Roswell Story*, Paraview-Pocket Books, 2005
2. *The Flying Saucer*, Bernard Newman, Gollancz, 1948;
The Mystic and the Spy: Two Early British UFO Writers, Philip Taylor, *Magonia*, No. 61, November 1997, and http://www.magaonia.demon.co.uk
3. *The Ogden Enigma*, Gene Snyder, Playboy Press, 1981
4. *Majestic*, Whitley Strieber, Putnam's, 1989
5. *Whitley Strieber's Unknown Country*, http://www.unknowncountry.com
6. *Whitley's Journal, The Scum Rises: Peter Jennings on UFOs* http://www.unknowncountry.com/journal/?id=177
7. *Alien Rapture: The Chosen*, Edgar Rothschild Fouche & Brad Steiger, Galde Press, Inc., 1998; http://www.ufocongress.com
8. *Stratagem*, Jacques Vallee, Documatica Research, LLC, 2007; http://www.jacquesvallee.net/stratagem.html
9. *Jacques F. Vallee*, http://www.jacquesvallee.net/
10. *Revelations*, Jacques Vallee, Ballantine, 1991
11. *Magonia Monthly Supplement*, No. 31, September 2000
12. Ibid.
13. Ibid.

Chapter 9: *The UFO That Never Was*

1. *The Flying Saucer*, http://www.en.wikipedia.org/wiki/The_Flying_Saucer

2. *Film Actor Finds Flying Disc, But Press Agent Doubts Tale*, Dayton, Ohio *Journal Herald*, September 14, 1949

3. *Remote Viewers*, Jim Schnabel, Bantam Doubleday Dell Publishing Group, 1997

Chapter 10: *Sci-Fi, Scientology, and the FBI*

1. *L. Ron Hubbard: The Founder of Scientology*, http://www.aboutlronhubbard.org;

L. Ron Hubbard: Scientology's Esteemed Founder, Michael Crowley, *Slate*, July 15, 2005;

L. Ron Hubbard: A Profile, http://www.lronhubbardprofile.org/profile/index.htm

L. Ron Hubbard: Founder of Dianetics and Scientology, http://www.theta.com/goodman/lrh.htm

2 *Battlefield Earth (novel)*, http://en.wikipedia.org/wiki/Battlefield_Earth_ (novel)

3. *Sex and Rockets*, John Carter, Feral House, 2000

4. *Jack Parsons and the Curious Tale of Rocketry in the 1930s*, George Pendle, *The Naked Scientists*, March 2006, http://www.thenakedscientists.com/ HTML/articles/article/georgependlecolumn1.htm/

5. *Books by L. Ron Hubbard*, http://www.biblio.com/author_ biographies/2098631/L_Ron_Hubbard.html;

Babalon, http://en.wikipedia.org/wiki/Babalon;

JPL -- The Occult Roots of NASA, http://www.bariumblues.com/jpl.htm;

Hubbard's Magic, Craig Branch, *Watchman*, http://www.watchman.org/Sci/ hubmagk2.htm

Jack Parsons, http://en.wikipedia.org/wiki/Jack_Parsons

John Whiteside Parsons, Colin Bennett, *Fortean Times*, March 2000

6. *The Bare Faced Messiah Interviews*, http://www.cs.cmu.edu/~dst/Library/ Shelf/miller/interviews/himmel.htm

7. *Dianetics*, http://www.dianetics.org;

Dianetics, http://en.wikipedia.org/wiki/DMSMH

What is Dianetics?, http://www.scientologytoday.org/Common/question/ pg06.htm

Dianetics: Understanding the Mind, http://www.essentialdianetics.org/

8. *Scientology*, *New World Encyclopedia*, http://www.newworldencyclopedia.org/entry/Scientology;

Wonder's Child, Jack Williamson, Benbella Books, 2005

9. *History of Dianetics*, http://en.wikipedia.org/wiki/History_of_Dianetics

10. *Psychologists act Against Dianetics*, Lucy Freeman, *New York Times*, Sep-

tember 9, 1950
11. *Church of Scientology*, http://www.scientology.org;
Scientology (The Church of Scientology), http://www.forf.org/news/2004/
scientology.html
12. *L. Ron Hubbard*, http://en.wikipedia.org/wiki/L._Ron_Hubbard
13. *The Mysterious Death of L. Ron Hubbard*, http://home.earthlink.
net/~snefru/deathoflrh/
The Death of L. Ron Hubbard, http://www.xenu.net/archive/hubbardcoroner/
14. *L. Ron Hubbard: Scientology's Esteemed Founder*, Michael Crowley, *Slate Magazine*, July 15, 2005

Chapter 11: *Weapons of Mass Destruction*

1. *War of the Worlds*, H.G. Wells, Modern Library, 2002
2. *Goldfinger*, http://www.imdb.com/title/tt0058150/
3. *Star Trek*, http://www.startrek.com
4. *American Heritage Dictionary*, http://www.bartleby.com/61/17/R0061750.html
5. *Aliens*, http://www.imdb.com/title/tt0090605/
6. *Babylon 5*, http://babylon5.warnerbros.com
7. *Resident Evil 3*, http://en.wikipedia.org/wiki/Resident_Evil_3
8. *Star Wars*, http://www.starwars.com
9. *Tesla Biography*, http://www.teslasociety.com/biography.htm;
Nikola Tesla, http://en.wikipedia.org/wiki/Nikola_Tesla;
Tunguska - A Tesla Connection?, http://www.tfcbooks.com/articles/tunguska.htm;
Tesla Wireless and the Tunguska Explosion, http://www.frank.germano.com/tunguska.htm;
Tesla: Free Energy, The Tunguska Explosion, http://prometheus.al.ru/english/phisik/onichelson/onichelson.htm;
Nikola Tesla and Tunguska, http://www.reformation.org/tesla-and-tunguska.html;
Mysterious Tunguska Explosion of 1908 in Siberia may be linked to Tesla's experiments of wireless transmission, http://www.teslasociety.com/tunguska.htm
10. *The Death Ray: The Secret Life of Harry Grindell Matthews*, Jonathan Foster, http://www.harrygrindellmatthews.com/
Harry Grindell Matthews, http://en.wikipedia.org/wiki/Harry_Grindell_Matthews;
Harry Grindell Matthews of Winterbourne, http://www.frenchaymuseu-

marchives.co.uk/Archives/PagesBiogy/Matthews_HG.htm;
Grindell "Death Ray" Matthews, Dr. David Clarke & Andy Roberts, *Fortean Times*, October 2003
11. *Hump-Day: The Tizard Committee*, http://etherwave.wordpress.com/2008/11/12/hump-day-history-the-tizard-committee/
12. *Sky Crash*, Jenny Randles, Brenda Butler & Dot Street, Neville Spearman, 1984
13. *R.V. Jones*, http://www.spartacus.schoolnet.co.uk/2WWjonesRV.htm; *Most Secret War*, R.V. Jones, Combined Publishing, 1998
14. *United Press Release*, June 6, 1934
15. *Modern Mechanix*, http://blog.modernmechanix.com/2007/06/07/inventor-hides-secret-of-death-ray/
16. *Popular Science*, February 1940
17. *Hitler's Suppressed and Still-Suppressed and Still-Secret Weapons, Science and Technology*, Henry Stevens, Adventures Unlimited Press, 2007
18. *America's New Ray Guns*, Taylor Dinerman, *The Space Review*, January 3, 2006, http://blog.modernmechanix.com/2007/06/07/inventor-hides-secret-of-death-ray/
19. *Connecting the Dots*, Robert Howard, Welcome Rain, 2009

Chapter 12: *Lightning Conspiracies*

1. *On the Banks of Plum Creek*, Laura, Ingalls Wilder, Harper-Collins, 1994
2. *Dark Rivers of the Heart*, Dean Koontz, Bantam 2000
3. *Sinister Barrier*, Eric Frank Russell, Del Rey, 1985
4. *Journey to the Center of the Earth*, Jules Verne, Simon & Schuster, 2008
5. *Unidentified Flying Objects*, Project 'Grudge,' *Technical Report*, Air Materiel Command, U.S. Air Force, 1949
6. *Survey of Kugelblitz Theories for Electromagnetic Incendiaries*, W.B. Lyttle & C.E. Wilson, December 1965, for the New Concepts Division/Special Projects, Edgewood Arsenal, Maryland
7. *From out of the Blue*, Jenny Randles, Inner Light-Global Communications, 1991
8. *Left at East Gate*, Larry Warren & Peter Robbins, Cosimo, 2005
9. *Edgewood Arsenal Experiments*, http://en.wikipedia.org/wiki/Edgewood_Arsenal_experiments
10. *Like Ball Lightning: In Memory of Ralph Noyes*, Dennis Stacy, http://www.anomalist.com/milestones/noyes.html

Chapter 13: *Big Brother is Watching*

1. *Aldous Huxley, The Literature Network*, http://www.online-literature.

com/aldous_huxley/;

Aldous Huxley, http://www.huxley.net/ah/aldoushuxley-biography.html;

Aldous Huxley: The Author and His Times: http://somaweb.org/w/huxbio. html;

Brave New World: A Defense of Paradise-Engineering, http://www.huxley. net/;

Brave New World, http://en.wikipedia.org/wiki/Brave_New_World

2. *Biography of George Orwell*, http://www.george-orwell.org/l_biography. html;

George Orwell, The Literature Network, http://www.online-literature.com/ orwell/;

1984: Plot Overview, http://www.sparknotes.com/lit/1984/summary.html;

3. *Amusing Ourselves to Death: Public Discourse in the Age of Show Business*, Neil Postman, Penguin Books, 1986

4. *CIA, Movie Producer*, http://www.defensetech.org/archives/002229.html

Chapter 14: *Secrets of The War Game*

1. *The War Game, The Museum of Broadcast Communications*, http://www.museum.tv/archives/etv/W/htmlW/wargamethe/wargamethe.htm

2. *The Day After*, http://www.imdb.com/title/tt0085404/

3. *Threads*, http://en.wikipedia.org/wiki/Threads

4. *The War Game, The Museum of Broadcast Communications*, http://www.museum.tv/archives/etv/W/htmlW/wargamethe/wargamethe.htm

5. *War Plan UK*, Duncan Campbell, Burnett Books, 1982

6. Ibid.

7. Ibid.

8. *Churchill Gagged BBC on H-Bomb*, Alan Travis, *Guardian*, August 20, 1999

9. *Meeting the Threat of Surprise Attack*, Technological Capabilities Panel, February 14, 1955

10. *Churchill Gagged BBC on H-Bomb*, Alan Travis, *Guardian*, August 20, 1999

Chapter 15: *Alien Invaders and Iron Mountain*

1. *War of the Worlds, Orson Welles, and the Invasion from Mars*, http://www.transparencynow.com/welles.htm;

War of the Worlds Radio Broadcast, http://www.war-ofthe-worlds.co.uk/war_worlds_orson_welles_mercury.

htm;
The War of the Worlds (radio),
http://en.wikipedia.org/wiki/The_War_of_the_Worlds_(radio)
2. *Sideslip*, Ted White & Dave van Arnam, Pyramid, 1968
3. *The Adventures of Buckaroo Banzai across the 8th Dimension*, http://www.imdb.com/title/tt0086856/
4. *The X-Files, War of the Coprophages*, Season 3, Episode 12, 1996
5. *War of the Worlds*, http://www.imdb.com/title/tt0094578/
6. *Behold a Pale Horse*, William Cooper, Light Technology Publications, 1991
7. *Report from Iron Mountain*, Philip Coppens, *Conspiracy Times*, http://www.philipcoppens.com/ironmountain.html
8. *Report from Iron Mountain*, Free Press, 1996
9. *Report from Iron Mountain*, *Museum of Hoaxes*, http://www.museumof-hoaxes.com/hoax/Hoaxipedia/Report_From_Iron_Mountain/;
Report from Iron Mountain, Philip Coppens, *Conspiracy Times*, http://www.philipcoppens.com/ironmountain.html;
Report from Iron Mountain, http://www.wingtv.net/ironmountain.html
10. *The JFK 100*, "The Organizing Principle of any Society is for War," http://www.jfk-online.com/jfk100lewin.html;
The Collected Works of Col. L. Fletcher Prouty, http://www.prouty.org/cdrom.html
11. *The Report from Iron Mountain*, http://en.wikipedia.org/wiki/The_Report_From_Iron_Mountain
12. *Cast of Characters*, http://www.acts1711.com/cast.htm
13. *A Cause for Fear*, Wall Street Journal, May 9, 1995
14. *News of War and Peace You're not Ready for*, Herschel McLandress, *Washington Post, Book World*, November 26, 1967
15. *Peace - It could be Horrible*, Eliot Fremont-Smith, *New York Times, Book of the Times*, November 20, 1967
16. *The New Revolutionaries*, Garry Wills, *The New York Review of Books*, Vol. 42, No. 13, August 10, 1995, http://wwww.nybooks.com/articles/article-preview?article_id=1829
17. *Report from Iron Mountain*, Free Press, 1996

Chapter 16: The Andromeda Strain: Fact or Fiction?

1. *Fort Detrick*, http://www.globalsecurity.org/military/facility/fort-detrick.htm
A History of Fort Detrick, Maryland, Norman Covert, http://www.detrick.army.mil/cutting_edge/index.cfm

2. *The Andromeda Strain*, Michael Crichton, Ballantine Books, 1992
3. Interview, 4 January, 2003
4. *A History of Fort Detrick, Maryland*, Norman Covert, http://www.detrick. army.mil/cutting_edge/index.cfm
5. *Majestic 12, 1st Annual Report*, http://www.majesticdocuments.com/pdf/ mj12_fifthannualreport.pdf
6. Ibid.
7. *Aids as a Biological Weapon*, http://cambodia.usembassy.gov/biological_ weapon.html
8. *A Life in Black*, V.L. Durov, 2004 (original manuscript, publication pending)
9. *The Last Man*, Mary Wollstonecraft Shelley, Dodo Press, 2009
10. *The Shape of Things to Come*, H.G. Wells, Penguin Classics, 2006
11. *I am Legend*, Richard Matheson, Bantam, 1964
12. *A Choice of Catastrophes*, Isaac Asimov, Ballantine Books, 1981
13. *It's Been a Good Life*, Isaac Asimov & Janet Jeppson Asimov, Prometheus Books, 2002
14. *The Matrix*, http://www.imdb.com/title/tt0133093/

Chapter 17: The Strange Tale of Solarcon-6

1. *Philip K. Dick, 1928-1982*, Lawrence Sutin, http://www.philipkdick.com/ aa_biography.html
2. *Exegesis (Book)*, http://en.wikipedia.org/wiki/Exegesis_(book)
3. *An Interview With America's Most Brilliant Science-Fiction Writer* (*Philip K. Dick*), by Joe Vitale, *The Aquarian*, No. 11, October 11-18, 1978, http:// www.philipkdick.com/media_aquarian.html
4. *Excerpts from Philip K. Dick's FBI File*, http://www.alphane.com/moon/ PalmTree/fbi.htm
5. *An Interview With America's Most Brilliant Science-Fiction Writer* (*Philip K. Dick*), by Joe Vitale, *The Aquarian*, No. 11, October 11-18, 1978, http:// www.philipkdick.com/media_aquarian.html
6. *Excerpts from Philip K. Dick's FBI File*, http://www.alphane.com/moon/ PalmTree/fbi.htm
7. Ibid.
8. *How* Jeet *Heer Betrayed Philip K. Dick Admirers to Marxist Literary Critics*, Frank C. Bertrand, http://www.philipkdickfans.com/frank/jeetheer.htm

Chapter 18: Science fiction Secrets in the White House

1. *E.T.: The Extra-Terrestrial*, 1982

2. *A Young Stephen Spielberg Meets the President*, Grant Cameron, http://www.presidentialufo.com/reagan_spielberg.htm;
Ronald Reagan's Obsession with an Alien Invasion, A. Hovni, *UFO Universe*, September 1988;
What did Reagan Know About UFOs?, Douglas Bower, http://www.presidentialufo.com/reagan_spielberg.htm
3. *Stephen Spielberg: A Biography*, Joseph Mcbride, Da Cap Press, 1999
4. *Presidential UFOs - Ronald Reagan to Back Kunich?*, Brenda Burton, *American Chronicle*, November 2, 2007, http://www.americanchronicle.com/articles/view/41932
5. *A Young Stephen Spielberg Meets the President*, Grant Cameron, http://www.presidentialufo.com/reagan_spielberg.htm
6. *Presidential UFOs - Ronald Reagan to Back Kunich?*, Brenda Burton, *American Chronicle*, November 2, 2007, http://www.americanchronicle.com/articles/view/41932
7. *A Young Stephen Spielberg Meets the President*, Grant Cameron, http://www.presidentialufo.com/reagan_spielberg.htm
8. *Ronald Reagan and Russian Leader Gorbachev Promoted a Future "UFO Alien" False Flag Invasion*, Alfred Lambremont Webre, *Examiner*, http://www.examiner.com/x-2912-Seattle-Exopolitics-Examiner~y2009m2d17-Ronald-Reagan-and-Russian-leader-Gorbachev-promoted-a-future-UFO-alien-false-flag-invasion
9. *UFOs Changed Communist World History*, George Filer, *UFO Research Center*, February 6, 2008, http://www.uforc.com/database/UFOs-Changed-History_George-Filer_020908.htm
10. *Hilary Clinton UFO*, http://www.hillaryclintonufo.net/otherquotes.html
11. *President Reagan*, Lou Cannon, Perseus Publishing, 2000
12. *A Young Stephen Spielberg Meets the President*, Grant Cameron, http://www.presidentialufo.com/reagan_spielberg.htm

Chapter 19: *A False Prophet and the Science fiction Scientist*

1. *Cosmos: A Personal Voyage*, PBS/KCET, 1980
2. *Contact*, Carl Sagan, Simon & Schuster, 1985
3. www.carlsagan.com; *Carl Sagan*, http://en.wikipedia.org/wiki/Carl_Sagan
4. *Deep Impact*, http://www.imdb.com/title/tt0120647/
5. *Armageddon*, http://www.imdb.com/title/tt0120591/
6. *US planned one big Nuclear Blast for Mankind*, Antony Barnett, *Observer*, May 14, 2000

Chapter 20: *Novel Secrets*

1. National Archive file: Admiralty 131/119;
W.P. Drury, http://openlibrary.org/a/OL160404A/W.-P.-Drury;
2. *Dennis Wheatley: An Introduction*, http://www.denniswheatley.info/denniswheatley.htm;
Dennis Wheatley, http://www.fantasticfiction.co.uk/w/dennis-wheatley/;
Biographical and Bibliographical note on Dennis Wheatley, http://www.abfar.co.uk/bibliogs/dw_bib.htm
3. *Star of Ill-Omen*, Dennis Wheatley, Hutchinson, 1963
4. *The Gerald Heard Official Website*, http://www.geraldheard.com/biblio.htm
5. Letter, November 29, 1983
6. *Star of Ill-Omen*, Dennis Wheatley, Hutchinson, 1963
7. *On the Trail of the Saucer Spies*, Nick Redfern, Anomalist Books, 2006
8. *From Outer Space to You*, Howard Menger, Saucerian Books, 1959;
Howard Menger Research by Timothy Good, *Plan B from the Bacardi Room*, http://planbfromthebacardiroom.blogspot.com/2009/03/howard-menger-research-by-timothy-good.html
9. *A Secret Property*, Ralph Noyes, Quartet Books, 1986
10. *Left at East Gate*, Larry Warren & Peter Robbins, Cosimo, 2005;
Sky Crash, Jenny Randles, Brenda Butler & Dot Street, Neville Spearman, 1984;
You Can't Tell the People, Georgina Bruni, Pan Books, 2001;
From out of the Blue, Jenny Randles, Inner Light-Global Communications, 1991;
UFO Crash Landing?; Jenny Randles, Blandford, 1998
11. *Out of the Shadows*, Dr. David Clarke & Andy Roberts, Piatkus, 2002
12. *UFO Brigantia*, No. 41, May 1991

Chapter 21: *Thunder Child*

1. *By Space Ship to the Moon*, Gavin Gibbons, Blackwell Publishers, 1958
2. *Fire on the Mountain*, Andy Roberts, published privately, 1998
3. *UFO Magazine*, September/October 1996
4. *History of Porton Down*, http://www.mod.uk/issues/portondownvolunteers/history.htm
5. *Open Skies, Closed Minds*, Nick Pope, Simon & Schuster, 1996
6. *The Uninvited*, Nick Pope, Simon & Schuster, 1997
7. *Operation Thunderchild*, Nick Pope, Simon & Schuster, 1999
8. Interview, November 14, 1999

9. *Operation Thunderchild*, Nick Pope, Simon & Schuster, 1999
10. *Invasion Earth*, BBC Television, 1998
11. Interview, November 14, 1998

Chapter 22: *9-11*

1. *The Lone Gunmen*, http://en.wikipedia.org/wiki/Lone_Gunmen; *The Lone Gunmen*, http://www.mightyponygirl.com/television/lgm/index.html
2. Ibid.
3. *The Lone Gunmen's Pilot Episode*, http://killtown.911review.org/lonegunmen.html
4. *9/11: What did Rupert Murdoch Know*, Christopher Bollyn, October 3, 2003,
http://www.rumormillnews.com/cgi-bin/archive.cgi?read=37543
5. Ibid.
6. Ibid.
7. *The Lone Gunmen Episode 1: Pilot*, Jeffrey King, http://www.plaguepuppy.net/public_html/Lone%20Gunmen/The_Lone_Gunmen_Episode_1.htm

Chapter 23: *Project Teleport*

1. *Star Trek*, http://www.startrek.com
2. *Teleportation*, http://dic.academic.ru/dic.nsf/enwiki/36664
3. *Quantum Teleportation*, IBM,
http://www.research.ibm.com/quantuminfo/teleportation/
4. *Edward Page Mitchell*, http://en.wikipedia.org/wiki/Edward_Page_Mitchell
5. *The Disintegration Machine*, Sir Arthur Conan Doyle, Kessinger Publishing, 2005
6. *World of Null-A*, A.E. van Vogt, Orb Books, 2002
7. *Rogue Moon*, Algis Budry, Fawcett Publications, 1963
8. *The Fly*, George Langelaan, *Playboy*, June 1957;
The Fly (1958), http://www.imdb.com/title/tt0051622/;
The Fly (1986), http://www.imdb.com/title/tt0091064/
9. *Teleportation Physics Study*, Eric W. Davis, Warp Drive Metrics, for the Air Force Research Laboratory, Air Force Materiel Command, Edwards Air Force Base
10. *The Official Website of Gregory Benford*, http://www.gregorybenford.com/bio.php; *Gregory Benford*, http://en.wikipedia.org/wiki/Gregory_Benford
11. *Air Force report calls for $7.5M to study psychic teleportation*, Dan Ver-

gano, *USA Today*, November 5, 2004, http://www.usatoday.com/tech/
news/2004-11-05-teleportation_x.htm
12. Ibid.
13. Ibid.

Chapter 24: *Science fiction Special-Effect or Secret Evidence?*
1. *Good Morning with Anne and Nick*, BBC, January 13, 1995
2. *Alien Autopsy: FAQ*, James Easton, September 21, 1996, http://www.dark-conspiracy.com/alienufo/autopsy/faw/txt
3. *Beyond Roswell*, Michael Hesemann & Philip Mantle, Marlowe, 1997
4. Ibid.
5. Interview, January 22, 1997
6. *Open Skies, Closed Minds*, Nick-Pope, Simon & Schuster, 1996
7. *Eamonn Investigates: The Alien Autopsy*, http://video.google.com/videoplay?docid=-7039109606537272722
8. *Alien Autopsy*, http://en.wikipedia.org/wiki/Alien_autopsy
9. Ibid.
10. *I made the Roswell alien*, BBC, June 27, 2006, http://www.bbc.co.uk/manchester/content/articles/2006/04/07/070406_alien_interview_feature.shtml
11. Ibid.
12. *UFO*, http://en.wikipedia.org/wiki/UFO_(TV_series)
13. Interview, March 28, 1997
14. *The UFO Crash Retrieval Syndrome*, Leonard H. Stringfield, published privately, 1980
15. *UFO Crash/Retrievals: Is the Cover-Up Lid Lifting?* Leonard H. Stringfield, published privately, 1989
16. *Body Snatchers in the Desert*, Nick Redfern, Paraview-Pocket Books, 2005
17. *Alien Autopsy Inquest*, Philip Mantle, Publish America, 2007
18. *Disney, UFOs and Disclosure*, Grant Cameron, http://www.rense.com/general27/dis.htm, July 11, 2002
19. *Alien Autopsy Inquest*, Philip Mantle, Publish America, 2007

Chapter 25: *Serpo and the Science fiction Spy*
1. *Serpo.org: The Zeta Reticuli Exchange Program*, http://www.serpo.org/
2. *UFO*, February 2006
3. *Project Beta*, Greg Bishop, Paraview-Pocket Books, 2005

4. *Fortean Times*, May 2006

5. *Above Top Secret*, http://www.abovetopsecret.com/forum/single. php?post=1966952

6. *James Tiptree, Jr.*, http://en.wikipedia.org/wiki/James_Tiptree,_Jr; *Author Biography and Bibliography*, http://www.scifi.com/scifiction/classics/classics_archive/tiptree2/tiptree2_bio.html; *The Secret Science Fiction Life of Alice B. Sheldon*, http://www.npr.org/templates/story/story.php?storyId=6468136 *James Tiptree, Jr.*, Julie Phillips, Picador, 2007

7. *UFO*, February 2006

8. Ibid.

9. *Project Beta*, Greg Bishop, Paraview-Pocket Books, 2005

10. *The X-Files*, *Paper Clip*, http://www.imdb.com/title/tt0751174/

11. *SERPO Was A Big Fat Fake*, Greg Bishop, *UFO Mystic*, http://www.ufomystic.com/wake-up-down-there/serpo-was-disinformation/

INDEX